Sung-Un Yang

Reputation Management for Organizations

Sung-Un Yang

Reputation Management for Organizations

Effects of Organization-Public Relationships

VDM Verlag Dr. Müller

ISBN: 978-3-8364-2916-0

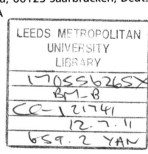

DEDICATION

I dedicate this book to my loving wife, Minjeong, who has been a soulmate sharing

moments of joy and sorrow, and my loving daughter, Danielle. This work could have not

been completed without their love and support.

iii
ACKNOWLEDGEMENTS

First, I thank God, the Father in heaven, who always cares about me and my family from the beginning to the end.

I have to mention many people who supported completing this book. Without help, support, and encouragement from several persons, I would never have been able to finish this work.

Above of all, I would like to Dr. James Grunig for his constant support and his invaluable comments during the whole work. His priceless editorial advice was essential to the completion of this book and has taught me invaluable insights on the working of academic research in general. I also give a special thanks to Dr. Larissa Grunig, Dr. Elizabeth Toth, Dr. Linda Aldoory, and Dr. Gregory Hancock, for their loving encouragement of my study and valuable advice for this work. Dr. Larissa Grunig has been a mentor and my role model for rigorous, persistent, and ambitious scholarship. Knowing Dr. Toth has enriched my works. She has always been very supportive of my works and especially encouraged this work. Dr. Aldoory was my Master's advisor who first inspired me for my academic rigor and has influenced my works with her insightful guidance. It is Dr. Hancock from whom I mostly have learned quantitative research methods for my research works.

My thanks also goes to my colleagues at the Department of Communication, University of Maryland. They have been my teachers, mentors, friends, and family members. Also, I am very grateful for my fellow faculty members at S. I. Newhouse School of Public Communications, Syracuse University.

iv

My highest thanks goes to my family. Especially, I thank Minejong, my loving wife, for her love, endurance, and support.

Newhouse, Syracuse

September, 2007

Sung-Un Yang

TABLE OF CONTENTS

LIST OF TABLES

LIST OF FIGURES

CHAPTER I: Introduction

Over the last decade, public relations scholars have increased their focus on relationship management (Bruning & Ledingham, 1999, 2000; Griffin, 2002; J. Grunig & Hung, 2002; L. Grunig, J. Grunig, & Dozier, 2002; Ledingham, 2001; Ledingham & Bruning, 1998, 2000; Yang & J. Grunig, 2005). For example, Ledingham and Bruning (2000) viewed relationship management as a new "paradigm" for public relations scholarship and practice in their book, "Public Relations as Relationship Management." Summarizing the results of the IABC Excellence study, L. Grunig et al. (2002) suggested quality relationships as the key indicator of effective public relations practice.

Practitioners, on the other hand, have expanded their efforts into reputation management. *PR Week*, in an editorial, described how rampant the growth of reputation management has been in the field of public relations: "In fact, with everyone jumping on the reputation bandwagon these days, reputation management products are becoming as ubiquitous as hot-dog vendors in Manhattan" ("PR Week," 1999, November 15). Another example comes from Christopher Carfi, a co-founder of Cerado, Inc., who said: "Ultimately, reputation and trust are everything. Whether we are talking about music, books, web sites, products, or people, reputation is critical" ("Reputation Management," 2004, June 23).

The primary venue for reputation management appears to be media relations, such as management of corporate web sites and media content analysis. For example, Biz360 performs analysis of LexisNexis content to ensure "how reputation, brands, and messages are perceived positively in the marketplace" ("Biz360," n.d.). Another example includes Bonner Consultants, Inc., which claims that its specialty is "persuasive communications," including positioning, crisis management, strategies, and leveraging reputation. More specifically, image and reputation management are described as follows: "Test whether reputation follows performance. Assess perceptions of key internal and external audiences, including the news media, to measure credibility and address shortcomings. Create a public relations plan that reinforces the desired reputation" ("Bonner," n.d.). Last, regarding reputation management on corporate web sites, Jakob Nielson introduced software for an online reputation manager called *Alexa*, which offers 1) "reputation statistics (for most sites on the Web showing how frequently they [web sites] are visited and how popular they are)" and 2) "recommendation links (to good other sites that are related to the current page)" ("The Reputation Manager," 1998, February 8).

However, in discussing practitioners' concentration on the reputation concept, Verčič (2000) stated in a presentation to the IABC International Conference in Vancouver: "For nearly a century, the public relations profession has been trying to disassociate itself from the image of being a profession about image-making. It is therefore a pity that it tries to redefine itself as reputation management—which is basically the same as image-making" (p. 4; cited in J. Grunig & Hung, 2002, p. 3). Also, being concerned about inconsistent reputation measures, Capelin (1999) criticized the trend of public relations toward reputation management as follows: "I applaud the 'hot ticket' status of reputation management that has engulfed PR Week's pages … But while there is clearly a place for a consistent system to evaluate corporate status, it is not the Holy Grail of reputation management" ("PR Week," 1999, November 15).

Why do practitioners and scholars embrace such concepts, as "relationships" or "reputation," in the field of public relations? Public relations professionals have increasingly faced the challenge of demonstrating the value of public relations to their organizations (Hon, 1997). Consequently, both public relations professionals and scholars have long strived to find the key concept to demonstrate public relations effectiveness at the organizational level (e.g., Griffin, 2002; Hon & J. Grunig, 1999; Huang, 1997, 2001; Hung, 2002; Hutton, Goodman, Alexander, & Genest, 2001; Jo, 2003; Kim, 2000, 2001; J. Grunig & Hung, 2002; L. Grunig, J. Grunig, & Dozier, 2002; Ledingham & Bruning, 2000).

In contemporary public relations research and practice, therefore, organization-public "relationships" and organizational "reputation" have been suggested as focal concepts to establish that public relations has value to an organization. The concept of organization-public relationships plays a pivotal role in measuring public relations effectiveness at the organizational level (J. Grunig & Hung, 2002; Huang, 1997, 2001; Hung, 2002; Jo, 2003; Kim, 2000, 2001; Ledingham & Bruning, 2000; Yang & J. Grunig, 2005) and at the societal level (e.g., J. Grunig & L. Grunig, 1996, 2001; Ledingham, 2001). Griffin (2002) and Hutton, Goodman, Alexander, and Genest (2001) pointed out that public relations professionals have widely embraced "reputation management" to show the economic effects of public relations.

Purpose of the Study

The purpose of this study was to investigate the effects of organization-public relationships on organizational reputation from the perspective of publics. Several authors of the public relations literature have observed that scholars and public relations professionals have generally embraced different concepts to assess public relations effectiveness (e.g., Hutton et al., 2001; J. Grunig & Hung, 2002). Practitioners generally have attempted to prove the bottom-line value of public relations in terms of the effect of favorable reputation on the organization's financial performance, assuming the viable role of public relations in creating favorable reputation (J. Grunig & Hung, 2002). In contrast, scholars often have suggested that public relations obtains value by helping organizations reduce organizational costs, associated with issues, crises, regulation, litigation, and bad publicity, by means of cultivating quality relationships with strategic publics (L. Grunig, J. Grunig, & Dozier, 2002).

However, I contend that the concepts of organization-public relationships and organizational reputations are so closely intertwined that such divergent approaches are not necessary in demonstrating the value of public relations. Furthermore, I propose that an integrative framework involving both concepts is a more effective way to capture the nature of public relations effectiveness than separate focuses on each of the concepts.

Likewise, many public relations theorists have suggested that organization-public relationships affect organizational reputation (e.g., Coombs, 2000; Coombs & Holladay, 2001; J. Grunig, 1993; J. Grunig & Hung, 2002; L. Grunig, J. Grunig, & Dozier, 2002). For example, J. Grunig and Hung (2002) theorized the link between relationships and reputation: "... reputation is a direct product of organization-public relationships and relationships should be the focal variable for measuring the value of public relations" (p. 1). Along the same lines, L. Grunig, J. Grunig, and Dozier (2002) explained the results of the IABC Excellence study:

> In a nutshell, we show that the value of public relations comes from the
> relationships that communicators develop and maintain with publics. We show
> that reputation is a product of relationships and that the quality of relationships

and reputation result more from the behavior of the organization than from the
messages that communicators disseminate." (xi)

Despite these strong suggestions, minimal empirical research has dealt with the
effect of organization-public relationships on organizational reputation in public
relations. Therefore, even with recent developments in measuring public relations
effectiveness by focusing on either organization-public relationships (e.g., Huang, 1997,
2001; Hon & J. Grunig, 1999; Ledingham & Bruning, 2000) or organizational reputation
(e.g., Hutton, Goodman, Alexander, & Genest, 2001; Kim, 2001), I believe that there still
remains a critical research problem that public relations scholars should delve into: the
effect of organization-public relationships on organizational reputation. Thus, the purpose
of this study was to investigate the link between organization-public relationships and
organizational reputations. In particular, I aimed to examine the causal effects of
organization-public relationships on organizational reputation.

From the perspective of publics, this study proposed a causal model in which I
hypothesized that the quality of organization-public relationship outcomes and
organization-public relationship types (communal and exchange relationships) will
predict organizational reputation. In developing a causal model, I considered external
influences of additional variables such as communication behaviors of publics, predictor
variables for communication behaviors (problem recognition, constraint recognition, self
involvement, and communication involvement), familiarity, and experience with the
organizations studied. Methodologically, I used structural equation modeling (SEM) to
test the hypothesized causal paths between variables of interest in the proposed model

and to validate the model across four different types of the organizations that I intended to study.

To delimitate this study, I focused on the perspective of publics in modeling the link between organization-public relationships and organizational reputation. Public relations scholars have recommended that organization-public relationships be assessed by both sides of relational parties, between an organization and its publics (e.g., Broom & Dozier, 1990; Hon & J. Grunig, 1999; J. Grunig & Hunt, 1984; L. Grunig, J. Grunig, & Dozier, 2002).

Theoretical Framework

Major theoretical concepts, framing this study, included organization-public relationships, organizational reputation, cognitive representations, communication behaviors of publics, and familiarity and experience. First, since Ferguson (1984) called for more research on the concept of "relationships" between organizations and publics, public relations scholars and professional researchers have increasingly focused on organization-public relationships as their primary research area.

The IABC Excellence study provided another important influence on public relations research about relationship management. Before the IABC Excellence study, the question of how to demonstrate the value of public relations remained largely unanswered. The key finding of the IABC Excellence study suggested that public relations can be valuable to an organization by 1) "identifying the strategic publics that develop because of the consequences that organizations and publics have on each other" and 2) "using symmetrical communication programs to develop and maintain quality relationships with these strategic publics" (L. Grunig, J. Grunig, & Dozier, 2002, p. 548).

Likewise, for the last decade, many public relations scholars (e.g., Broom, Casey, & Ritchey, 2000; Hon & J. Grunig, 1999; Huang, 1997, 2001; Hung, 2002; J. Grunig & Hung, 2002; Ledingham & Bruning, 2000; L. Grunig, J. Grunig, & Dozier, 2002; Rhee, 2004; Toth, 2000) have defined the concept of (organization-public) relationships, identified dimensions of the concept, developed measurement instruments, and applied the concept in a variety of research contexts. Among them, I used theoretical concepts and measurement instruments of "organization-public relationship outcomes" (Huang, 1997; J. Grunig & Huang, 2000) and "organization-public relationship types" (Hon & J. Grunig, 1999) as important constructs in the hypothesized causal model. Public relations scholars have widely used such constructs (i.e., organization-public relationship outcomes and organization-public relationship types) to assess organization-public relationships in global contexts including the United States, Taiwan, China, and South Korea (e.g., Hon & J. Grunig, 1999; Han, 2002; Huang, 1997, 2001; Hung, 2002; Jo, 2003; J. Grunig & Hung, 2002; Jo & Kim, 2003; Yang & J. Grunig, 2005).

In conceptualizing organizational reputation, previous research of J. Grunig and Hung (2002) and Bromley (1993, 2000, 2002) influenced this current study mostly. In particular, such studies guided relevant theories, operationalization, and measurement instruments of the reputation concept for the current study. Unlike common closed-end measures of organizational reputation, this study used an open-end measure to investigate organizational reputation as "cognitive representations" that individual members of publics hold of the organizations studied. For the operationalization of organizational reputation, this study gauged the *distribution* and *valence* of cognitive representations in the open-end measure. Additionally, the perspectives of cognitive and social psychology

8

(e.g., Anderson, 1983, 1996, 2000; Ashcraft, 2002; Carlston & Smith, 1996; Smith, 1998) suggested useful theoretical frameworks in studying elements of cognitive representations and the mechanism of human memory. Additionally, I found that person impression research in psychology (e.g., Bromley, 1993; Hamilton, 1981; Hamilton, Katz, & Leirer, 1980) can be analogical to research on organizational reputation.

Business scholars (e.g., Fombrun, 1996; Fombrun & Gardberg, 2000; Fombrun & Shanley, 1990; Fombrun & Van Riel, 1997, 2003) have studied corporate reputation and its precursors, such as familiarity of strategic constituents with a corporation (e.g., Fombrun & Van Riel, 2003) and organizational visibility in the media (e.g., Deephouse, 2000; Fombrun & Shanley, 1990; Rindova & Kotha, 2001; Pollack & Rindova, 2002). In the hypothesized model, I posited organizational reputation to be predicted by familiarity and experience with the organizations studied.

In addition, J. Grunig and Huang's (2000) chapter shed light on an important antecedent of organization-public relationships: "communication behaviors of publics with organizations." Along with familiarity and experience of publics, I proposed that communication behaviors of publics be one of the important precursors of organization-public relationships from the perspective of publics. J. Grunig's situational theory of publics (e.g., J. Grunig, 1997; J. Grunig & Hunt, 1984) served as the foundation of indicators to measure communication behaviors as well as predictor variables of communication behaviors in this study.

With regard to organization-public relationship types, I have consulted the literature of public relations, such as Hon and J. Grunig (1999) and L. Grunig, J. Grunig, and Dozier (2002), which suggests that a communal relationship is an important predictor of quality organization-public relationship outcomes. In this study, I posited that two types of organization-public relationships, including exchange relationships and communal relationships, predict the quality of organization-public relationship outcomes and organizational reputation.

In summary, based on the above theoretical frameworks, I hypothesized a causal model between organization-public relationships and organizational reputation. In the model, I hypothesized that the quality of organization-public relationships affects organizational reputation and that such a causal link was also influenced by additional factors such as organization-public relationship types, communication behaviors of publics, familiarity, and experience.

Method and Research Design

For this study, I used the results of a survey for data analysis. I selected a metropolitan city in South Korea, Gwangju city, as the sampling universe because of convenience and economy of data collection. I also limited the sampling area to one city to enhance homogeneity among survey respondents (Bromley, 1993, 2000). Bromley suggested that a researcher should assure homogeneity of survey respondents to study organizational reputation as collective representations of an organization.

For a method of data collection, I used quota sampling to mitigate sampling bias caused by nonprobability sampling. Quota sampling ensures representations of sampling elements of interest in the final sample although it is still nonprobability sampling (Nardi, 2003). In this study, I did not attempt to generalize the findings beyond the immediate sample I studied. Thus, I consider that quota sampling can be a relevant method for the purpose of this study: analyzing theory-derived relations among constructs of interest in a causal model, rather than describing data for a specific sample.

I initially planned to collect around 300 questionnaires. 16 research assistants (after four assistants ended participation) gathered questionnaires from participants following the assigned segments of the quota. Returned questionnaires totaled 305 with a 45 percent response rate: 684 potential participants were contacted; 305 questionnaires were finally collected. The original sample was reduced to 294 ($N = 294$) by 11 participants who did not sign the consent form in the returned questionnaires.

I selected participants between the ages of 20 and 49 years, replicating the proportions of sex and age in the population of the survey. I chose these criteria because I considered that publics within this age range are most likely to have experience with the organizations studied and hence to be able to answer questions in the questionnaire. After two pretests and a survey, I selected four South Korean-based organizations to study (Samsung Electronics, Sony Korea, the Korea Football Association, and the Korean National Red Cross). The purpose of organization selection was to diversify types of the organizations studied to validate the hypothesized model across different types of organizations.

This study departed from previous research in that I investigated the causal effects of organization-public relationships on organizational reputation. Despite the significance of the research problem, there has been minimal research investigating effects of organization-public relationships on organizational reputation in the literature of public relations, except for Coombs and Holladay (2001), J. Grunig and Hung (2002), Hagan (2003), Lyon and Cameron (2004), and Yang and J. Grunig (2005). Although these studies contributed to a body of knowledge in public relations, I consider that these scholars did not test causal effects of (organization-public) relationships on (organizational) reputation, except for Coombs and Holladay's (2001) experimental study and Yang and J. Grunig's (2005) study using structural equation modeling. In addition, only few studied (J. Grunig and Hung, 2002; Yang & J. Grunig, 2005) studied communication behaviors of publics, which I consider are key antecedents of organization-public relationships and organizational reputation as J. Grunig and Huang (2000) pointed out.

I considered that key constructs in this study, such as organization-public relationships and organizational reputation, are difficult to manipulate in experimental research. Experimental research is generally not feasible, if not completely impossible, to study "behavioral" relationships built between an organizations and its publics. Consequently, Coombs and Holladay's (2002) research was limited to effects of a symbolic approach to crisis situation on organizational reputation; they found significant effects of only *negative* relationship history on organizational reputation.

In this study, I used structural equation modeling (SEM), which makes it possible to test causal links between variables of interest using "nonexperimental" data (Kline, 1998). Also, by including experience of survey participants and their communication behaviors in the model, I reflected past behavioral interactions between the organizations studied and the participants, which took a step further after Yang and J. Grunig's (2005) study.

Significance of the Study

This proposed study should have the following implications for the study and practice of public relations.

This study can contribute to a theoretical body of knowledge in public relations about organization-public relationships and organizational reputation. Public relations scholars and practitioners alike have focused on relationships and reputation to demonstrate public relations effectiveness; several public relations theoreticians suggested a close link between such concepts. Nonetheless, there has been minimal research on this topic in the literature of public relations. This study can have value by suggesting empirical findings on the effect of (organization-public) relationships on (org) reputation.

Additionally, the findings of this study can contribute to public relations practice. Recently, public relations professionals have widely embraced reputation management to show the economic value of their practice, whereas scholars have generally emphasized relationship management within the framework of strategic management of public relations. Meanwhile, even if behavioral relationship outcomes (e.g., trust, satisfaction, and commitment) often serve as critical dimensions of common reputation measures, management scholars tend to marginalize public relations as a technical function used to manipulate symbolic reputations through media relations (e.g., Dowling, 2001; Fombrun, 1996). I consider that public relations professionals will find the results of this study useful in understanding the effect of organization-public relationships on organizational reputation as well as precursors of such concepts from the perspective of publics.

In next sections of this study, I will define and explain key theories and concepts guiding this study. First, I will describe public relations research on public relations effectiveness including the IABC Excellence study and other research on the topic of relationships and reputation. This section will be the introductory part of the conceptualization chapter in the sense that I will discuss theoretical and practical reasons why research on relationships and reputations has emerged to be dominant in the field of public relations. Then, I will explicate the notion of "effectiveness" at different levels of analysis. More specifically, I will begin this section by 1) describing why public relations scholars and practitioners alike have long searched for key concepts to demonstrated public relations effectiveness, 2) showing definitions of organizational effectiveness, 3) discussing levels of analysis in public relations effectiveness, 4) reviewing variables explaining public relations effectiveness found in the Excellence study, and finally 5) discussing the findings of public relations research on public relations effectiveness other than the Excellence study.

Secondly, I will define the notions of "strategic publics" and the "symmetrical model of public relations" because I consider that such notions play critical roles in conceptualizing organization-public relationships and organizational reputation. As several scholars (e.g., Hon & J. Grunig, 1999; L. Grunig et al., 2002) have suggested, organizations need to cultivate good relationships with their strategic publics using symmetrical communication to demonstrate the value of public relations.

In this section, I also will discuss the distinction between stakeholders and publics in terms of communication behaviors; I will explain the situational theory of publics and models of public relations in a brief manner. Variables of the situational theory of publics serve as indicators and predictors of communication behaviors of publics in this study.

Thus, explaining each independent and dependent variable of the theory is necessary to elaborate constructs of the proposed model.

Third, before giving details about organization-public relationships and organizational reputation, I will describe how scholars and professional researchers have explained the value of such concepts for public relations effectiveness. In this section, I will discuss common assumptions in reputation research, non-financial values of organization-public relationships, and the contrast of symbolic and behavioral relationships.

In conceptualizing organization-public relationships, first, I will define the terms "publics," "organizations," "relationships" respectively to explicate the notion of "organization-public relationships." Then, I will explain attributes of the concept of relationships. Next, I will explain models of organization-public relationships and elaborate each part of J. Grunig and Huang's (2000) model, such as antecedents of organization-public relationships, relational cultivation strategies, and relationship outcomes. Finally, I will explicate indicators of organization-public relationship outcomes (control mutuality, trust, commitment, and relational satisfaction) and organization-public relationship types (communal and exchange relationships). I will also introduce additional relationship types suggested by Hung (2002).

Likewise, in conceptualizing organizational reputation, I will define the concept of "reputation" from several perspectives, explain the nature and attributes of reputation, discuss the distinction between primary and secondary reputation as well as the distinction between reputation and similar concepts (e.g., image, identity, and impression), and finally summarize measurement issues facing most current reputation measures (e.g., sampling issues, reliability and validity in measurement, and problems in a reputation ranking system).

Then, I will explain a new measure of reputation based on cognitive representations shared by publics, suggested by Bromley (1993, 2000, 2002) and J. Grunig and Hung (2002), by using definitions of "cognition" and "representations" respectively to explicate the notion of "cognitive representation." Additionally, I will describe relevant concepts related to cognitive representations, such as associative network models of representations, spreading activation in cognitive representations, and components in impression formation.

Finally, to explain theoretical reasons for the links among constructs in the model, I will first look at theories and empirical findings on the link between organization-public relationships and organizational reputation from the perspectives of public relations, social psychology, and business. After I discuss theoretical links among the quality of organization-public relationship outcomes, organization-public relationship types, and organizational reputation, I will explain antecedents of such constructs as communication behaviors, familiarity, and experience with an organization. Then, I will summarize research questions and hypotheses.

CHAPTER II: Conceptualization

Public Relations Effectiveness

Assessment of Public Relations Value

Public relations professionals and scholars have long been searching for key concepts to assess the value of public relations. According to J. Grunig and Hung (2002), "Throughout the history of public relations, practitioners and scholars have attempted to identify and name a single concept that defines the value of public relations" (p. 2). Likewise, L. Grunig, J. Grunig, and Dozier (2002) also said: "For at least 25 years, public relations professionals and researchers have struggled to develop measures that would establish that public relations is effective or adds value" (p. 90).

Public relations professionals have attempted to measure public relations effectiveness as they increasingly have faced the challenge of demonstrating the value of public relations to their organizations (Hon, 1997). For example, Kim (2001) described practitioners' challenge from their organizations as follows: "CEOs' demands for accountability [of public relations] have become more tenacious than ever" (p. 5) because of recent budget cuts in the public relations industry. Ledingham and Bruning (1998) put it as follows: "Scholars have the luxury to deliberate the nature of public relations but practitioners deal on a daily basis with the immediate problem of justifying the value of their programs" (p. 61).

However, despite the critical nature of demonstrating public relations value at the organizational level, a common belief is that the value of public relations is difficult to measure since most of its elements are intangible. Moreover, the function of public relations traditionally has been considered to be a means of reducing costs rather than as a means of generating organizational revenues.

L. Grunig, J. Grunig, and Dozier (2002) described the dilemma of assessing public relations value in detail:

> The question of the value of public relations has been of great concern to professional communicators for many years because of the perception among both communicators and other managers that public relations is an intangible management function in comparison with other functions whose value can be described, measured, and evaluated through systematic research. Because of its intangibility, public relations often has been believed to suffer at budget time and particularly during financial crises, because there is no way to demonstrate its worth. (p. 90)

Consequently, public relations scholars and professionals have long strived to seek out the key concept to demonstrate public relations value and to develop measures of the concept (e.g., Hon & J. Grunig, 1999; Huang, 1997, 2001; Hung, 2002; Hutton, 1999; Hutton, Goodman, Alexander, & Genest, 2001; Jo, 2003; Kim, 2000, 2001; J. Grunig & Hung, 2002; L. Grunig, J. Grunig, & Dozier, 2002; Ledingham & Bruning, 2000). J. Grunig and Hung (2002) illustrated this trend as "the search for the Holy Grail" (p. 2) because the search for such key concepts has become prevalent in public relations. J. Grunig and Hung added that public relations has adopted one faddish term after another, beginning with publicity in the early history of public relations: "First it was image, then identity and image together. Now the popular terms are reputation and brand" (p. 2). The result of "the search for the Holy Grail" (J. Grunig & Hung, 2002, p. 2) appears, at this time, to be that organization-public relationships and organizational

reputation have become the central focus in the study and practice of public relations

(Bruning & Ledingham, 1999; J. Grunig & Hung, 2002). Additionally, as leading

scholars defined public relations as a management function in textbooks of public

relations (e.g., Cutlip, Center, & Broom, 2000; J. Grunig & Hunt, 1984), scholars and

professionals now regularly use the terms "relationship management" or "reputation

management" to describe public relations practice.

More specifically, first, about relationships, the concept of relationships plays a

pivotal role in measuring the value of public relations at the organizational level (J.

Grunig & Hung, 2002; Huang, 1997, 2001; Hung, 2002; Jo, 2003; Kim, 2000, 2001;

Ledingham & Bruning, 2000) and at the societal level (e.g., J. Grunig & L. Grunig, 1996,

2001; Ledingham, 2001). For example, Broom et al. (2002) described the popularity of

the relationship concept in the field of public relations as follows: "Many scholars and

practitioners say that public relations is all about building and maintaining an

organization's relationships with its publics" (p. 4). Also, Ledingham and Bruning (2000)

maintained that relational management now is the dominant "paradigm" in public

relations scholarship and practice since Ferguson (1984), about two decades ago, called

for a paradigmatic shift of public relations research to relationships between

organizations and publics.

Secondly, about reputation, Griffin (2002) and Hutton et al. (2001) have pointed

out that public relations professionals have widely embraced "reputation management" to

demonstrate the economic viability of the public relations function. Specifically, Kim

(2000, 2001) maintained that the accountability of public relations at the organizational level could be demonstrated well by showing the effect of reputation on financial performance of the organization.

Indeed, public relations practitioners advocate reputation management more than professionals in any other field. According to Hutton et al. (2001), "… major international public relations agencies have embraced the concept of reputation management in varying degrees" (p. 248). Deephouse (2002) depicted how rampant reputation management is in public relations practice. According to Deephouse, among 31 members of the Reputation Institute, public relations firms make up the "majority." Members of the Institute other than public relations firms include two corporate advertising agencies, one brand consulting service, and four market research firms. This may indicate that the profession of public relations drives the development of reputation measures and research.

In next section of this chapter, I will review the results of the IABC Excellence study. Business scholars have studied the reputation concept and developed measures of reputation. In the field of public relations, it was the IABC Excellence study that first elucidated factors contributing to public relations effectiveness and, specifically, the importance of relationship management.

An Overview of the IABC Excellence Study

Before the IABC research project on excellence in public relations and communication management (called the IABC Excellence study), the question of how to demonstrate the value of public relations was largely unanswered. The IABC Excellence study was a landmark study on public relations effectiveness; it continued for about 15 years and was conducted by leading researchers and practitioners in public relations.

The key findings of the IABC Excellence study suggested that public relations can provide the value to an organization by 1) "identifying the strategic publics that develop because of the consequences that organizations and publics have on each other" and 2) "using symmetrical communication programs to develop and maintain quality relationships with these strategic publics" (L. Grunig, J. Grunig, & Dozier, 2002, p. 548). For this reason, after I review the findings of the Excellence study briefly, I will elaborate the notions of "strategic publics" and "symmetrical model of public relations" and discuss how they are related to relationship management.

The IABC Research Foundation initially requested a research proposal on "how, why, and to what extent communication affects the achievement of organizational objectives" (L. Grunig, J. Grunig, & Dozier, 2002, p. ix). According to L. Grunig, J. Grunig, and Dozier (2002), the research team expanded this question into two major research questions to guide the Excellence study:

1. The "effectiveness" question: How does public relations make an organization more effective, and how much is that contribution worth economically?

2. The "excellence" question: What are the characteristics of a public relations function that are most likely to make an organization effective? (pp. 4-5)

Next, I will summarize the key approaches of organizational effectiveness identified by the Excellence research team, discuss levels of analysis of public relations effectiveness, and introduce factors contributing to public relations effectiveness found in the Excellence study.

Organizational Effectiveness

First, to answer the "effectiveness" question, the Excellence research team identified the following four approaches from organizational theory (J. Grunig and Huang, 2000)[1]:

1. The *goal attainment* approach: Organizations are effective when they meet their goals. The goal-attainment approach is limited, however, because it cannot explain effectiveness when an organization has multiple goals and different stakeholders of an organization have conflicting goals. It also cannot explain the role of the environment[2] in organizational effectiveness.

2. The *systems* approach: Organizations are effective when they survive in their environment and successfully bring in resources necessary for their survival. The systems approach, therefore, adds the environment to the equation of organizational effectiveness, but it is limited because survival is an extremely weak goal. The systems approach also defines the environment in vague terms. It does not answer the question of how an organization determines what elements of the environment are important for its success.

3. The *strategic constituencies* approach: This approach puts meaning into the term 'environment' by specifying the parts of the environment that are crucial for organizational survival and success. Strategic constituencies are the

---

[1] L. Grunig, J. Grunig, and Ehling (1992) explained theories of organizational effectiveness in more detail (pp. 70-80).

[2] According to Daft (2001), organizations are "social entities that are goal-oriented, deliberately structured activity systems linked to the external environment" (p. 200). Daft's definition of organizations suggests the reason why the role of the environment is critical in explicating the concept of organizations.

elements of the environment whose opposition or support can threaten the organization's goals or help to attain them. Taken broadly the environment is both external and internal so employee groups and management functions can be strategic constituencies as much as can external groups.

4. The *competing values* approach: This approach provides a bridge between strategic constituencies and goal. It states that an organization must incorporate the values of strategic constituencies into its goals so the organization attains the goals of most value to its strategic constituencies. Thus, different organizations with different goals, and their effectiveness will be defined in different ways. (pp. 30-31)

Organizational theorist Daft (2001) defined *organizational effectiveness* as "the degree to which an organization realizes its goals" (p. 26). Daft differentiated "effectiveness" from "efficiency." According to him, "Effectiveness is a broad concept. It implicitly takes into consideration a range of variables at both the organizational and departmental levels. Effectiveness evaluates the extent to which multiple goals—whether official or operative—are attained" (p. 26). For this reason, I consider that Daft's definition of organizational effectiveness falls into the *goal attainment* approach identified by the IABC research team. To explain how the term *organizational efficiency* is different from organizational effectiveness, Daft added: "Efficiency is a more limited concept that pertains to the internal workings of the organization. Organizational efficiency is the amount of resources used to produce a unit of output. It can be measured as the ratio of inputs to outputs" (p. 26).

After identifying four approaches to organizational effectiveness, the Excellence research team conducted both quantitative and qualitative research across several countries and extracted factors contributing to effective public relations (i.e., the answer to the "Excellence" question).

Before I introduce characteristics of excellent public relations, I will explain levels of analysis in public relations effectiveness. Levels of analysis are an important issue in discussing both organizational effectiveness and public relations effectiveness. This is because, according to L. Grunig, J. Grunig, and Dozier (2002), "Effectiveness at a lower level contributes to effectiveness at higher levels, but organizations cannot be said to be truly effective unless they have value at the highest of these levels" (p. 8). In other words, levels of analysis in public relations effectiveness can suggest that, to be effective, organizations should engage in quality relationship management at the societal level. Public relations itself can be effective by contributing to quality relationship management at the program and functional levels and also be eventually effective at the organizational and societal levels by means of such contribution. I believe that this is why relationship management is important in demonstrating the value of public relations.

Levels of Analysis in Public Relations Effectiveness

To clarify the ways to demonstrate the value of public relations, L. Grunig, J. Grunig, and Dozier (2002) explained levels of analysis in public relations effectiveness at the program level, the functional level, the organizational level, and the societal level as follows:

1. The *program* level: Individual communication programs such as media relations, community relations, or customer relations are successful when they

affect the cognitions, attitudes, and behaviors of both publics and members of the organization—that is, the cognitive, attitudinal, and behavioral relationships among organizations and their publics.

2. The *functional* level: The public relations or communication function as a whole can be audited by comparing the structure and processes of the department or departments that implement the function with the best practices of the public relations function in other organizations or with theoretical principles from scholarly research.

3. The *organizational* level: To show that public relations has value to the organization, we must be able to show that effective communication programs and functions contribute to organizational effectiveness.

4. The *societal* level: Organizations have an impact beyond their own bottom line. They also affect other organizations, individuals, and publics in society. As a result, organizations cannot be said to be effective unless they also are socially responsible; and public relations can be said to have value when it contributes to the social responsibility of organizations. (pp. 91-92)

L. Grunig et al.'s (2002) discussion of levels of analysis in public relations effectiveness suggests another critical point to consider. According to L. Grunig, J. Grunig, and Dozier (2002), "The program level has been the traditional focus of evaluative research in public relations. However, effective communication programs may or may not contribute to organizational effectiveness; many operate independently of the organization's mission and goals" (p. 91). This means that public relations effectiveness at the program level alone cannot ensure the value of public relations at the organizational level, although effectiveness at the program level is the starting point of effectiveness. Thus, for public relations to have value to organizations, public relations professionals need to consider higher levels of analysis in effectiveness—relationship management with strategic publics—than short-term outputs or outcomes at the program level.

Based on the findings of the Excellence study, Hon and J. Grunig (1999) suggested that the value of public relations is in "relationships" that an organization develops and maintains with strategic publics. This is because organizations become effective when achieving their goals; by means of quality relationships, organization can achieve goals because they choose goals valued by strategic publics (J. Grunig & Hung, 2002; L. Grunig, J. Grunig, & Dozier, 2002).

In addition to the focus on the value of public relations at the organizational level, public relations scholars have also extended the value of public relations to society in general based on the relationship concept (e.g., J. Grunig & L. Grunig, 1996, 2001; Ledingham, 2001; Starck & Kruckeberg, 2001). Starck and Kruckeberg (2000), for example, called for a *communitarian* approach in public relations. They explained that the role of public relations is to restore and maintain a sense of community that "had been lost because of the development of modern means of communication/transportation" (p. 58). They suggested this view initially in Kruckeberg and Starck (1988) and reaffirmed this view in Starck and Kruckeberg (2001). Also, from a study of government-citizen relationships, Ledingham (2001) found that public relations contributes to community by cultivating quality relationships.

I consider that Starck and Kruckeberg's (2001) "a sense of community," or Ledingham's (2001) "community building," fundamentally begin with the idea of a relationship: An organization often has consequences beyond its own bottom-line and affects general members of society through relationships (J. Grunig, 2000; J. Grunig & L. Grunig, 2001). Also, in a reciprocal sense, organizations can be effective when their publics have good relationships with them—when publics trust organizations and their products or services, when publics are satisfied with organizational performance, when publics commit themselves to relationships with an organization, when publics agree with the degree of mutual control in interactions, and so forth.

Because of quality relationship management between an organization and its publics, effective organizations can select goals valued by publics; consequently, they can achieve their goals because publics support them (Hon & J. Grunig, 1999). However, as J. Grunig and Hung (2002) pointed out, "... ineffective organizations cannot achieve their goals, at least in part, because their publics do not support and typically oppose management efforts to achieve what publics consider illegitimate goals" (p. 10). Thus, as J. Grunig and L. Grunig (2001) concluded, for an organization to be effective, it should behave ethically and be socially responsible, which means that an organization engages in "quality relationship management" with its publics.

Based on the findings of the literature on organizational effectiveness and conceptualization of levels of analysis in public relations effectiveness, the Excellence research team (1992) concluded: Effective organizations achieve their goals and public relations has value to an organization when it helps an organization select and achieve organizational goals that create less conflicts with strategic constituencies in the

environment (J. Grunig & Repper, 1992; J. Grunig & Huang, 2000).

In next section, I will introduce the empirical findings that the Excellence

research team found about public relations effectiveness.

Excellent Characteristics of Public Relations

To find characteristics of public relations effectiveness, the Excellence research

team conducted empirical research across several countries, including the United States,

Canada, and the United Kingdom. The research team initially identified 14 characteristics

of excellent public relations programs and three effects of those programs (L. Grunig, J.

Grunig, & Dozier, 2002)[3]:

    I. *Program level*

       1. Managed strategically.

   II. *Departmental level*

       2. A single or integrated public relations department.

       3. Separate function from marketing.

       4. Direct reporting relationship to senior management.

       5. Two-way symmetrical model.

       6. Senior public relations person in the managerial role.

       7. Potential for excellent public relations, as indicated by:

          a) Knowledge of symmetrical model.

          b) Knowledge of managerial role.

          c) Academic training in public relations.

---

[3] This is adopted from Table 1.1, titled "Characteristics of Excellent Public Relations
Program, in L. Grunig, J. Grunig, and Dozier (2002, p. 9).

      d) Professionalism.

    8. Equal opportunity for men and women in public relations.

III. *Organizational level*

    9. Worldview for public relations in the organization reflects the two-way symmetrical model.

    10. Public relations director has power in or with the dominant coalition.

    11. Participative rather than authoritarian organizational culture.

    12. Symmetrical system of internal communication.

    13. Organic rather than mechanical organizational structure.

    14. Turbulent, complex environment with pressure from activist groups.

IV. *Effects of excellent public relations*

    1. Programs meet communication objectives.

    2. Reduce costs of regulation, pressure, and litigation.

    3. Job satisfaction is high among employees. (p. 9)

Dozier, L. Grunig, and J. Grunig (1995), in the second book of the Excellence study series, summarized these characteristics of excellence into three factors: 1) departmental expertise in sophisticated communication practices, 2) shared expectation with the dominant coalition about communication, and 3) qualities of organizational culture.

J. Grunig and Repper (1992) suggested that such characteristics of excellent public relations help the public relations function to be effective as well as contribute to overall organizational effectiveness. In summary, the key attributes of excellent public relations include the following practices: 1) identifying "strategic publics" from the environment and 2) practicing a "symmetrical" model of public relations to cultivate

quality relationships with these strategic publics (L. Grunig, J. Grunig, & Dozier, 2002).

After the Excellence study shed light on public relations effectiveness, a number

of scholars have extended the Excellence theory to specific topics of research. Next, I

will review other research on public relations effectiveness in a brief manner.

Other Research on Public Relations Effectiveness

Many public relations scholars have studied public relations effectiveness in a

variety of contexts: for example, conflict resolution (Plowman, 1995, 1998), relationship

measurement and the implication of organization-public relationships for conflict

resolution (Huang, 1997, 2001), models of public relations in global settings (Kim &

Hon, 1998; Rhee, 2002; Sriramesh, Kim, & Takasaki, 1999), and global public relations

(Wakefield, 1997, 2000). Some scholars (e.g., Hon, 1997, 1998; Gordon & Kelly, 1999;

Kim, 2000, 2001; Sriramesh, J. Grunig, & Dozier, 1996) have directly focused their

studies on public relations effectiveness.

By exploring public relations effectiveness in qualitative research, Hon (1997)

found that practitioners and organization heads believe that effective public relations can

be defined in many ways. In general, the results of her research supported the Excellence

theory as follows:

When probed for specific examples, practitioners and CEOs easily could associate

effectiveness in public relations with value-added contributions for their

organization. This seamless connection suggests extraordinary implications for

scholars and practitioners. Although the purpose of this research was not to test a

specific theory, these anecdotal reports provide rich information that augments J.

Grunig et al.'s (1992) conceptualization of public relations' impact on

organizations. (p. 26)

Hon (1998), then, explored how practitioners evaluate public relations as a means of

demonstrating public relations effectiveness to their organizations. She found that many

practitioners conduct informal evaluation because of lack of resources and difficulty.

Sriramesh, J. Grunig, and Dozier (1996) studied the link between organizational

culture and excellence in public relations. Sriramesh et al. found that participatory culture

and the nature of internal communication in public relations are strongly correlated,

which suggests "symmetrical internal communication may be the entry point for public

relations practitioners to affect organizational culture and, in turn, to begin an incremental

process toward excellence in public relations" (p. 230).

As another extension of the Excellence study, Gordon and Kelly (1999) also tried

to identify characteristics predicting which public relations departments are most likely to

contribute to organizational effectiveness. They found that public relations effectiveness

was correlated with departments having high potential to practice the two-way

symmetrical model, enact a managerial role, and participate in strategic planning.

Additionally, they also found that traditional craft models, such as one-way models and

the technician role, is a foundation for effective public relations.

As I noted previously, the key finding of the Excellence study was that public

relations can have value to organizations when it helps organizations cultivate quality

relationships with strategic publics using symmetrical public relations programs. For this

reason, I will discuss the notions of "strategic publics" and the "symmetrical model of public relations" in the following section. To define strategic publics, I will first explain the terms "stakeholders" and "publics" and discuss the situational theory of publics.

The situational theory of publics is useful to identify strategic publics, first, because active publics are in general strategic publics. That is, active publics are most likely to affect an organization's goal achievement and to be affected by organizational outcomes. Secondly, the situational theory of publics helps to predict communication behaviors of publics and hence to identify active publics (i.e., publics with active communication behaviors).

Strategic Publics and Symmetrical Public Relations

In this book, I conceptualized *strategic* publics as "those publics who maintain *active* communication behaviors to deal with their problems and those with whom an organization needs to develop relationships" (Hon & J. Grunig, 1999; J. Grunig & Hunt, 1984; J. Grunig et al., 1992; J. Grunig & Hung, 2002; L. Grunig, J. Grunig, & Dozier, 2002). This is because, as I discussed previously, an organization needs to develop quality relationships with publics engaging in active communication behaviors to attain organizational goals.

I will define the term "publics" prior to explaining characteristics of *strategic* publics. To this end, first, I will discuss the difference between stakeholders and publics briefly. According to J. Grunig and L. Grunig (2000) and J. Grunig and Repper (1992), the terms "stakeholders" and "publics" are often used synonymously in the public relations literature. However, J. Grunig and Repper (1992) explained that a subtle difference between these terms "helps to understand strategic planning of public relations" (p. 125).

Stakeholders

The key characteristic of stakeholders is the *linkage* with an organization resulting from *consequences*, or "stakes" (Clarkson, 1991; Coombs, 2000; Daft, 2001; Freeman, 1984; J. Grunig & Repper, 1992; J. Grunig & L. Grunig, 2000; Wood, 1991). J. Grunig and Repper (1992) pointed out that stakeholders and an organization are linked because "they and the organization have consequences on each other" (p. 126). J. Grunig and L. Grunig (2000) defined stakeholders as "those who are affected by decisions of an organization, or those who affect the organization by their decisions" (p. 312). Similarly, Daft (2001) defined a stakeholder as "any group within or outside an organization that has a stake in the organization's performance" (p. 30).

About the implications of stakeholders for an organization's management, Coombs (2000) said as follows: "It is taken for granted in the management literature that organizations have stakeholders and that the management of these stakeholders affect the organization's viability" (p. 75).

Publics

J. Grunig and Hunt (1984) defined a public as "a group of people who face a problem, are divided on its solution, and organize to discuss it" (p. 145). The term "publics" refers to people in a more *active* stage of interactions with an organization than "stakeholders" (J. Grunig & Repper, 1992; J. Grunig and Huang, 2000). In other words, publics are some "active" stakeholders who organize to deal with problems through their active communication behaviors; publics engage in active communication based on their situations (J. Grunig & Hunt, 1984). Citing Blumer (1946, 1948), Dewey (1927), and J. Grunig and Hunt (1984), Vasquez and Taylor (2001) also explained, "the term public generally refers to a situational collection of individuals who emerge and organize in response to a problem" (p. 140).

J. Grunig and Hunt (1984) explained more details about Blumer and Dewey's definition of a public. According to J. Grunig and Hunt, Blumer defined a public "as a group of people who 1) are confronted by an issue, 2) are divided in their ideas as to how to meet the issue, and 3) engage in discussion over the issue" (p. 143). Likewise, Dewey defined a public "as a group of people who 1) face a similar problem, 2) recognize that the problem exists, and 3) organize to do something about the problem" (J. Grunig & Hunt, 1984, pp. 143-144).

In explicating the concept of publics, J. Grunig and Hunt (1984) concluded: 1) "behavior is the key" and 2) "consequences create publics" (p. 144). According to them, "... publics consist of individuals who detect the same problems and plan similar behaviors to deal with those problems" (p. 144). Organizational consequences create problems and lead publics to form. In turn, organizations have a public relations problem because of the presence of such publics.

Distinction Between Stakeholders and Publics

J. Grunig and Repper (1992) clearly distinguished publics from stakeholders as follows:

> People are stakeholders because they are in a category affected by decisions of an organization or if their decisions affect the organization. Many people in a category of stakeholders—such as employees or residents of a community—are passive. The stakeholders who are or become more aware and active can be described as publics." (p. 125)

More specifically, J. Grunig and Repper (1992) conceptualized *three stages of strategic management of public relations* in their model:

1. The *stakeholder* stage: An organization has a relationship with stakeholders when the behavior of the organization or of a stakeholder has consequences on the other.

2. The *public* stage: Publics form when stakeholders recognize one or more of the consequences as a problem and organize to do something about it or them.

3. The *issue* stage: Publics organize and create issues out of the problems they perceived. (p. 124)

In conclusion, publics are different from stakeholders in that they have active communication behaviors to deal with their problems with organizations and hence are more conducive to organization-public relationship building because of their "repeated communications" with an organization (Rhee, 2004).

Next, I will elaborate the situational theory of publics. J. Grunig and Hunt (1984) described the purpose of the theory: "Grunig has developed such a theory to explain when and how people communicate and when communications aimed at people are most likely to be effective" (p. 148). Therefore, I used this theory to model causes of active communication behaviors of publics as well as indicators of such communication behaviors in this study. Many public relations scholars found the theory useful to predict communication behaviors of publics (e.g., Heath, Bradshaw, Lee, 2002; Major, 1998).

Situational Theory of Publics

To identify situational attributes of *active* publics, J. Grunig developed a situational theory of publics based on decades of research (J. Grunig & Hunt, 1984). J.

Grunig's situational theory has been used to explain when publics are most likely to communicate actively with organizations.[4]

As a result, I believe that the theory accounts for a critical aspect of the antecedents for the formation of organization-public relationships, in particular from the perspective of publics. This is because communication behaviors of publics are required to *initiate* and *cultivate* relationships between publics and an organization. In other words, to form and maintain a solid relationship with an organization, a member of a public needs to have active communication behavior (Rhee, 2004). An organization, in a reciprocal manner, is more likely to cultivate quality relationships with these active publics because of potential consequences on the organization's ability to achieve its goals (J. Grunig & Huang, 2000).

In the situational theory of publics, J. Grunig (e.g., 1978, 1983a, 1983b, 1989a, 1997; J. Grunig & Childers (a.k.a., Hon), 1988; J. Grunig & Hunt, 1984) identified three independent variables that predict communication behaviors of publics: 1) *problem recognition*: the degree to which people detect that something should be done about a situation and stop to think about what to do, 2) *constraint recognition*: the extent to which people perceive obstacles in a situation that limit their ability to do anything about the situation, and 3) *level of involvement*: the extent to which people connect themselves with a situation (J. Grunig & Hunt, 1984; J. Grunig, 1997).

---

[4] J. Grunig and Hunt explained how publics can be segmented on the basis of their situational behaviors: "... communication behaviors of publics can be best understood by measuring how members of publics perceive situations in which they are affected by such organizational consequences as pollution, quality of products, hiring practices, or plant closings" (p. 148).

In theorizing a situational theory of publics, J. Grunig considered the search for information as a dependent variable and has attempted to identify what kinds of decision situations would motivate people to engage in different types of communication behavior. He theorized two types of communication behaviors: *information seeking* (i.e., active search for information) as active communication behavior in genuine decision-making situations and *information processing* (i.e., passive attention to information) in nondecision situations. Publics are more likely to be active in communication when they perceive *high* level of involvement, *high* problem recognition, and *low* constraint recognition (J. Grunig, 1997).

Among three independent variables of communication behaviors, J. Grunig first identified problem recognition using Dewey's (1938) concept of problem recognition. Then, he added constraint recognition and finally Krugman's (1965) level of involvement.

Problem Recognition

J. Grunig used problem recognition to explain the reasons for people's rational behavior, or genuine decision behavior, and habitual behavior depending on situations. Dewey defined problem recognition as "the perception that something is lacking in a situation" (J. Grunig & Repper, 1992, p. 135). People engage in rational behavior when they recognize a situation as problematic; otherwise, they engage in habitual behavior (J. Grunig and Repper, 1992).

About communication behaviors, J. Grunig theorized that, when people face habitual situations, they would need less information than in genuine situations. In other words, people are more likely to *actively* search for information in *genuine* decision situations. When publics recognize problems but lack information, or have little previous decision-making experience, they would exercise rational behavior and search for information.

However, J. Grunig suggested that, even after recognizing problems, publics would not be likely to engage in active communication behaviors if they recognize that their ability to solve the problem is limited, which is the second variable in the theory.

Constraint Recognition

The concept of constraint recognition refers to a situation in which people's active communication behavior is discouraged by barriers to their behaviors. According to J. Grunig and Hunt (1984), people do not engage in active communication behavior to solve their problems because they believe they can do little in the situation; people are less likely to engage in active communication behavior when they believe they have limited personal efficacy to solve problems.

After constraint recognition, J. Grunig added a third variable, level of involvement, as an independent variable explaining communication behavior. When people believe organizational behaviors could affect them (i.e., a genuine decision situation), J. Grunig theorized that people would actively search for information.

Level of Involvement

As the last independent variable, J. Grunig (1976a, 1979; J. Grunig & Disbrow, 1977) added Krugman's (1965) concept of level of involvement in his situational theory to explain active information search in genuine decision situation but passive attention to information in nondecision situations.

J. Grunig (1997) pointed out that high problem recognition and low constraint recognition will increase both information seeking and information processing behaviors. However, unlike such variables, level of involvement increases information seeking but seldom affects information processing. In other words, unless publics are involved in situations—or they believe organizational behaviors affect them personally, they are unlikely to seek information.

J. Grunig and Childers (a.k.a. Hon) (1988) isolated two types of involvement: 1) *internal* involvement: "ego involvement, as defined by Sherif, Sherif, and Nebergall (1965)" and 2) *external* involvement: "situational connections, as defined by Krugman (1965) and more recently by Petty and Cacioppo (1986)" (p. 136). Although publics may not perceive both types of involvement in every situation, internal and external involvement alike increases publics' active communication behaviors (J. Grunig & Repper, 1992).

J. Grunig and L. Grunig (2000) pointed out that *active* publics, or at least potentially active publics, are most likely to be strategic publics for an organization. Therefore, L. Grunig, J. Grunig, and Dozier (2002) said that organizations should work to cultivate high quality relationships with strategic publics, or active publics, using symmetrical communication programs so as to get publics' support for attaining organizational goals. Also, the goals of a public must also be a part of an organization's goals once both relational parties, an organization and its strategic publics, cultivate quality relationships. J. Grunig and Huang (2000) added as follows: "Public relations makes organizations more effective by building relationships with strategic publics. Strategic publics are publics with which organizations need relationships—that is, they possess the antecedent characteristics [active communication behaviors] in the model we are developing" (p. 30).

Now that I have elaborated the concept of "strategic publics," I will explain the "symmetrical model of public relations" in the next section. In summarizing the results of the Excellence study, L. Grunig, J. Grunig, and Dozier (2002) said: "If we were to choose a few keywords to describe the Excellence theory in this book and previously in J. Grunig (1992) and Dozier with L. Grunig and J. Grunig (1995), we would list five: Excellent public relations is *managerial, strategic, symmetrical, diverse,* and *ethical*" (p. 306). They added that the term *symmetrical* underlies such terms as diverse and ethical: "When public relations practice is based on *symmetrical* values, it also brings both *diverse* perspectives and *ethical* considerations into organizational decisions and behavior" (p. 306).

Symmetrical Model of Public Relations

Along with the notion of strategic publics, *symmetrical* public relations is a key concept elucidating the value of public relations (Huang, 1997; J. Grunig et al., 1992; L. Grunig, J. Grunig, & Dozier, 2002). For public relations to have value to an organization and to society in general, the public relations function needs to balance the interests of an organization with the interests of publics and society (J. Grunig, 2000). In addition to having a symmetrical system to communicate with external publics, the Excellence study found that effective public relations departments also have a symmetrical system of internal communication (J. Grunig et al., 1992). Rather than top-down or one-way communication, a symmetrical system of internal communication ensures interactive communication among employee groups and management functions based on mutual interests.

For years, J. Grunig and L. Grunig (1989, 1992) have developed models of public relations that J. Grunig and Hunt (1984) initially proposed. J. Grunig and Hunt (1984) developed models of public relations to describe the historical development of public relations in the United States and to suggest models of contemporary public relations practice. Their four models of public relations were press agentry or publicity, public information, two-way asymmetrical, and two-way symmetrical.

First, the press agentry/publicity and public information models are one-way models (L. Grunig, J. Grunig, & Dozier, 2002):

1. *Press agentry* or *publicity* model: Practitioners of press agentry seek attention for their organization in almost any way possible.

2. *Public information* model: Practitioners are journalists-in-residents who disseminate accurate, but usually only favorable, information about their organizations. (p. 308)

Two-way models include the two-way asymmetrical and two-way symmetrical models of public relations (L. Grunig, J. Grunig, & Dozier, 2002):

1. *Two-way asymmetrical* model: Practitioners conduct scientific research to determine how to persuade publics to behave in the way the client organization wishes.

2. *Two-way symmetrical* model: Practitioners use research and dialogue to bring about symbiotic changes in the idea, attitudes, and behaviors of both the organization and its publics. (p. 308)

Initially, J. Grunig and Hunt (1984) developed a *contingency* approach in which they said that different public relations models could be effective depending on an organization's structure and environment. J. Grunig (1989b) and J. Grunig and L. Grunig (1989, 1992), in later works, dropped the contingency approach, suggesting that the two-way symmetrical model or, at least, Murphy's (1991) *mixed-motive* model could "almost always increase the contribution of public relations to organizational effectiveness" (L. Grunig, J. Grunig, & Dozier, 2002, p. 309).

In the third Excellence book, L. Grunig et al. (2002) decided that the two-way symmetrical model and the mixed-motive model were the same model. Murphy (1991) developed a mixed-motive model of public relations from game theory. In a mixed-motive model, an organization tries to satisfy its own interests while helping a public satisfy its interest. According to L. Grunig, J. Grunig, and Dozier (2002), she misunderstood the symmetrical model to consist of games of pure cooperation. L. Grunig, J. Grunig, and Dozier (2002) contended:

1. The two-way symmetrical model of public relations has never been conceptualized as such pure-cooperation or a total accommodation of publics' interests.

2. What Murphy described as a mixed-motive model is the same as the two-way symmetrical model of public relations. (L. Grunig et al., 2002)

Based on models of public relations (J. Grunig, 1989; J. Grunig & Hunt, 1984; J. Grunig & L. Grunig, 1989, 1992), J. Grunig, L. Grunig, and colleagues have developed specific theories and tested models in various contexts: focus groups for two-way symmetrical model (L. Grunig, 1992, 1993); collectivism, collaboration, and societal corporatism (J. Grunig, 2000); symmetrical model of public relations (J. Grunig, 1989, 2001); and models of public relations in global settings (e.g., J. Grunig, L. Grunig, Sriramesh, Lyra, & Huang, 1995; Rhee, 2002; Sriramesh, Kim, & Takasaki, 1999).

In conclusion, the Excellence study suggests that public relations can have value to an organization by cultivating high quality relationships with strategic publics. After the Excellence study, public relations scholars and practitioners have increasingly considered relationship management as one of the focal public relations activities to foster public relations effectiveness. At the same time, many public relations practitioners have widely embraced reputation management, believing that they can show bottom-line effects of public relations to management by means of reputation management.

In the following section, therefore, I will describe the implications of relationships and reputation for public relations effectiveness. After giving a brief overview of a divergent approach about the value of public relations, I will 1) discuss common assumptions in reputation research by reviewing the supposed value of reputation management, 2) review the non-financial value of public relations in the light of relationship management, and 3) explain symbolic and behavioral relationships.

The Value of Relationships and Reputation for Explaining the Effectiveness of Public Relations

As I discussed previously, public relations theories and research suggest that the value of public relations is in the *relationships* built between organizations and their *strategic* publics, publics maintaining *active* communication behaviors with organizations (e.g., Hon & J. Grunig, 1999; L. Grunig, J. Grunig, & Dozier, 2002; Yang & J. Grunig, 2005). This is largely because quality organization-public relationships enable public relations to not only be effective at the program and functional levels, but also contribute to effectiveness at the organizational and societal levels (J. Grunig et al., 1992; J. Grunig & L. Grunig, 1996, 2001; L. Grunig, J. Grunig, & Dozier, 2002).

Nonetheless, despite the prominence of the *relationship* concept in the contemporary literature of public relations, many scholars and public relations professionals have embraced different concepts to demonstrate the value of public relations (e.g., Heath, 2001; Hutton, Goodman, Alexander, & Genest, 2001; J. Grunig & Hung, 2002). For example, in the *Handbook of Public Relations*, Heath (2002) described the overall divergence between public relations scholars and practitioners in addressing the value of public relations: "Academic discussions tend to address public policy issues relevant to advancing harmony between organizations and publics, whereas practitioners spend the bulk of their time dealing with other dynamics of the marketplace" (p. 2).

Professionals often have attempted to demonstrate the economic value of public relations through the effect of favorable reputation on financial performance (e.g., Griffin, 2002; J. Grunig & Hung, 2002; Kim, 2000, 2001). In contrast, scholars often have suggested that organizations save the costs associated with issues, crises, regulation, litigation, and bad publicity by cultivating quality relationships with strategic publics (e.g., L. Grunig, J. Grunig, & Dozier, 2002).

L. Grunig, J. Grunig, and Dozier (2002, p. 91), who advocated the importance of "relationships," were critical of the emphasis on reputation:

Recently, public relations practitioners and firms have been on a quest to develop a single indicator of the value of organizational reputation that they believe will establish that communication has a measurable monetary return that can be

attributed to the public relations function. (p. 91)

L. Grunig et al. continued, "... this quest for a magic number to demonstrate the overall

value of public relations by estimating the value of reputation is fraught with difficulty

and is not likely to provide a valid and reliable measure of the value of public relations"

(p. 91).

Next, I will review common assumptions in reputation research. Business and

organizational psychology scholars have studied reputation extensively, whereas public

relations practitioners are the dominant advocates of reputation management. After I

discuss such common assumptions in reputation research by describing the proposed

value of reputation management, I will discuss why non-financial indicators of public

relations, such as "relationships," can explain the value of public relations better than

reputation.

Common Assumptions in Reputation Research

A common assumption underlying the study of reputation in public relations is

that public relations can have economic value to organizations through reputation

management, since developing a favorable reputation contributes to the organization's

financial returns.

Public relations researchers recently have attempted to demonstrate the bottom-

line effect of public relations by looking at the association between public relations

expenditures and a company's favorable reputation (Hutton, Goodman, Alexander, &

Genest, 2001; Thomas L. Harris/Impulse Research, 1999) and, furthermore, the link between spending on public relations and financial returns of the company through the mediation of favorable reputation (Kim, 2000, 2001).

Fortune magazine and business scholars studying reputation initially made the assumption that there is a link between a firm's reputation ranking and its financial returns. Following the lead of the *Fortune* survey, business scholars (e.g., Fombrun, 1996; Fombrun & Van Riel, 2003) have attempted to establish "corporate reputation" as a new intangible asset for strategic management of a corporation. To prove that reputation is a firm's strategic asset, business scholars (e.g., Fombrun, 1996; Fombrun & Van Riel, 2003) and *Fortune* magazine itself have calculated the monetary value of reputation by investigating the link between reputation rankings, such as in the *Fortune* list or in Fombrun et al.'s *Reputation Quotient*, and corporate revenues. For example, Fombrun (1996) attempted to calculate the value of corporate reputation to five companies that have been visible in their product categories since 1923. Fombrun (1996) coined the term "Reputational Capital" to emphasize the reputation concept as an intangible corporate asset and defined it as "the amount by which the company's market value exceeds the liquidation value of its assets" (p. 92).

As I noted previously, a common belief about demonstrating the value of public relations is that the value of public relations cannot be measured because most of its elements are intangible (Lesley, 1991). Thus, to public relations practitioners, efforts to investigate the link between reputation and financial returns of the organization are attractive (Griffin, 2002). They believe that they can prove the worth of public relations to managers and client organizations by showing that public relations affects reputation (J. Grunig & Hung, 2002; Kim, 2000, 2001). Public relations agencies also have used reputation management as a new product to develop comparative advantages over other

agencies. According to Yang and Mallabo (2003), "The new service [reputation

management] also allowed public relations firms with additional offerings to provide

client companies seeking novel tactics in the economic expansion of the mid-to late

1990s" (p. 4).

For this reason, public relations firms and researchers have studied the link

between spending on public relations and reputation to demonstrate the bottom-line value

of public relations (Hutton, Goodman, Alexander, & Genest, 2001; Thomas L.

Harris/Impulse Research, 1999) and the link between spending on public relations and

financial returns of the company through the mediation of reputation (Kim, 2000, 2001).

However, several scholars, in specializing research methods, have warned that

correlational research does not imply causation (e.g., Campbell & Stanley, 1963;

Hancock, 2004; Judd, Smith, & Kidder, 1991; Shadish, Cook, & Campbell, 2002). I

consider that such correlational research (Hutton, Goodman, Alexander, & Genest, 2001;

Thomas L. Harris/Impulse Research, 1999), between public relations expense and

reputation, does not establish the bottom-line "effect" of public relations on reputation

because correlation exists, unless they are grounded in theoretically developed causal

models. Therefore, these researchers can only show the association between corporate

reputation and the company's spending on communication activities, not the bottom line

"effect" of public relations on reputation.

J. Grunig and Hung (2002) pointed out an important issue regarding the sample of

the *Fortune* survey. According to J. Grunig and Hung (2002), "Although the

Fortune/Roper research on reputations now includes a similar survey of the 'general public,' these studies discussed here were based only on the original survey of CEOs, corporate directors, and financial analysts" (p. 7). Likewise, Bergen (2001) pointed out that the *Fortune* ranking is flawed because the participants mostly have financial expertise. Among the eight attributes of the *Fortune* rankings, survey respondents (i.e., financial analysts) are asked to rate the financial performance of the companies in thee indicators (i.e., value as a long-term investment, soundness of financial position, and wise use of corporate assets).

In Kim's (2001) study, as J. Grunig and Hung (2002) pointed out, these three indicators of financial performance were three of the five "highest" coefficients for the reputation composite. Therefore, J. Grunig and Hung (2002) said:

> Since ratings of financial performance make up a substantial component of the
> reputation index and a large proportion of the sample consists of financial analysts,
> it is not surprising that this measure of reputation correlated with financial
> performance. To a large extent, the predictor variable (reputation rating of
> financial performance) measures the same thing as the variable predicted (actual
> financial performance). (p. 7)

Another critical issue is the influence of company size on the link between public relations expense and reputation ranking. Hutton et al. (2001) replicated the Harris/Impulse study a year later. When they controlled for company size, they found the correlation between reputation and public relations expenses dropped from .24 to .11. Therefore, they concluded: "In other words, there was a modest correlation between reputation and spending on communication activities, but most of that was accounted for by the fact that larger companies—which presumably benefit from greater visibility—

tended to have better reputations" (p. 252). Additionally, they also found *negative*

correlations between reputation and other specific types of spending such as spending on

social responsibility ($r = -.19$) and corporate advertising ($r = -.19$).

To claim the bottom line effect of public relations, Kim (2000, 2001) went a step

further by investigating the link between spending on public relations and financial

returns of the company through the mediation of favorable reputation. Methodologically,

Kim (2001) used structural equation modeling to test the hypothesized causal

relationships. Hancock and Mueller (2004) said that a structural equation model can be

challenged by alternative explanations beyond the structural relations imposed in his

model. Despite his claim of causations, Kim's (2001) study can also be challenged by

alternative explanations. For example, the company's revenues may determine public

relations expense, which is the opposite causation from Kim's (2001) model. Hutton et al.

(2001) also argued against Kim's (2001) causal claims: "Indeed, he concluded that an

increase in communication spending caused both an increase in reputation and an

increase in revenues, and that an increase in revenues caused an increase in market

share—simply assuming that correlation equaled causality, in each case" (p. 253).

Many public relations scholars have suggested that non-financial indicators of

public relations can explain the value of public relations better than financial indicators

such as reputation (e.g., Hon & J. Grunig, 1999; Huang, 1997; J. Grunig & Huang, 2000;

J. Grunig & Hung, 2002; L. Grunig, J. Grunig, & Dozier, 2002; Jackson, 2000). For

example, L. Grunig, J. Grunig, and Dozier (2002) introduced the totality of the concept of

value and said: "We reject any simplistic notion that the only relevant contribution public

relations makes is a monetary one, directly to the bottom line. We consider this kind of cause-effect, linear thinking to be overly narrow" (p. 97). Advocating non-financial

indicators of the value of public relations, former leading practitioner Jackson (2000)

suggested that public relations value, assessed by non-financial indictors, will eventually

contribute to the bottom line of an organization (cited in L. Grunig, J. Grunig, and Dozier,

2002, p. 100).

Therefore, next I will explain why public relations scholars and practitioners

consider that non-financial values of public relations are critical in demonstrating public

relations effectiveness and how relationships can serve as an important indicator of public

relations' non-financial values.

Toward Non-Financial Values of Public Relations: The Value of Relationships

After reviewing public relations research on the link between reputation and

public relations expenses, and between public relations expenses and corporate revenues,

J. Grunig and Hung (2002) pointed out: "… these attempts to demonstrate that spending

on public relations improves a company's reputation either have failed or are subject to

alternative explanations largely because researchers have not conceptualized how and

why reputation creates value, have used gross indicators of public relations activities, and

have used equally gross measures of reputation" (p. 9). Therefore, J. Grunig and

colleagues (e.g., J. Grunig & Hung, 2002; L. Grunig, J. Grunig, & Dozier, 2002)

suggested: 1) Non-financial values of public relations can demonstrate public relations

effectiveness better than financial indicators and 2) organization-public relationships can

serve as an important indicator of non-financial values of public relations.

To explain the importance of non-financial values of public relations, L. Grunig et al. (2002) first reviewed what Jeffries-Fox Associates summarized as the value of reputation (Jeffries-Fox Associates, 2000b[5]; cited in J. Grunig & Hung, 2002):

1. Increasing market share

2. Lowering market costs

3. Lowering distribution costs

4. Being able to charge a premium

5. Avoiding over-regulation

6. Being able to weather bad times

7. Greater employee alignment and productivity

8. Being able to attract and retain talent

9. Being able to attract investors

10. Being able to gain access to new global markets

11. Gaining more favorable media coverage (pp. 9-10)

About such possible benefits of reputation, L. Grunig, J. Grunig, and Dozier (2002) said: "Public relations professionals tend to use the term 'reputation' as a surrogate for what we have called 'relationships' in the Excellence study" (p. 101). This is because, for the most part, they believe that the value of reputation is included in the value of relationships.

L. Grunig, J. Grunig, and Dozier (2002) described the value of relationships as follows:

---

[5] According to J. Grunig and Hung (2002), "In their study for the Council of Public Relations Firms, Jeffries-Fox Associates (2000b) searched the business, public relations, and marketing literature for explanations of why reputation has value for an organization" (p. 9).

1. Relationships (and their product reputation) provide a context for behavior by consumers, investors, employees, government, the community, the media, and other strategic constituencies—but they do not determine this behavior alone. The behavior of these constituencies affects financial performance; but many other factors, such as competition and the economic environment, also affect that performance.

2. Relationships save money by preventing costly issues, crises, regulation, litigation, and bad publicity. It is not possible, however, to determine the cost of something that *did not happen* or even to know that the negative event or behavior *would have happened* in the absence of excellent public relations

3. The return on relationships is delayed. Organizations spend money on relationships for years to prevent events or behaviors such as crises, boycotts, or litigation that *might* happen many years down the road.

4. The return on relationships usually is lumpy. Good relationships with some constituencies such as consumers may produce a continuing stream of revenue, but for the most part the return comes all at once—e.g., when crises, strikes, boycotts, regulation, litigation, or bad publicity are avoided or mitigated. Similarly, relationships with potential donors must be cultivated for years before a donor makes a major gift. As a result, it is difficult to prorate the delayed returns on public relations to the monies invested in the function each year. (p. 105)

Next, I will introduce J. Grunig's (1993) discussion of symbolic and behavioral relationships, which I consider elucidates the value of relationships. To gain greater value from organization-public relationships, J. Grunig suggested that an organization needs to build good *behavioral* relationships, rather than just symbolic relationships.

Symbolic and Behavioral Relationships

According to J. Grunig (1993), a paradigm struggle in public relations has occurred "between practitioners who use only superficial symbolic activities—the quest for positive images—and those who build substantive behavioral relationships between organizations and publics" (p. 121). J. Grunig pointed out that public relations scholars and practitioners use the term image so broadly that "it has been used as a synonym for such concepts as message, reputation, perception, cognition, attitude, credibility, belief, communication, or relationship" (p. 124). J. Grunig (1993) distinguished symbolic relationships (e.g., image, reputation, or other associated terms) from behavioral relationships, a type of relationships that organizations build with publics through long-term behaviors.

For public relations to have value to an organization, as J. Grunig (1993) suggested, public relations practitioners should demonstrate public relations effectiveness at two levels: 1) at the *micro* level, practitioners focus on symbolic relationships to derive objectives for communication programs and to develop measures to evaluate their effectiveness and 2) at the *macro* level, practitioners demonstrate their efforts contribute to organizations' goals by building long-term behavioral relationships with strategic publics. Although he said that symbolic and behavioral relationships are "intertwined like the strands of a rope" (p. 136), J. Grunig (1993) added that behavioral relationships with strategic publics contributes more to the value of public relations over the long term.

In the next parts of this chapter, I will define and explain the concepts of relationships and reputation along with popular measurement systems. Then, I will discuss how I hypothesize the link between organization-public relationships and organizational reputation with some precursors of those concepts in the proposed structural equation model.

Organization-Public Relationships

After the Excellence study (J. Grunig et al., 1992; Dozier et al., 1995; L. Grunig et al., 2002), public relations scholars have studied the relationship concept in a variety of contexts (e.g., J. Grunig & Hung, 2002; Huang, 1997, 2001; Hung, 2002; Jo, 2003; Ledingham & Bruning, 2000; Rhee, 2004; Toth, 2000). About the preeminence of the relationship concept in the literature of public relations, Bruning and Ledingham's (1999) said: "An increasing number of scholars are adopting the perspective that public relations should be viewed as the management of a relationship between an organization and publics" (p. 157). Later, in a book titled "Public Relations as Relationship Management," Ledingham and Bruning (2000) said that they considered organization-public relationship management to be "a paradigm for public relations scholarship and practice" (p. xiii). Broom, Casey, and Ritchey (2000) also said: "Many scholars and practitioners say that public relations is all about building and maintaining an organization's relationships with its publics" (p. 4).

Ferguson (1984) played a significant role in initiating public relations research on organization-public relationships. She suggested that the unit of study in public relations should be the "relationships" between organizations and their publics. To develop better public relations theories, Ferguson (1984) suggested that the field of public relations needs a paradigm focus, and that organization-public relationships should be that focus for research on and the practice of public relations.

Definitions of Organization-Public Relationships

To establish organization-public relationships as a paradigm in public relations, Ferguson (1984) suggested as follows:

> We will have to come to agreement as to what we mean by our most basic terms: public, relationships, organization, communication and public issues. Beyond this basic first step, we also will need to begin to identify what we believe to be the important attributes of public relationships. (p. 27)

Recently, scholars have identified attributes of the quality of organization-public relationship outcomes (Bruning & Ledingham, 1999, 2000; Huang, 1997, 2001; J. Grunig & Huang, 2000; Ledingham & Bruning, 1998) and types of organization-public relationships (Hon & J. Grunig, 1999; Hung, 2002). This study used indicators of relationship outcomes and relationship types identified by J. Grunig and colleagues (e.g., J. Grunig & Huang, 2000; Huang, 1997; Hon & J. Grunig, 1999).

Before I discuss dimensions and measurement systems of organization-public relationships, I will define organization-public relationships by explicating definitions of "organization," "publics," and "relationships" respectively. I will briefly define publics here because I have already defined the term in a previous part of this chapter.

Defining Publics

The term "public" originated from "the Latin phrase poplicus or populus, meaning the people" (Price, 1992; cited in Vasquez & Taylor, 2001, p. 140). J. Grunig and Hunt (1984) defined a public as "a group of people who face a problem, are divided on its solution, and organize to discuss it" (p. 145). People become stakeholders because of interdependence with an organization. Stakeholders organize into publics because of problems they have with an organization or problems they want an organization to solve (J. Grunig & Huang, 2000; J. Grunig & Hunt, 1984). Publics engage in *active* communication behavior to solve such problems with an organization (J. Grunig, 1997; J. Grunig & L. Grunig, 2000; J. Grunig & Repper, 1992).

Defining Organizations

Organizational theorist Daft (2001) defined organizations as "1) social entities that 2) are goal directed, 3) are designed as deliberately structured and coordinated activity systems, and 4) are linked to the external environment" (p. 5). Daft suggested that organizations become effective by managing relationships with strategic publics:

> The key element of an organization is not a building or a set of policies and procedures; organizations are made up of people and their relationships with one another. An organization exists when people interact with one another to perform essential functions that help attain goals… An organization cannot exist without interacting with customers, suppliers, competitors, and other elements of the external environment. (p. 5)

Defining Relationships

O'Hair et al. (1995) defined relationships as "the interdependence of two or more people" (p. 10). Coombs (2000) connected this definition, from the perspective of interpersonal communication, with stakeholder theory. People are *interdependent* with one another when they need others for some reason; consequently, people engage in a relationship based on such a linkage (Coombs, 2000). Likewise, in the context of org-

stakeholder relationships, organizations have a relationship with stakeholders when they have a connection with stakeholders (Coombs, 2000).

To define relationships between organizations and their publics, Broom et al. (2000) reviewed definitions of organization-public relationships from such perspectives as interpersonal communication, psychotherapy, inter-organizational relationships, and systems theory. I will introduce some useful definitions reviewed in Broom et al.'s (2000) chapter.

First, from the perspective of interpersonal communication, Surra and Ridley (1991) defined a relationship as "moment-to-moment interaction events" and "inter-subjectivity" or "cognitive interdependence" (p.37). Anderson (1993) also noted the interdependence of relational participants: "Relationships are the combined product and producers of both the interpersonal interactions and the cognitive activities of the interactancts" (p. 2). Secondly, from the perspective of psychotherapy, Gelso and Carter (1994) defined the counselor-client relationship as "the feelings and attitudes that counseling participants have toward one another, and the manner in which these are expressed" (p. 297). Third, from the perspective of an inter-organizational relationship, organizational behavior is a focal aspect to conceptualize relationships: "Theoretically, organizations enter relationships because of their dependence on other organizations for resources" (Broom et al., 2000, p. 11). According to Broom et al., inter-organizational relationships are generally studied from the perspectives of *resource dependency theory*[6]

---

[6] According to Broom et al. (2000), "According to resource dependency theory, relationships from in response to an organization's need for resources. Satisfying the need for resources allows an organization to survive, to grow, and to achieve other goals. Relationships consist of the transactions involving the exchange of resources between organizations" (p. 12).

(e.g., Aldrich, 1976; Lincoln & McBride, 1985) and *exchange theory*[7] (e.g., Cook, 1977; Levine & White, 1961; Stearns, Hoffman, & Heide, 1987). Finally, the systems perspective suggests that communication, as the primary exchange in social systems, can "serve as a major determinant of both relationships and the overall functioning of most systems" (Broom et al., 2000, p. 13).

Based on the previous discussion of definitions of "organization," "publics," and "relationships," I will define organization-public relationships as "the interdependence of an organization and its publics and the consequences of such interdependence." Next, I will review how public scholars define organization-public relationships. Then, I will describe the nature of organization-public relationships.

Defining Organization-Public Relationships

Despite the common use of the term "relationship" by both scholars and practitioners in explaining the value of public relations, "neither scholars nor practitioners have defined the concept carefully or have developed reliable measures of relationships outcomes" (J. Grunig & Huang, 2000, p. 25). Broom, Casey, and Richey (2000) also pointed out the absence of relationship definitions as follows: "Even though the public relations function builds and maintains organizations' relationships with publics, we found few definitions of such relationships in public relations literature" (p. 3).

After reviewing definitions of relationships in several perspectives, Broom et al. (2000) described relationships between organizations and publics: "Organization-public

---

[7] Broom et al. (2000) described exchange theory as "Similarly, exchange theory suggests that voluntary transactions result from knowledge of domain similarity and lead to mutual benefit, as well as to mutual goal achievement. It should be noted that exchange theorists define relationships in terms of the voluntary transactions and of the mutuality of interests and rewards." (p. 13).

relationships are represented by the patterns of interaction, transaction, exchange, and linkage between an organization and its publics" (Broom et al., 2000, p. 18). Bruning and Ledingham (1998) defined organization-public relationships as the "states which exist between an organization and its key publics in which the actions of either entity impact the economic, social, political, and/or cultural well-being of the other entity" (p. 62).

Whereas Broom et al. (1997) defined organization-public relationships as processes of relationship formation, and Bruning and Ledingham (1998) defined it as broad consequences, Huang (1997) and J. Grunig and Huang (2000) defined organization-public relationships focusing on relationship attributes, or relationship outcomes. Huang (1997) examined organization-public relationships based on two underlying assumptions: 1) relationships consist of more than one fundamental feature, and 2) four relational features represent the construct of organization-public relationships (control mutuality, trust, commitment, and satisfaction). Later, along the same line of conceptualization, Huang (1998) defined organization-public relationships as "the degree that the organization and its publics trust one another, agree on one has rightful power to influence, experience satisfaction with each other, and commit oneself to one another" (p. 12).

As I noted previously, I defined organization-public relationships as "the interdependence of an organization and its publics and the consequences of such interdependence." Rhee's (2004) definition improves my definition by adding a significant aspect of organization-public relationships: "communication behaviors between an organization and its publics to cultivate a relationship." Rhee (2004) defined an organization-public relationship as "a connection or association between an organization and a public that results from behavioral consequences an organization or a public has on the other and that necessitates repeated communication" (p. 9).

The Nature of Organization-Public Relationships

Ferguson (1984) suggested the following attributes of organization-public relationships:

1. The degree to which the relationship is a dynamic versus a static one, or the degree to which the relationship is open versus closed.

2. The attributions of those who are party to the relationships (i.e., an organization and its public).

3. The degree to which one or both participants are satisfied with the relationship.

4. The degree to which power is distributed in the relationship.

5. The degree to which the parties to the relationship are tightly coupled or loosely coupled. (pp. 19-20)

Huang (1997) reviewed the literature about relational features that have been suggested at the interpersonal and inter-organizational levels. At the interpersonal level, according to Huang, scholars (e.g., Canary & Cupach, 1988; Canary & Stafford, 1992; Canary & Spitzberg, 1989; Hendrick, 1988; Stafford & Canary, 1991) have adopted the following concepts consistently to study the nature of relationships: "control mutuality, trust, commitment, intimacy, liking, and relationship satisfaction" (p. 49).

At the organizational level, scholars (e.g., Aldrich, 1975, 1979; Ferguson, 1984; L. Grunig, J. Grunig, & Ehling, 1992) also have studied the relationship concept. For example, Aldrich (1975, 1979) identified four factors of organizational relationships:

1. *Formalization*: The extent to which the organizations recognize the relationship and assign intermediaries (such as public relations practitioners) to coordinate the relationship.

2. *Intensity*: The extent to which organizations commit time and money to the relationship.

3. *Reciprocity*: The extent to which all organizations devote resources to the relationship and mutually determine how interaction will take place.

4. *Standardization*: The extent to which interaction becomes fixed. (cited in L. Grunig, J. Grunig, & Ehling, 1992, p. 83)

Huang (1997) listed seven characteristics as the nature of organization-public relationships:

1. Organization-public relationships can be regarded as relationships between a corporate person and another corporate person or between a corporate person and a group of individuals.

2. Both a relationship and conflict in that relationship often are experienced and perceived subjectively.

3. Conflict in organization-public relationships, ranging from "entirely relationship-damaging" to "entirely relationship-enhancing" (Levinger & Rubin, 1994, p. 205), is driven by one or more underlying motives, i.e., cooperation, competition, or both.

4. The ways in which communication representatives interact with their constituents could affect the organization-public relationships.

5. Whether mass media or outside audiences are involved could influence the development of relations between an organization and its publics.

6. Various resources, at both interpersonal and inter-organizational levels, could be exchanged in organization-public relationships.

7. Although the resources to be exchanged may not be exactly the same at interpersonal and inter-organizational levels, the notions of trust, control mutuality, commitment, and satisfaction can be used as relational features to represent organization-public relationships. In other words, these four features have universal characteristics applicable to interpersonal, inter-organizational and organization-public relationships. (pp. 59-60)

From the above discussion on the nature of organization-public relationships, I conclude: 1) A relationship can be studied either by *processes* of relationship formation, such as antecedents and consequences of the relationship, or by *properties* of the relationship; 2) *subjective perceptions* of relational parties determine the assessment of properties of a relationship; and 3) relational features at the interpersonal level can be also applied across *broader* units of analysis, such as the inter-organizational level or combination between interpersonal and inter-organizational levels.

Now that I have discussed the nature of relationships, I will explain models of organization-public relationships. In the literature of public relations, Broom et al. (2000) and J. Grunig and Huang (2000) developed models of organization-public relationships.

Models of Organization-Public Relationships

By developing quality relationships with strategic publics, public relations can have long-term value to organizations (L. Grunig, J. Grunig, & Dozier, 2002). About attributes of good relationships, L. Grunig et al. (2002) suggested:

Good relationships between organization and their publics are two-way and symmetrical—that is, the relationships balance the interests of the organization with the interests of publics on which the organization has consequences and that have consequences on the organization. (p. 11)

To build quality relationships, world-views of public relations also play an important role (J. Grunig & White, 1992). For public relations to be effective, J. Grunig and White (1992) suggested: "... public relations must viewed as symmetrical, idealistic and critical, and managerial" (p. 31). L. Grunig, J. Grunig, and Dozier (2002 summarized such world-views of public relations:

1. The *symmetrical* worldview: Organizations have the worldview that public relations practitioners serve the interests of both sides of relationships while still advocating the interests of the organizations that employ them.

2. The *idealistic* and *critical* worldview: Public relations practitioners have the freedom to advocate the interests of publics to management and to criticize management decisions that affect publics adversely.

3. The *managerial* worldview: Public relations fulfills the managerial role of negotiating and mediating the conflict that occurs between management and strategic publics. When organizations practice public relations in accordance with this worldview, organizations can serve the interests of society, consisting of publics, as well as the interests of organizations. (p. 11)

63

In addition to such underlying attributes of quality organization-public relationships,

Broom et al. (2000) and J. Grunig and Huang (2000) developed models of organization-

public relationships in the literature of public relations.

Three-Stage Model of Organization-Public Relationship

Broom et al. (2000) proposed a model of *antecedents* and *consequences* of

organization-public relationships. This model is useful to explain why publics and

organizations come to form a relationship (i.e., antecedents), what properties

relationships have (i.e., the relationship concept), and what consequences relationships

can bring to both parties of the relationship (i.e., consequences).

Broom et al. (2000) defined each stage of the model as follows:

1. *Antecedents*: The perceptions, motives, needs, behaviors, and so forth, posited

    as contingencies or as causes in the formation of relationships.

2. *Relational properties*: Properties of exchange, transactions, communications,

    and other interconnected activities.

3. *Consequences*: The outputs that have the effects of changing the environment

    and of achieving, maintaining, or changing goal states both inside and outside

    the organization. (p. 16)

Antecedents of Relationships, PR Strategies, and Relationship Outcomes

J. Grunig and Huang (2000) took a step further from Broom et al.'s (2000) three-

stage model by examining *relationship cultivation strategies*, following Stafford and

Canary (1991) from the perspective of interpersonal relationships. In this model, J.

Grunig and Huang (2000) conceptualized: 1) the *antecedents* that describe the publics with which organizations need relationships, 2) the *strategies* used to cultivate those relationships, and 3) the consequences or *outcomes* of those strategies.

Antecedents of Organization-Public Relationships

The Excellence theory and J. Grunig and Hunt's (1984) situational theory of publics can explain the antecedents of organization-public relationships. *Strategic publics* are those whom organizations need to build relationships with because consequences on the other (J. Grunig & Huang, 2000). In detail, J. Grunig and Huang added:

> Organizations have a public relations problem (a reason to develop a public
>
> relations program) when management decisions have consequences on non-
>
> management people inside or outside of the organization (publics) or when the
>
> behavior of these publics has consequences on the success with which the
>
> decision can be implemented. (p. 33)

In other words, when there are *behavioral consequences* on the other, between an organization and its publics, the organization and its publics engage in a relationship.

Two additional aspects to be considered are that, first, the antecedents of relationships are *situational* and *behavioral*. According to J. Grunig and Huang (2000), "… the antecedents of relationships are situational, just as publics are situational. That is, publics come and go and change as situations change. In addition, consequences stem from the behaviors of both organizations and publics" (p. 35). Secondly, organizations typically face *multiple* publics with different interests and conflicting goals (J. Grunig & Huang, 2000; Hung, 2002; Verčič, 1997[8]). In addition to a single organization or a

---

[8] Regarding the implications of multiple publics in relationship management, Verčič (1997) stated: "… the problem of managing multiple stakeholder relationships become

public, there could be coalitions of both organizations and publics or the combination between a relationship party and coalitions.[9]

Relational Cultivation Strategies

J. Grunig and Huang (2000) explicated strategies to cultivate organization-public relationships, whereas Broom et al. (2000) did not explicate properties of the relationship concept in the middle stage of their model. Hon and J. Grunig (1999) suggested that most successful organization-public relationships are *two-way* and *symmetrical* relationships. Successful relationships between organizations and publics are cultivated by a *two*-way communication process with effects on both parties in the relationship, whereas the most common way to evaluate the effects of communication is *one*-way from organizations to publics (Hon & J. Grunig, 1999). Additionally, Hon and J. Grunig said that *symmetrical* relationships are another key attribute of successful relationship cultivation: "... the most productive relationships in the long run are those that benefit both parties in the relationship rather than those designed to benefit the organizations only" (p. 11).

On these points, J. Grunig (2002) suggested two-way communication and symmetrical communication as key components of relationship cultivation strategies. J. Grunig (J. Grunig & Huang, 2000) initially named their model's middle-stage as relationship maintenance strategy; recently, he suggested renaming the stage to "relationship cultivation strategy" (J. Grunig, 2002), influenced by Baxter's (1994) dialogic approach. J. Grunig (2002) said as follows: "Cultivation strategies are the communication methods that public relations people use to develop new relationships

---

particularly difficult when an organization is squeezed between two (or more) groups of stakeholders/publics with opposing needs and/or wants" (p. 265).

[9] For more details, see Table 2.1 in J. Grunig and Huang (2000, p. 34).

with publics and to deal with the stresses and conflicts that occur in all relationships" p.

5).

Interpersonal communication scholars have studied communication strategies that

participants of relationships use to maintain desired relationships (e.g., Baxter & Dindia,

1990; Bell et al., 1987; Canary & Stafford, 1992; Stafford & Canary, 1991). In particular,

Stafford and Canary (1991) studied how romantic couples maintain their relationships

and explored the association between perceptions of maintenance behaviors and such

salient relational features as control mutuality, commitment, liking, and relational

satisfaction. Canary and Stafford (1992) studied the association between equity in

marriage and maintenance strategies. About the assumption underlying such studies,

Stafford and Canary (1991) explained: "One guiding research assumption of this study is

that the actor's assessment of the relationship is strongly determined by perceptions of

the partner's efforts to maintain the relationship" (p. 223).

Stafford and Canary (1991) used a series of factor analyses to extract non-

redundant items and found five discrete maintenance strategies such as positivity,

openness, assurance, networks, and sharing tasks. Hon and J. Grunig (1999)[10] applied

those relationship maintenance strategies to the context of organization-public

symmetrical relationships and added one more dimension of access:

---

[10] Regarding the application of Stafford and Canary's (1991) findings on interpersonal
relationships to public relations, Hon and J. Grunig (1999) explained: "Research on
interpersonal relationships and conflict resolution suggests several strategies that
organizations can use to maintain relationships with strategic constituencies. All of the
concepts from research on interpersonal relationships can be applied to maintaining
symmetrical public relations, or those that benefit both the organization and publics" (p.
14).

1. *Positivity*: Anything the organization or public does to make the relationship more enjoyable for the parties involved.

2. *Openness*: Openness of thoughts and feelings among parties involved.

3. *Assurance*: Attempts by parties in the relationship to assure the other parties that they and their concerns are legitimate. This strategy also might involve attempts by the parties in the relationship to demonstrate they are committed to maintaining the relationship.

4. *Networking*: Organizations' building networks or coalitions with the same groups that their publics do, such as environments, unions, or community groups.

5. *Sharing of tasks*: Organizations' and publics' sharing in solving joint or separate problems. Examples of such tasks are managing community issues, providing employment, making a profit, and staying in business, which are in the interest of either of the organization, the public, or both.

6. *Access*: Members of publics or opinion leaders provide access to public relations people. Public relations representatives or senior managers provide representatives of publics similar access to organizational decision-making processes. (p. 14)

In addition to symmetrical relationship maintenance strategies, J. Grunig and Huang (2000) also emphasized strategies of *conflict resolution* identified by Huang (1997) and Plowman (1995). J. Grunig and Huang added integrative strategy, distributive strategy, and dual concern strategy from the conflict resolution perspective and concluded that symmetrical and integrative strategies are more effective in maintaining organization-public relationships than asymmetrical and distributive strategies. Hon and J. Grunig (1999) summarized key differences between integrative and distributive strategies in the context of the asymmetrical/symmetrical distinction:[11]

1. *Integrative* strategy: These approaches are symmetrical because all parties in a relationship benefit by searching out common or complementary interests and solving problems together through open discussion and joint decision-making. The goal is a win-win solution that values the integrity of a long-term relationship between an organization and its publics.

2. *Distributive* strategy: These strategies are asymmetrical because one party benefits at the expense of another by seeking to maximize gains and minimize losses within a win-lose or self-gain perspective. (p. 16)

Dual concern strategies, identified from conflict resolution by Plowman (1995), are relevant in relationship cultivation strategies of public relations. J. Grunig and Huang (2000) said that the dual role of balancing the interests both of an organization and its publics fits well with symmetrical model of public relations.

Hon and J. Grunig (1999) pointed out that some dual concern strategies are asymmetrical "because they emphasize the organization's interest over the public or vice versa" (p. 16), such as contending and avoiding: 1) *contending*: "the organization tries to convince the public to accept its position" and 2) *avoiding*: "the organization leaves the conflict, either physically or psychologically" (J. Grunig & Huang, 2000, p. 40).

Additionally, J. Grunig and Huang (2000) considered accommodating and compromising strategies equally ineffective because such strategies accommodate the

---

[11] Canary and Cupach (1988) also reviewed the literature on conflict strategies: integrative strategies, distributive strategies, and avoidance (see pp. 306-308).

public's interests at the expense of the organization: 1) *accommodating*: "the organization yields, at least in part, on its position and lowers its aspirations" and 2) *compromising*: "the organization meets the public part way between their preferred positions, but neither party is completely satisfied with the outcome" (p. 40).

Finally, J. Grunig and Huang (2000) suggested the following three strategies as truly symmetrical strategies: 1) *cooperating*: "both organization and the public work together to reconcile their interests and to reach a mutually beneficial relationship," 2) *being unconditionally constructive*: "the organization should do whatever it thinks is best for the relationship, even if it means giving up some up of its position and even if the public does not reciprocate," and 3) *saying win-win or no deal*: "if the organization and the public cannot find a solution that benefits both, they agree or disagree" (p. 40).

J. Grunig and Huang (2000) proposed that the effects of relational cultivation strategies can be measured by the outcomes of relationships. Traditionally, practitioners use short-term outputs or outcomes of specific programs to evaluate public relations effectiveness. Unlike such short-term measures, J. Grunig and colleagues consider organization-public relationships as "long-term" outcomes of relationship cultivation strategies (Hon & J. Grunig, 1999; J. Grunig & Huang, 2000).

According to Hon and J. Grunig (1999), "… outputs are usually the immediate results of a particular PR program or activity," whereas outcomes measure whether target audience groups received, attended, understood, and retained the messages directed at them (p. 2). Because short-term outputs and outcomes explain the effectiveness of only particular public relations program or event, Hon and J. Grunig (1999) suggested that the effectiveness of overall public relations can be best explained by organization-public relationship outcomes.

Likewise, Bruning and Ledingham (2000) also noted the change of public relations evaluation from measuring short-term outputs to long-term outcomes, which measurement of relationships have catalyzed. Bruning and Ledingham (2000) said as follows: "As the profession of public relations continues to come under intense pressure to justify its existence and demonstrate accountability, the movement from measuring communication outputs to linking public relations activities to key public members' symbolic and behavioral outcomes continues to gain momentum" (p. 88).

Organization-public Relationship Outcomes & Relationship Types

Huang (1997, 2001) and J. Grunig and Huang (2000) identified four indicators of the quality of organization-public relationship outcomes: control mutuality, trust, satisfaction, commitment, and satisfaction. Also, Ledingham and Bruning (1998, 2000) identified five dimensions of organization-public relationship outcomes: trust, commitment, openness, investment, and involvement. About organization-public relationship types, Hon and J. Grunig (1999) have identified two types of relationships, exchange and communal relationships, from the perspective of social psychology. Later, Hung (2002) identified more types of organization-public relationships: communal (one-sided versus mutual), exchange, covenantal, contractual, exploitive, manipulative, and symbiotic relationships.

For this study, I focused on the indicators of organization-public relationship outcomes and organization-public relationship types identified by J. Grunig and colleagues (e.g., J. Grunig and Huang, 2000; Huang, 1997; Hon & J. Grunig, 1999).

Huang (2001) maintained that the four indicators of the quality of relationship outcomes (control mutuality, trust, satisfaction, commitment, and satisfaction) occur consistently in the literature of relationships, and that these four features represent the essence of organization-public relationships. In light of organization-public relationship types, I will use the indicators of relationship types identified by Hon and J. Grunig (1999).

Public relations scholars have most widely used these indicators of relationship quality and relationship type to measure organization-public relationships (e.g., Hon & J. Grunig, 1999; Huang, 1997, 2001; Hung, 2002; Jo, 2003; J. Grunig & Hung, 2002; Jo & Kim, 2003; Yang & J. Grunig, 2005). In the next parts of this section, I will discuss each indicator of relationship quality and relationship type.

Indicators of Organization-public Relationship Outcomes and Relationship Types

Control Mutuality

Huang (1997) found that control mutuality and trust are two major dimensions of organization-public relationships in her study. Coming from different perspectives, Huang (1997) said that scholars have identified control mutuality to study relationships in terms of the following similar concepts: "bilateral control" (Kelly, 1979[12]), "mutual legitimacy" (Bruning & Ledingham, 1999), "reciprocity" (Aldrich, 1975, 1979; L. Grunig, J. Grunig, & Ehling, 1992), "distribution of power in the relationship" (Ferguson, 1984), "power" (Millar & Rogers, 1976), and "empowerment" (Mooer, 1986). For instance, Ferguson (1984) explained as follows:

---

[12] According to Stafford and Canary (1991), "This concept is similar to Kelly's (1979) notion of bilateral control, wherein both partners decide their goals and behaviors. Bilateral, or mutual, control is distinguished from unilateral attempts to control the partner (Kelly, 1979)" (p. 224).

Other variables related to the relationship might be how much control both parties to the relationship believe they have, how power is distributed in the relationship, whether the parties to the relationship believe they share goals, and whether there is mutuality of understanding, agreement, and consensus. (p. 20)

Stafford and Canary (1991) defined control mutuality as "the degree to which partners agree about which of them should decide relational goals and behavioral routines" (p. 224). Morton, Alexander, and Altman (1976) defined mutuality of control as "consensus about which partner has rightful power to influence the other" (cited in Stafford & Canary, 1991, p. 224).

Previous research has found, according to J. Grunig and Huang (2000), that unilateral attempts to achieve control are associated with decreases in perceptions of communicator competence, decreases in relational satisfaction (Bochner, Kaminski, & Fitzpatrick, 1977; Canary & Cupach, 1988), and increases in levels of activism (L. Grunig, 1992).

In the context of public relations, Hon and J. Grunig (1999) defined control mutuality as "the degree to which parties agree on who has rightful power to influence one another" (p. 13). According to J. Grunig and Huang (2000), power asymmetry is natural in reality and occurs in one of the following three situations:

1. One party is completely powerless.

2. If the power difference is only slight, the result is likely to be a power struggle in which neither party does well.

3. When the power asymmetry is reasonably large, it would be appropriate to involve a mutually trusted third party to balance power, insomuch as the third

party likely would favor the weaker party in order to provide balance and

come to an equitable resolution. (p. 43)

The sense of control mutuality, or a norm of reciprocity, among relational parties

is important to stable and quality organization-public relationships even if power

asymmetry is inevitable in any relationship (Huang, 1997, 2001; J. Grunig & Huang,

2000; L. Grunig, J. Grunig, Ehling, 1992). I consider that control mutuality is critical in

conceptualizing and measuring organization-public relationships. This is because power

and resource asymmetry often occur in the case of organization-public relationships.

Consequently, understanding mutual interests in asymmetrical conditions is important to

foster reciprocity, an important attribute of successful organization-public relationships.

Trust

Scholars have widely studied trust in conceptualizing a relationship across

different perspectives: for example, interpersonal relationships (Canary & Cupach, 1988;

Millar & Rogers, 1976; Larzelere & Huston, 1980), risk communication (McCallum,

Hammond, & Covello, 1991; Trumbo & McComas, 2003), relationship marketing

(Anderson & Narus, 1990; Morgan & Hunt, 1994), and organizational communication

(Becerra, 1998; Bruning & Ledingham, 1999; Huang, 1997, 2001; Jo, 2003; Jo & Kim,

2003; Ledingham & Bruning, 1998).

In the topoi of relational communication, Burgoon and Hale (1984) explained that

trust is a complex concept to define:

Trust includes both 'trusting' behaviors (indications of one's vulnerability and

dependence) and 'trustworthy' actions (indications that one will not exploit

another's vulnerability and will not betray the trust that one is given). It entails the qualities associated with the character of credibility—sincerity, dependability,

honesty, respect, and the like. (p. 205)

Canary and Cupach (1988) conceptualized trust as "a willingness to risk oneself

because the relational partner is perceived as benevolent and honest" (p. 308). Morgan

and Hunt (1994), from the perspective of relationship marketing, conceptualized trust "as

existing when one party has confidence in an exchange partner's reliability and integrity"

(p. 23). Moorman, Deshpande, and Zalman (1993) added the behavioral intention of

"willingness" to this definition and defined trust as "a willingness to rely on an exchange

partner in whom one has confidence" (p. 82).

In the context of public relations, Hon and J. Grunig (1999) defined trust as "one

party's level of confidence in and willingness to open oneself to the other party" (p. 19).

As Burgoon and Hale (1984) suggested, trust is a complicated concept; Hon and J.

Grunig (1999) defined the following underlying dimensions: 1) *integrity*: "the belief that

an organization is fair and just," 2) *dependability*: "the belief that an organization will do

what it says it will do," and 3) *competence*: "the belief that an organization has the ability

to do what it says it will do" (p. 19).[13] Also, as Ledingham and Bruning (1998)

conceptualized, "… trust essentially refers to a feeling that those in the relationship can

---

[13] See more details about these three dimensions of trust in Hung (2002). In summary, Hung (2002,) reviewed the literature on trust and defined it as follows: 1) *dependability*: "inconsistencies in words and behaviors decrease levels of trust," 2) *competence*: "the ability a party has to capably perform his or her duties and obligations," and 3) *integrity*: "related to parties' sense of justice and whether the parties' behaviors are consistent with their words" (pp. 74-76). In addition to these dimensions, Hung (2002) also reviewed *faith* (i.e., the confidence one party has in another to face an unknown future), and *benevolence* (i.e., individuals consider the needs and welfare of others) as additional dimensions of trust.

rely on the other. Dependability, forthrightness and trustworthiness are key components" (p. 58).

About possible effects of trust in relationships, Canary and Cupach (1988) suggested that trust should be strongly associated with control mutuality and intimacy (i.e., knowledge of the other) and that trust is related to relational growth much like intimacy and control mutuality. In other words, Canary and Cupach (1988) said: "… trust appears to be essential to the promotion and maintenance of a relationship, whereas suspicion undermines such growth (Larzelere & Huston, 1980)" (p. 308).

Commitment

According to Morgan and Hunt (1984), and Stafford and Canary (1991), commitment has been extensively studied from the perspective of social exchange. Cook and Emerson (1978) conceptualized commitment as "a variable we believe to be central in distinguishing social from economic exchange" (p. 728). Additionally, McDonald (1981) said as follows: "Clearly, the major differentiation of these exchange relationship types[14] … is the mutual social trust and the resultant commitment on the part of the individuals to establish and maintain exchange relationships" (p. 836).

Morgan and Hunt (1994) maintained that commitment, as a form of brand loyalty, is crucial in relationship marketing and organization-buyer behavior. From the perspective of relationship marketing, Morgan and Hunt (1994) defined commitment as "an exchange partner believing that an ongoing relationship with another is so important as to warrant maximum efforts at maintaining it; that is, the committed party believes the

---

[14] The communal/exchange distinction, conceptualized by Clark and Mills (e.g., Clark & Mills, 1979, 1993; Mills & Clark, 1994), is defined more narrowly than exchange relationships referring to mutually rewarding interaction.

relationship is worth working on to ensure that it endures indefinitely" (p. 23). Morgan

and Hunt (1994) also quoted Moorman et al. (1992, p. 316), in which commitment is

defined as "an enduring desire to maintain a valued relationship" (p. 23). After reviewing

the literature on commitment, Morgan and Hunt (1994) concluded: "Parties identify

commitment among exchange partners as key to achieving valuable outcomes for

themselves, and they endeavor to develop and maintain this precious attribute in their

relationships" (p. 23).

In the context of public relations, Hon and J. Grunig (1999) defined commitment

as "the extent to which one party believes and feels that the relationship is worth

spending energy to maintain and promote" (p. 20). Ledingham and Bruning (1998)

conceptualized commitment: "… commitment involves the decision to continue a

relationship. It adds the element of responsibility by suggesting that successful

relationships involve facing relational difficulties together" (p. 58).

According to Meyer and Allen (1984), there are two types of commitment:

continuance commitment (i.e., a certain line of affection) and *affective* commitment (i.e.,

an emotional orientation). Mowday, Steers, and Porter (1979) described characteristics of

affective commitment as: "1) a strong belief in and acceptance of the organization's goals

and values, 2) a willingness to exert considerable effort on behalf of the organization, and

3) a strong desire to maintain membership in the organization" (p. 226). Meyer and Allen

(1984) defined continuance commitment as "the extent to which employees feel

committed to their organizations by virtue of the costs that they feel are associated with

leaving" (p. 375).

Commitment has been found to be strongly associated with other relational features. For example, commitment is positively associated with relational satisfaction and investment in the relationship (Rusbult, 1983), equity and expectations for a relational partnership (Sabatelli, 1984), and relational stability (Lund, 1985; Sabatelli & Cecil-Pigo, 1985).

Relational Satisfaction

Satisfaction is most commonly studied as relational features (Ferguson, 1984; Huang, 1997, 2001; Millar & Rogers, 1976; Stafford & Canary, 1991). Citing Kelley and Thibaut (1978), Stafford and Canary (1991) explained relational satisfaction: "From a social exchange perspective, a satisfying relationship is one in which the distribution of rewards is equitable and the relational rewards outweigh the cost" (p. 225).

In the context of public relations, like Stafford and Canary (1991), Hon and J. Grunig (1999) also conceptualized the cost/reward framework and defined relational satisfaction as follows:

The extent to which one party feels favorable toward the other because positive expectations about the relationship are reinforced. Or, a satisfying relationship, is one in which the benefits outweigh the costs. Satisfaction also can occur when one party believes that the other party's relationship maintenance behaviors are positive. (p. 20)

Another key characteristic of relational satisfaction is that satisfaction also includes affection and emotion, unlike control mutuality and trust that involve cognitive dimensions (J. Grunig & Huang, 2000). For instance, along the same conceptualization of

Hon and J. Grunig (1999), Hecht (1978) pointed out that relational satisfaction brings out

a favorable affective response to the reinforcement of positive expectations.

Finally, about the implication of satisfaction for relational maintenance strategies,

Safford and Canary (1991) said: "Moreover, relational satisfaction is probably the

hallmark of effective relational maintenance" (p. 225). Previous research has found that

there is a strong association between relational maintenance behaviors and satisfaction

(Bell, Daly, & Gonzalez, 1987).

Organization-public Relationship Types

Clark and Mills (1979) first distinguished *communal* relationships from *exchange*

relationships. Initially, they adopted sociologist Goffman's (1961) concepts of social

exchange and economic exchange.[15] Since 1979, Clark and Mills have extensively

studied the distinction between communal and exchange relationships: interpersonal

attraction in communal and exchange relationships (Clark & Mills, 1979); the difference

between communal and exchange relationships (Clark, 1984; Clark & Mills, 1993; Mills

& Clark, 1982, 1994); perceptions of exploitation in communal and exchange

relationships (Clark & Waddell, 1985); evidence for the effectiveness of manipulations of

communal and exchange relationships (Clark, 1986); needs in communal and exchange

relationships (Clark, Mills, & Powell, 1986); recipient's mood, relationship type, and

helping (Clark, Ouellette, Powell, & Milberg, 1987); needs and inputs of friends and

---

[15] According to Mills and Clark (1994), they replaced Goffman's term economic exchange with their term exchange relationships because "many of the benefits people give and receive do not involve money or things for which a monetary value can be calculated" (p. 30).

strangers (Clark, Mills, & Corcoran, 1989); and reactions to and willingness to express emotion in two types of relationships (Clark & Taraban, 1991).

Clark and Mills (e.g., Clark, 1984; Clark & Mills, 1993; Mills & Clark, 1982, 1994) distinguished communal and exchange relationships "based on the rules of norms that govern the giving and receiving of benefits" and defined each concept: 1) in *exchange* relationships, "benefits are given with the expectation of receiving a comparable benefit in return or as repayment for a benefit received previously" and 2) in *communal* relationships, benefits are given "in response to needs or to demonstrate a general concern for the other person" (Clark & Mills, 1993, p. 684).

The major distinction between communal and exchange[16] relationships lies in that a communal relationship "does not create a specific debt or obligation to return a comparable benefit, as it does in an exchange relationship" (Clark & Mills, 1993, p. 684). About the importance of the distinction of communal and exchange relationships, Mills and Clark (1994) said as follows:

> We believe that the distinction between a communal and exchange relationship is a fundamental one, and that relationships in which there is a concern for the welfare of the other are different in important ways from relationships in which people benefit one another in order to receive specific benefits in return. (p. 30)

---

[16] Clark and Mills (1993) said that they used the term exchange in accord with the "dictionary definition" of exchange (i.e., giving or taking one thing in return for another); the term exchange is broadly defined in social psychology as mutually rewarding interaction.

Another distinct feature of a communal relationship[17] is in its varying strength.

Unlike exchange relationships, communal relationships can vary in strength (Clark &

Mills, 1993; Mills & Clark, 1994). According to Clark and Mills (1993), "… the greater

the motivation to be responsive to the other person's needs, the stronger the communal

relationship" (p. 685). They cited examples of such varying strength of communal

relationships: "The communal relationship with one's best friend is typically stronger

than that with one's own friends. The communal relationship with one's child is typically

stronger than that with one's best friend" (p. 685).

In the context of public relations, Hon and J. Grunig (1999) defined communal

and exchange relationships: 1) in an *exchange* relationship, "one party gives benefits to

the other only because the other has provided benefits in the past or is expected to do so

in the future" and 2) in a *communal* relationships, "both parties provide benefits to the

other because they are concerned for the welfare of the other—even when they get

nothing in return" (pp. 20-21). Exchange is the essence of marketing relationships

between organizations and customers and the key concept in marketing theory; however,

theorists of relational marketing also have pointed out that profit organizations need

communal relationships with customers (Hon & J. Grunig, 1999).

Because publics expect communal relationships (e.g., organizations to do things

for the community for which organizations get little or nothing in return), organizations

can be effective by building communal relationships with strategic publics (L. Grunig, J.

---

[17] Clark and Mills (1993) suggested that there can be one-sided communal relationships.
On this point, Clark and Mills stated as follows: "At the beginning of our work on
communal/exchange distinction, our focus was on communal relationships that are
mutual (Clark & Mills, 1979). Later (Mills & Clark, 1988), we discussed one-sided
communal relationships, such as the relationship between a parent and an infant or young
child" (pp. 684-685).

Grunig, & Dozier, 2002). In particular, Hon and J. Grunig (1999) described implications

of communal relationships for organizational effectiveness:

1. Communal relationships are important if organizations are to be socially

   responsible and to add value to society as well as to client organizations.

2. Communal relationships reduce the likelihood of negative behaviors from

   stakeholders such as litigation, regulation, strikes, boycotts, negative

   publicity, and the like. (p. 21)

However, as Clark and Mills (1993) explained, most relationships begin as

exchange relationships and then developed to communal relationships as they mature. In

this regard, L. Grunig et al. (2002) said that exchange relationships are not bad for

organizations; relatively, communal relationships are more strongly associated with

organizational effectiveness than exchange relationships.

Along the same line, Hon and J. Grunig (1999) suggested the effect of communal

relationships on organization-public relationship outcomes: "Exchange relationships

never develop the same levels of trust and the other three relationship indicators that

accompany communal relationships" (p. 21). Likewise, L. Grunig, J. Grunig, and Dozier

(2002) explained the effects of communal relationships: "Nevertheless, a measure of the

degree to which a public perceives that it has a communal relationship with an

organization is perhaps the purest indicator of the success of the public relations

management function" (p. 553).

Additional Organization-public Relationship Types

In addition to communal and exchange relationships, Hung (2002) identified more

types of organization-public relationships: communal (one-sided versus mutual), covenantal, contractual, and exploitive relationships: 1) *exploitive* relationships: "arise when one takes advantage of the other when the other follows the communal norms or one does not fulfill his/her obligation in an exchange relationship" (pp. 45-46), 2) *covenantal* relationships[18]: "both sides commit to a common good by their open exchange and the norm of reciprocity" (p. 46), and 3) *contractual* relationships: "start when parties agree on what each should do in the relationships" (p. 46).

After conducting research, Hung (2002) found two additional types of relationships in the context of organization-public relationships: 1) a *symbiotic* relationships which "happens when organizations, realizing the interdependence in the environment, work together with certain publics with the common interest of surviving in the environment" (p. 319) and 2) a *manipulative* relationships which "happens when an organization, with the knowledge of what publics want, applies asymmetrical or pseudo-symmetrical approaches to communicate with publics to serve its own interests" (p. 320).

In the following section, I will discuss the concept of reputation and its measurement systems. Then, I will explain why an open-end measure of reputation is necessary to improve the validity and reliability of measurement systems of the reputation concept. Finally, I will 1) introduce J. Grunig and Hung's (2002) typology of cognitive representations to measure reputation and 2) connect their typology with concepts and models of cognitive representations and person impression in the literature of psychology.

---

[18] According to Hung (2002), mutual communal relationships are different from covenantal relationships, in which "the latter emphasizes open exchanges between two parties, while the former emphasizes the psychological intention to protect the welfare of the other" (p. 326).

Organizational Reputation

Despite popular surveys to measure reputations (Deephouse, 2000, 2002; Fombrun, 1996; Hall, 1992) following the lead of *Fortune* magazine, several issues have been raised over definitions and measurement systems of organizational reputation. In particular, several scholars have repeatedly pointed out 1) inconsistency in definitions and failure to distinguish reputation from similar concepts (e.g., Bromley, 1993, 2000, Caruana & Chircop, 2000; Fombrun, 1996; Fombrun & Van Riel, 1997; J. Grunig & Hung, 2002; Pruzan, 2001) and 2) discrepancy between the theoretical concept of reputation and its operationalization in measurement systems (e.g., Bergen, 2001; Bromley, 1993, 2000, 2002; Caruana & Chircop, 2000; Fryxell and Wang, 1994; Fombrun, 1996; Fombrun & Van Riel, 2003; Fombrun & Gardberg, 2000; J. Grunig & Hung, 2002; Hutton et al., 2001; Schultz, Mouritsen, & Gabrielsen, 2001; Yang & J. Grunig, 2005). Before I address such issues in reputation measurement, I will first discuss the nature of organizational reputation and definitions of organizational reputation.

The Nature of Reputation

In a search for key attributes of reputation, Bromley (1993) reviewed 122 quotations on reputation from Bartlett (1980), Benham (1948), Stevenson (1949, 1974), and the Oxford Dictionary of Quotations (Oxford University Press, 1979). Among the propositions that Bromley extracted, I found that the following attributes of reputation are relevant in this study:

1. It is difficult to make and keep up a good reputation or to repair a damaged one, whereas a good reputation is easily lost or damaged.

2. It is immoral deliberately to seek to establish reputation, and reputations that are deliberately cultivated are more vulnerable than those that are not.

3. Popular (widespread) and rapidly acquired reputations are short lived.

4. Reputations are determined not only by the actions of an entity but also by the consequences of those actions, the entity's relationships and qualities, and by many other factors. (pp. 9-11)

With regard to the nature of organizational reputation, I consider that Bromley's above quotes suggest the following key aspects of organizational reputation related to organization-public relationships: 1) An organization needs to manage long-term quality relationships with publics rather than attempt to manipulate reputation for short-term outputs; and 2) Organizational reputation is "superficial" and can be easily damaged by organizational behaviors, whereas organization-public relationships are more endurable than organizational reputation since cultivating quality relationships requires long-term devotion from both parties.

The Attributes of Successful Reputation Management

Fombrun and Foss (2001a, May) explained five attributes of successful corporate reputation management, which they learned from the Reputation Institute's measurement and analysis of corporate reputations. I consider that these attributes suggest how critical the role "communication" plays in successful reputation management, in particular the principle of *transparency*. I summarize Fombrun and Foss's attributes of reputation management:

1. The principle of *distinctiveness*: Strong reputations result when companies own a distinctive position in the minds of resource-holders.

2. The principle of *focus*: Strong reputations result when companies focus their actions and communications around a single core theme.

3. The principle of *consistency*: Strong reputations result when companies are consistent in their actions and communications to all resource-holders.

4. The principle of *identity*: Strong reputations result when companies act in ways that are consistent with espoused principles of identity.

5. The principle of *transparency*: Strong reputations result when companies are transparent in the way they conduct their affairs; transparency requires active communication. ("Five Principles of Reputation Management")

Definitions of Reputation

Depending on different perspectives, the concept of organizational reputation has been defined as assessments that multiple stakeholders make about the company's ability to fulfill their expectations (Fombrun & Van Riel, 2003), a collective system of subjective beliefs among members of a social group (Bromley, 1993, 2000, 2002), and representations in minds of multiple publics about an organization's past behaviors and related attributes (Coombs, 2000; J. Grunig and Hung, 2002). More specifically, from diverse business perspectives, corporate reputation has been defined as beliefs of market participants about a firm's strategic character (Weigelt & Camerer, 1988), salient attributes that observers ascribe to firms (Fombrun & Shanley, 1990), the esteem in which a firm is held by publics (Fombrun, 1996), collective beliefs that exist in the organizational field about a firm's identity and prominence (Rao, 1994; Rindova & Kotha, 2002), and media visibility and favorability gained by a firm (Deephouse, 2000).

Fombrun and Van Riel (1997), in the inaugural issue of the *Corporate Reputation Review*, maintained that reputation has been understudied because of "a problem of definitions" (p. 5). Fombrun and Van Riel (1997) introduced six distinct literatures that currently converge in their emphasis on reputation. I summarize the following six perspectives on reputation from Fombrun and Van Riel and their citations (pp. 6-10):

1. The *economic* view

   a) Game theory: Reputation of a player is the perception others have of the player's values (Weigelt & Camerer, 1988).

   b) Signaling theory: Managers can make strategic use of a company's reputation to signal its attractiveness such as their quality to the company's constituents (Shapiro, 1983).

   c) Capital and labor market: Companies rent the reputation of their agents to signal investors, regulators, and other publics about the firm's probity and credibility (Wilson, 1985).

2. The *strategic* view: Strategies call attention to the competitive benefits of acquiring favorable reputations (Rindova & Fombrun, 1999).

3. The *marketing* view: Reputation is often labeled as brand image; building brand equity requires the creation of a familiar brand that has favorable, strong and unique association (Keller, 1993).

4. The *organizational* view: Reputations are rooted in the sense-making experiences of employees; a company's culture and identity shape a firm's business practices as well as the kinds of relationships that managers establish with key stakeholders.

5. The *sociological* view: Reputation rankings are social constructions that come into being through the relationships that a focal firm has with its stakeholders in a shared institutional environment.

6. The *accounting* view: Intangible assets build higher reputational assessments among observers; reputation, as intangible assets, needs to be included in financial reporting standards.

From the review of the literature, Fombrun and Van Riel (1997) concluded that Fombrun and Rindova's (1996) definition captured the characteristics of reputation best: "A corporate reputation is a collective representation of a firm's past actions and results that describes the firm's ability to deliver valued outcomes to multiple stakeholders. It gauges a firm's relative standing both internally with employees and externally with its stakeholders, in both its competitive and institutional environments" (p. 10).

However, Fombrun himself has defined reputation inconsistently over time. Overall, I found that he defined reputation as collective assessment of a firm's past behavior and outcomes that depicts the firm's ability to provide valued results to multiple stakeholders. In his book, Fombrun (1996) defined corporate reputation as "the overall estimation in which a company is held by its constituents. A corporate reputation represents the 'net' affective or emotional reaction—good or bad, weak or strong—of customers, investors, employees, and the general public to the company's name" (p. 37).

On the website of the Reputation Institute (n.d.a.), the founder of the Institute, Fombrun, defined reputation as:

1. A corporate reputation is a cognitive representation of a company's ability to meet the expectations of its stakeholders.

2. A corporate reputation describes the rational and emotional attachment that stakeholders form with a company.

3. A corporate reputation describes the net image a company develops with all of its stakeholders. ("Q. What are Corporate Reputations?")

Recently, Fombrun and Van Riel (2003) also viewed reputation as perceptions of an organization: "Reputations reflect how companies are perceived across a broad spectrum of stakeholders" (p. xxvii). Fombrun and Van Riel (2003) differentiated reputation from brand: "Reputation, on the other hand, involves the assessments that multiple stakeholders make about the company's ability to fulfill their expectations" (p. 4). In summary, Fombrun has considered the construct of reputation to be both *cognitive* and *evaluative*.[19]

Likewise, Bromley (1993, 2000, 2002), from the perspective of psychology, conceptualized reputation as cognition that is often *evaluative* rather than neutral. According to Bromley (1993), "... social evaluation plays a prominent part in reputation" (p. 1); "... the concepts of 'reputation' and 'public image' are virtually identical. The main difference is that reputation usually implies an evaluation, whereas public image is a fairly neutral term" (p. 6). However, as J. Grunig and Hung (2002) suggested, Bromley (1993) also pointed out that reputation is not always evaluative. Bromley (1993) stated: "... the collective view of a person or other entity can be strongly evaluative (in a

---

[19] J. Grunig and Hung (2002) reviewed the definitions of reputation, given by Fombrun, and pointed out: "If we isolate the key components of these definitions, we can see that reputations contain both cognitions ("cognitive representations," "net image," "reflections of past) and attitudes (i.e., evaluations or valence such as "affective or emotional reaction," "attachments," "attractiveness," "prestige," and "status").

positive or negative way), or ambivalent or neutral" depending on the nature of interactions between reputational entities (p. 5).

Bromley (1993) defined reputation as "a collective system of subjective beliefs among members of a social group" (p. 15). Bromley (1993) quoted the *Concise Oxford Dictionary of Current English* (Skyes, 1976), in which reputation is defined as "what is generally said or believed about a person's or thing's character" (p. 1). From this definition, Bromley (1993, p. 1) pointed out several key characteristics of reputation: 1) Reputation is extensively said or believed in a social group (i.e., reputation refers to collective representations); 2) What is generally said or believed about a reputational entity may vary depending on different social groups (i.e., a reputational entity may have more than one reputation); 3) What is said may be different from what is believed (i.e., people can be mistaken in their appreciation of group opinion); and 4) Reputation of an entity often means the esteem or standing in its main social groups or, conversely, reflects general discredit or ill favor (i.e., reputation is usually evaluative).

More specifically, Bromley (2000, 2002) suggested that reputation should be conceptualized as a collective phenomenon. By a "collective phenomenon," Bromley (2000) stated:

> A key concept in the study of the practical aspects of corporate, or personal, reputation is that of 'consensus' (agreement, unanimity, trend of opinion). Reputation is a collective phenomenon, and consensus underpins collective action… Collective reactions, such as a boycott, demonstration, or strike, however, depend on 'consensus,' meaning total or substantial conformity in the distribution of beliefs and agreement on how to react. (p. 245)

Distinction Between Primary and Secondary Reputation

Bromley (1993) traced the origin of reputation study to person impression

theories from the perspective of social psychology and differentiated a *first*-order

individual impression from a *second*-order collective phenomenon in the context of

corporate reputation (Bromley, 1993, 2000). First, he said that first-order mental

representations refer to an individual's impression or belief about a firm (Bromley, 1993).

Individual persons form their impression of a company through direct experience of its

premises, products, services, or personnel (Bromley, 2000). Second, by contrast,

corporate reputation is *second*-order collective (social) representations that can be

constructed through individual representations (Bromley, 1993). In addition to first-order

impressions, individuals form their impressions through exposure to other's opinions and

influence (Bromley, 2000).

In terms of the distinction between *primary* and *secondary* reputations, Bromley

(1993) also reflected the distinction between first-order and second-order representations.

Bromley (1993) defined *primary* reputation as "the totality of opinions circulating within

a primary face-to-face group" (reputations based on direct, first-hand acquaintance) (pp.

42-43), whereas *secondary* reputation refers to "those opinions in circulation in an

extended social network that are not based on, or closely connected with, direct face-to-

face contact with the person concerned" (p. 44). Bromley (1993) explained that a primary

reputation can be more diffusely spread than a secondary reputation, meaning that

"direct, first-hand contact leads to highly individualized impressions, whereas indirect

contact based on hearsay leads to stereotyped impressions" (pp. 42-43). Consequently, secondary reputations are relatively "superficial, simple, and stylized" (p. 7) and "conforming to prevailing opinion" (p. 44).

Finally, Bromley (1993) emphasized the role of the mass media in the formation of *secondary* reputation as follows:

> First-hand, direct acquaintance and word of mouth are the usual ways of getting to know about people in small face-to-face social settings. The mass communication media, however, make it possible for large numbers of people to know about a person (or product or organizations) indirectly. (p. 7)

In this regard, Fombrun and Shanley (1990), Fombrun and Van Riel (2003), and Deephouse (2000), and Rindova and Kotha (2002) also said that media visibility (i.e., frequency of media reports) and favorability of media coverage play a critical role in reputation formation.

Bromley (2000) suggested that there are two basic questions in conceptualizing and measuring reputation:

1. What is a second-order collective phenomenon derived from a set of first-order individual impressions of a company?

2. How do such collective phenomena affect individual impressions? (p. 245)

In other words, the key question is how individual and collective impressions interact with each other. According to Bromley (2000), "Individual impressions (cognitive representations) of an organization are shared and modified through a complex social pooling process," depending on "transmission of information and influence throughout one or more social networks" (p. 245). When the free-description method of opinions and attributes are used to study reputations, individual impressions can be characterized as either "distributed" (the spread of differences between individual's impressions and the lack of overall consensus) or "undistributed" (the degree of conformity between individuals).

From the perspective of public relations, J. Grunig and Hung (2002) defined reputation as "the distribution of cognitive representations that members of a collectivity hold about an organization, representations that may, but do not always, include evaluative components" (p. 20). In addition, from the perspectives of stakeholder theory and neo-institutionalism, Coombs (2000) conceptualized reputation as the relational history (i.e., a collection of past events in a relationship) with multiple stakeholders.

In conceptualizing organizational reputation, J. Grunig and Hung (2002) suggested: 1) Reputations refer to *collective* representations in minds of multiple publics about organizations; 2) Cognitive representations are *not* always evaluative (either evaluative or neutral); 3) Cognitive representations consist of *objects*, *attributes*, the *connection* among them (objects-attributes), and behaviors; and 4) Operationalization of cognitive representations can be the *distribution* of such components in a free-description (open-end measure).

J. Grunig and Hung (2002), like Bromley (1993, 2000, 2002), also differentiated primary and secondary reputation based on prior experience with organizations; they used the terms "experiential" (first-order) and "reputational" (second-order) respectively. According to J. Grunig and Hung (2002), when publics are involved with an organization, they have *experiential* relationships with the organization and hold *experiential* cognitive representations about the organization. When publics are not involved with an organization and have no *experiential* relationship with an organization, they may still hold *reputational* cognitive representations about the organization based on

hearsay (i.e., what they hear from the media and others).

J. Grunig and Hung (2002) proposed that the effect of organization-public

relationships on organizational reputation is likely to be more influential for the former

type of publics, having experiential (i.e., first-order) relationships and cognitive

representations, than for the latter type of publics. In contrast, to publics without

experiential relationships with an organization (low-involvement publics), second-order

reputations may be the basis for speculation about second-order relationships with the

organization (Yang & Mallabo, 2003). However, the effect of organization-public

relationships on organizational reputation is more likely to affect organizational

effectiveness, than the effect of organizational reputation on organization-public

relationships, because publics with experiential relationships are often strategic publics

that can affect or be affected by an organization (J. Grunig & Hung, 2002).

Coombs (2000) also considered that prior experience affects the nature of

organizational reputation. On this point, Coombs (2000) said: "… a reputation is based

on a stakeholder's experiences with an organization. Both reputation and relational

history are built from past interactions between the organization and the stakeholder" (p.

76). According to Coombs (2000), a stakeholder holds reputations of organizations based

on past interactions with the organization; depending on the intensity of interactions with

the organization, reputation can be evaluative or neutral as Bromley (1993) and J. Grunig

and Hung (2002) pointed out. About neutral reputation, Coombs (2000) said as follows:

> … a neutral reputation is a result of either no meaningful interaction between
>
> organization and stakeholder or the organization doing just the minimum in

maintaining the relationships with stakeholders. Either way, the organization generates no strong effect for stakeholders. (pp. 81-82)

Distinction Between Reputation and Other Similar Conceptspts

Depending on different perspectives, some researchers (e.g., Bromley, 1993, 2000; Fombrun, 1996; Fombrun & Van Riel, 1997) have argued that reputation is a distinct concept; others (e.g., Caruana & Chircop, 2000; J. Grunig & Hung, 2002; Pruzan, 2001, Verčič, 2002) emphasized the association of reputation with similar concepts such as image, identity, brand, impression, and the like.

Bromley (2000) distinguished corporate identity and corporate image from reputation in the following manner:

1. Corporate *identity*: The way key members conceptualize their organizations.

2. Corporate *image*: The way an organization presents itself to its publics, especially visually.

3. Corporate *reputation*: The way key external stakeholder groups or other interested parties actually conceptualize that organization. (p. 241)

On the website of the Reputation Institute (n.d.b.), the founder Fombrun argued that people often confuse the words reputation, brand, and image. Fombrun (n.d.b.) said:

The point is this: A company has many different images and can have many brands. In contrast, a corporate reputation signals the overall attractiveness of the company to *all of its constituents*, including employees, customers, investors, reporters, and the general public. A corporate reputation therefore reconciles the many images people have of a company, and conveys the relative prestige and status of the company vis-à-vis rivals. ("Q. Brand, Image, or Reputation?")

In contrast, others (e.g., Caruana & Chircop, 2000; J. Grunig & Hung, 2002; Pruzan, 2001, Verčič, 2000) emphasized the association of reputation to other terms. For example, Caruana and Chircop (2000) analyzed the history of reputation research and described the interconnectedness of terms:

> Research on corporate *reputation* is rooted in earlier work on corporate *image, corporate identity* and *personality* ... Corporate reputation emerges from the images held by various publics of an organization ... Corporate reputation is closely related to *brand* equity.(p. 43)

Pruzan (2001) explained the role of corporate image in the emergence of coporate reputation: "There is no doubt that corporate reputation—in the sense of corporate image—is given more attention than ever before in the history of organized business activity ... Their concern is with the images they receive of corporate behavior and results" (p. 50).

J. Grunig and Hung (2002) found the confusing use of such terms as reputations, image, identity, brand, or impression in the literature on reputation. Jeffries-Fox Associates (2000a) conducted a content analysis of 1, 149 articles in 94 trade and academic publications and concluded that the terms reputation and brand are used interchangeably. According to J. Grunig and Hung (2002): "With the exception of identity, most of these terms describe essentially the same phenomenon: what publics think of an organization. Identity describes what an organization thinks of itself" (p. 2). In fact, among research firms offering reputation measures, Young and Rubicam, Market Facts, and Opinion Research Corporation called their reputation measures *The Brand*

Asset Valuator, *Brand Vision*, and *Brand Perceptions* respectively; Landor Associates called its reputation measure *Image Power* (Jeffries-Fox Associates, 2000b).

Likewise, Verčič (2000) pointed out that reputation is equivalent with image. Verčič (2000, p. 4) said as follows:

> For nearly a century, the public relations profession has been trying to disassociate itself from the image of being a profession about image-making. It is therefore a pity that it tries to redefine itself as reputation management—which is basically the same as image-making. (cited in J. Grunig & Hung, 2002, p. 3)

Operationalization of Organizational reputation

Capelin (1999) pointed out inconsistency of current reputation measures: "I applaud the 'hot ticket' status of reputation management that has engulfed PR Week's pages ... But while there is clearly a place for a consistent system to evaluate corporate status, it is not the Holy Grail of reputation management" ("PR Week," 1999, November 15). Fombrun and Foss (2001b, May) also pointed out: "Measuring corporate reputations accurately is crucial if they are to be managed. Yet measures of reputation proliferate, encouraging chaos and confusion about a company's reputational assets" (p. 1).

As I discussed previously, J. Grunig and Hung (2002) suggested that operationalization of reputation may be biased by 1) the use of specific samples of the *Fortune* survey, 2) the concentration of items on financial performance, and 3) the correlation between the *Fortune* ranking and financial performance. Therefore, J. Grunig and Hung (2002) argued as follows: "To a large extent, the predictor variable (reputation rating of financial performance) measures the same thing as the variable predicted (actual financial performance). From the following sections, I will discuss 1) sampling issues, 2) the validity and reliability of reputation measures, and 3) reputation ranking systems in detail.

Sampling Issues

Fombrun, Gardberg, and Sever (2000) pointed out general methodological limitations of surveys of reputations such as the *Fortune* survey: 1) biased sampling frames; 2) target firms selected by size of revenue; 3) restriction to publicly traded companies; 4) collusion because of the sector membership of respondents; 5) over-representation of senior managers, directors, and financial analysts in samples; 6) lack of direct experience relevance to some attributes (items in rating samples) by respondents; and 7) the use of mainly pen and paper mail surveys. Consequently, to overcome over-representation of specific samples,[20] Fombrun and associates used a representative group of stakeholders to measure corporate reputations on 20 underlying attributes in the Reputation Quotient.[21]

---

[20] Fombrun used a type of political polling to sample respondents for the Reputation Quotient, aided by Harris Interactive, in which online or phone interviews were conducted to nominate companies with the best and worst reputations in the initial stage, and another group of samples were interviewed to provide their overall assessments of the reputations of the nominated companies (Fombrun & Gardberg, 2000).

[21] According to Fombrun and Van Riel (2003) and Fombrun and Gardberg (2000), the 20 attributes in the Reputation Quotient are grouped into the following 6 dimensions: 1) *emotional appeal*: how much the company is liked, admired, and respected; 2) *products & services*: perceptions of the quality, innovation, value, and reliability of the company's products and services; 3) *financial performance*: perceptions of the company's profitability, prospects, and risk; 4) *vision & leadership*: how much the company demonstrates a clear vision and strong leadership; 5) *workplace environment*: perceptions of how well the company is managed, how it is to work for, and the quality of its employees; and 6) *social responsibility*: perceptions of the company as a good citizen in its dealing with communities, employees, and the environment.

Caruana and Chircop (2000) held that, depending on the samples, attributes of reputation measurement should have different weights. On this point, Caruana and Chircop said in the following manner:

Firms interact with a multitude of publics, each of which often gives different consideration to a common set of reputation attributes. Therefore, the firm often has not just one but an array of images that together shape its reputation. For example, in looking at corporate reputation, managers and stockholders are likely to place strong emphasis on financial performance… On the other hand, consumers are likely to attribute greater importance to consistently high quality. For consumers, the firm's financial performance may be of less important in assigning a reputation to a firm. (p. 44)

Bromley (2002) maintained that the difference between a "collection" of people and a "collective" is critical in sampling respondents for reputations surveys. According to Bromley (2002), "A 'collective' is a relatively homogenous group of people with a degree of common interests in a reputational entity, such as a company or a product or a person" (p. 36). Thus, Bromley (2002) argued that reputations should be studied "based on 'collectives,' not on heterogeneous 'collections' of people" (p. 36), because 1) reputations are socially shared impressions in a social group and 2) reputational entities "have as many reputations as there are distinct social groups that take an interest in them" (p. 36).

Reliability and Validity in Reputation Measurement

About the measurement of reputation in the *Fortune* survey, Caruana and Chircop (2000) said: "No reliability or validity testing of the instrument is reported" (p. 45). Of eight attributes on the Fortune survey,[22] Fryxell and Wang (1994) said that four of the eight items in the index refer to performance, whereas constructs such as innovation, corporate social responsibility, and measurement quality are being measured by single items. When Fryxell and Wang (1994) conducted confirmatory factor analysis, they found that all but one of the items (community and environmental responsibility) appear to be directly influenced by the raters' perception of the financial potential of the firm. Along the same line with J. Grunig and Hung's (2002) argument, therefore, Fryxell and Wang argued that the *Fortune* reputation index measures little beyond economic performance.

Reputation Rankings

Bromley (2002) compared methods of measuring corporate reputations, such as league tables, quotients, benchmarks, free-description, psychometrics, and case studies. Bromley pointed out the sampling issues in the method of league tables, which is best characterized by the *Fortune* reports. By league tables, Bromley meant the *Fortune* survey's use of a ranking system derived from respondents' rating companies.

In addition to the sampling issues, Bromley (2002) also raised methodological questions about the use of overall ratings to set reputation rankings. Bromley (2002) said: "In some *Fortune* reports, it is not entirely clear how the 'rankings' are derived from the 'ratings'" (p. 36). Therefore, Bromley (2002) traced the ways of how the rankings in league tables and the *Reputation Quotient* are calculated:

---

[22] The eight attributes in the Fortune survey includes 1) quality of management; 2) quality of products or services; 3) innovativeness; 4) long-term investment value; 5) financial soundness; 6) ability to attract, develop, and keep up talented people; 7) responsibility to the community and the environment; and 8) wise use of corporate assets (Caruana & Chircop, 2000).

1. The ratings of a set of items (attributes) appear to be added together and averaged.

2. These averaged scores are then summed across a sample of respondents rating the same set of companies.

3. The scores are then ordered from highest to lowest, providing a rank order for companies. (p. 36)

Then, Bromley (2002) pointed out issues in reputation rankings: "the idea of averaging a set of ranks is problematic, because a rank order is an ordinal scale, not ratio or interval scale… Using ranked data in elaborative multivariate statistical analyses is questionable" (p. 36). Besides, about the *Reputation Quotient*, Bromley (2002) explained that Fombrun does *not* calculate "any arithmetical quotient" and just uses averaging rankings, although "a 'quotient,' by definition, is a ratio between two numbers" (p. 37). If any arithmetic quotient is used (e.g., the ratio of the rating of a selected company to the rating of average company, multiplied by 100), it is still doubtful that these are quotients because the original data are ratings in ordinal scales (Bromley, 2002).

As an alternative for league tables such as the *Fortune* reports and the Reputation Quotient, therefore, Bromley (1993, 2000, 2002) suggested the *free-description* method to study reputations. This is basically the same as the method used by J. Grunig and Hung (2002) and the method that will be used in this study to measure organizational reputation.

The free-description method (i.e., an open-end measure) "enables respondents to list various attributions, based on their personal interests and experiences" (Bromley, 2002, p. 38). Rather than averaging the responses to calculate a single composite,

Bromley (1993, 2000, 2002) suggested that reputations can be measured by the distribution of attributions in the free-description method. By doing so, attributes are not restricted and are not directed to abstract and general terms imposed by the researchers (Bromley, 1993).

Bromley (1993) asked students to write a paragraph about their instructors, and found that the distribution of reputations can be accounted for by the association between the prevalence of an attribution (i.e., the number of respondents citing that attribute) and the number of different attributions at that prevalence. The distribution of attributes, according to Bromley (1993), is often a reversed-J frequency distribution; as the opinions are widely shared, the frequency distribution gets undistributed (i.e., the negative regression line becomes steeper; the intercept becomes higher).

Criticizing common reputation ranking systems, for possible operationalization of organizational reputation, Bromley suggested as follows:

1. The boundaries of the relevant social group or network have to be defined.

2. The total number of attributes from respondents (including those given by only one person) can be defined as reputation.

3. Reputations can be measured by either overall rating on attributes or the number of mentions of particular attributes. (p. 16, p. 233)

Toward a New Measure of Organizational reputation as Cognitive Representations

J. Grunig and Hung (2002) developed an open-end measure of cognitive representations that a member of publics has about on organization. Like Bromley's (1993) use of an open-end measure for a sample of students to investigate instructors' reputations, J. Grunig and Hung asked a sample of the general population to describe in a sentence or two "what comes to mind when they think of organizations studied." They found that their measure of reputation can be used for publics who mostly have reputational relationships with an organization as well as those who have experiential relationships.

Whereas Bromley (1993, 2000, 2002) limited the free-description of cognitive representations to attributes, J. Grunig and Hung (2002) went beyond Bromley's method and developed a taxonomy of cognitive representations that includes other types of representations, influenced by J. Grunig (1993), J. Grunig et al. (1985), Anderson (1996, 2000), Anderson and Lebiere (1998), Carter (1979), and Scott, Osgood, and Peterson (1979). J. Grunig and Hung (2002) developed the following taxonomy of cognitive representations:

1. An *object-attribute* representation: Objects and attributes associated through an isa[23] connection. For example, General Electric is a large company.

2. An *object-object* representation: Objects associated with other objects through an isa connection. For example, Bill Gates is president of Microsoft.

3. A *behavioral* representation: Agents or actors (one object) connected through an action or behavior to a recipient of that action (a second object). For example, AT & T fired 2,000 workers.

---

[23] According to J. Grunig and Hung (2002), "organization also can be linked to other objects and associated with attributes through what Anderson and Lebiere (1998) called an 'isa' statement (p. 23). For example, we might think that Microsoft *is a* part of the electronics industry (an object-object linkage)... or think that Microsoft *is a* profitable company (an object-attribute linkage)" (p. 22). Detailed information on the isa links will be offered later in this chapter.

4. An *evaluative* representation: An object-attribute, object-object, or behavioral
   cognitive representation that contains an evaluative[24] component or that
   consists of a pure attitudinal statement such as "Exxon is an evil company."
   (p. 23)

By defining organizational reputation as cognitive representations that publics
have of organizations, definitions and key concepts in "cognition" and "representations"
need to be explained here. I will review *cognition, memory,* and the *structure* of cognition
from the literature of cognitive psychology, and *person impression* (or perception) from
the literature of social psychology. Reputation research has been developed from research
on person impression in psychology (Bromley, 1993); consequently, the following review
of the literature is relevant. In a nutshell, the following review about cognitive
representations in the literature of psychology suggests that cognitive representations of
organizations would consists of objects, attributes, the relations between objects and
attributes, and evaluations. Indeed, this is consistent with J. Grunig and Hung's (2002)
taxonomy of cognitive representations that I reviewed the above.

Definitions of Cognition and Representation

Defining Cognition

Ashcraft (2002) defined cognition as "the collection of mental processes and
activities used in perceiving, remembering, thinking, and understanding, as well as the act
of using those processes." (p. 10). Therefore, Ashcraft said that cognition and memory
are inseparable, in which memory is defined as "the mental processes of acquiring and

---

[24] Citing Kruglanski (1989), J. Grunig and Hung (2002) suggested that some
representations are nonevaluative or nonaffective.

retaining information for later retrieval and the mental storage system that enables these processes" (p. 10).

About the use of memory, Schacter (1987, 1994) distinguished between explicit memory and implicit memory as follows: 1) *explicit* memory: the conscious or intentional recollection of prior experiences, and 2) *implicit* memory: effects produced by prior experiences that do not require any current intentional or conscious awareness of those experiences (cited in Smith, 1998, p. 392). Another useful distinction in memory includes semantic or episodic memory (Ashcraft, 2002): 1) *semantic* memory: the long-term memory component in which general world knowledge, including knowledge of language, is stored (p. 547), and 2) *episodic* memory: the long-term memory in which personally experienced information (i.e., autobiographical long-term memory) is stored (p. 542).

Defining Representation

According to Smith (1998), "Psychologists generally define a *representation* as an encoding of some information, which an individual can construct, retain in memory, access, and use in various ways. Thus, your impression of your Uncle Harry—your body of interrelated feelings about him and beliefs about what kind of person he is—is a mental representation on which you might draw to describe, evaluate, or make behavioral decisions about him" (p. 391). Smith (1998) introduced basic assumptions of associative network memory representations:

1. *Fundamental representational assumption*: Representations are constructed from discrete "nodes" connected by "links" of different types.

2. *Interpretation of nodes*: Nodes stand for preexisting concepts or are newly constructed, in which case they take their meaning from their pattern of linkages to other nodes.

3. *Formation of links through continuity*: Links are formed (or strengthened if they already exist) when the objects they link are experienced or though about together.

4. *Link strength*: Links can vary in strength, a property that is considered to change only slowly with time.

5. *Activation of nodes*: Nodes have a property termed activation, which can vary rapidly over time.

6. *Activation in long-term memory*: Memory retrieval amounts to raising a node's activation level above some threshold.

7. *Spread of activation*: When a node is activated because it is perceptually present or is actively thought about, other nodes to which it is linked also become active to some extent, as activation spreads across the links.

8. *Links as pathways for retrieval in free recall*: Because of the spread of activation, recall can be thought of as following links (the more links connecting to a particular node, the greater its probability of retrieval. (pp. 393-394)

In the next sections, I will elaborate on *associative networks* models and *spreading activation* related to cognitive representations.

Associative Network Models of Representations

Psychology scholars have widely used the associative network in modeling

cognition (e.g., Carlston & Smith, 1996; Smith, 1998). Collins and Quilian (1969) and

Collins and Loftus (1975) suggested associative network models; more recently,

Anderson (1983) developed "ACT theory." In the ACT theory, Anderson (1983) held that

a new fact is represented not simply by constructing a new link between existing concept

nodes, but by creating and linking a proposition node. For example, according to Ashcraft

(2002), "ROBIN is a member of the category, BIRD, that a ROBIN has a RED BREAST,

that a CANARY is YELLOW, and so on. Each of these simple connections records an

elementary fact or proposition, a relationship between two concepts" (p. 253). Another

example, provided by Carlston and Smith (1996), is "John is hostile" would be

represented by a new proposition node with a "subject" link to John and a "predicate"

link to hostility (p. 194).

In associative networks, first, association refers to "the links or pathways between

concept nodes, such as the *isa* pathway" (Ashcraft, 2002, p. 539). Second, network means

"an interrelated set of concepts or interrelated body of knowledge" (Ashcraft, 2002, p.

252). In associative network models, concepts are represented as *nodes* (a point or

location in the semantic space) and *links*, or *pathways*, (connections between concepts).

According to Carlston and Smith (1996), "… nodes are merely placeholders, without

internal structure, that derive meaning from their place in the network of interconnections

as a whole. Thus, the information that John is hostile would be represented by the

formation of a link between the node representing John and the node representing

hostility" (p. 193). Different types of links represent subset relations, conventionally termed "isa" links that Rumelhart, Lindsay, and Norman (1972) first contributed as meaning of "is a," as in "is a member of the category." Thus, the literature of associative network in cognition is clearly supportive of J. Grunig and Hung's taxonomy of cognitive representations, in particular the relations between objects and attributes.

Also, each link specifies a certain relationship and the direction of that relationship (Ashcraft, 2002). In terms of the isa links, for example, "ROBIN *is a* BIRD" means ROBIN is a member of the category of BIRD. In addition to the isa links, a *property* statement also functions in the networks of cognition. Using a *property* statement, for example, "BIRD has the property FEATHERS." According to Ashcraft (2002), the importance of the direction of the relationships is that the reversed direction is not true, such as "ALL BIRDS are ROBINS" (p. 253). If related concepts are connected using nodes, (isa) links, and properties, for example, "ROBIN *isa* BIRD *isa* ANIMAL *property* BREATHE" (Ashcraft, 2002, p. 255).

Smith and colleagues (Rips, Shoben, & Smith, 1973; Smith, Rips, & Shoben, 1974) have suggested *feature* lists in a feature comparison model, which is similar to *property* statements. Considering features as simple characteristics or properties of the concept, Smith et al. proposed two distinct types of features in terms of a hierarchical network model: 1) *defining* features: the essential feature at the top of the list, and 2) *characteristic* features: features that are common but not essential to the meaning of the concept.

Likewise, Anderson (2000, p. 149) conceptualized cognition as a propositional network, in which cognition is "a tangle of marbles connected by strings. The marbles represent the nodes, and the strings represent the links between the nodes" (cited in J.

Grunig & Hung, 2002, p. 21). Cognitive representations are "chunks" that are used to "encode objects in the environment" (Anderson & Lebiere, 1998, p. 23); chunks consist of the features of objects (Anderson, 1996, p. 359) and are used to recognize objects and classifies them into categories (cited in J. Grunig & Hung, 2002, pp. 21-22).

Spreading Activation in Cognitive Representations

Spreading activation is the key principle in the associative network structure (Anderson, 1983). Ashcraft (2002) defined spreading activation as "the mental activity of accessing and retrieving information from" the associative network (p. 252). Cappella and Jamieson (1997) explained spreading activation in easy terms to understand

> This principle holds that whenever a focal node is brought into conscious
>
> awareness (i.e., is activated), some of its activation is then transferred to nodes
>
> that are linked to the focal node. The stronger the association, the greater the
>
> likelihood that a neighboring node will also be brought into awareness. (p. 61)

Cappella and Jamieson (1997) suggested that spreading activation explains cognitive priming where "associates of the activated construct are made more accessible for later recall" (p. 61). Smith (1998) also explained that spreading activation is required for recalling implicit memory: "… the effect of an associative structure on explicit memory retrieval is modeled as a process of traversing associative links," whereas "… the effect of an associative structure on implicit memory measures is modeled as a result of spreading activation" (p. 402).

Components in Impression Formation

Cappella and Jamieson (1997) provided an example of associative networks in impression formation:

We assume that knowledge is stored as a network of associations between nodes where the linkages vary from no connection to strongly connected. Nodes can be concepts such as 'health reform' and 'HMO,' character traits such as 'aggressive' or 'intelligent,' and affective components such as 'liked' or 'enthusiastic.'(p. 61)

In addition to nodes, traits, and affective component, Hamilton and associates (Hamilton, 1981; Hamilton, Katz, & Leirer, 1980) added the target person's behaviors in the formation of person impression. Hamilton et al. proposed:

1. When the target person's behaviors fall into trait categories, impression formation results in the formation of a hierarchically structured associative networks.

2. As the perceiver notes the categorical structure, the person is presumed to connect the behaviors into trait-based clusters, with the traits in turn being linked directly to the person node.

As previously noted in Cappella and Jamieson's quote, affect, or evaluation, and behavior can be a component of cognitive representations, as in J. Grunig and Hung's (2002) taxonomy of cognitive representations. In detail, Carlston and Smith (1996) said as follows:

A number of theorists have suggested that affective responses play an important role in person perception... From a more cognitive perspective, affects can also be viewed as material that is stored in memory, retrieved, and interpreted in much the same way as other cognitive representations. (p. 187)

Carlston and Smith suggested that affect can be equivalent with evaluations: "... affective reactions associated with particular individuals are sometimes called evaluations... such evaluations are included in several general models of person perception" (p. 187).

In conclusion, applying such concepts related to cognitive representations in the literature of psychology, in particular person impression, cognitive representations that a member of publics has of organizations would consists of objects, attributes, the relation between objects and attributes, and evaluations, as suggested by J. Grunig and Hung (2002) in their taxonomy of cognitive representations.

In the next sections, I will discuss the link between organization-public relationships and organizational reputation from several perspectives, such as public relations, psychology, and business. Then, I will explain precursors of organization-public relationships and organizational reputation.

Link between Organization-public Relationships and Organizational reputation

The effect of organization-public relationships on organizational reputation has been widely suggested not only in the literature of public relations, but also in the literature of other fields such as business and psychology.

The Effects of Relationships on Reputation from Public Relations Research

In the literature of public relations, the results of the IABC Excellence study suggested the effect of organization-public relationships on organizational reputation (L. Grunig, J. Grunig, & Dozier, 2002). Other academic researchers recently have studied the link between organization-public relationships and organizational reputation (Coombs, 2000; Coombs & Holiday, 2001; J. Grunig & Hung, 2002; Hagan, 2003; Rhee, 2004; Yang & J. Grunig, 2005; S. K. Yang & S. U. Yang, 2003; Yang & Mallabo, 2003).

About the link between organization-public relationship and organizational reputation, J. Grunig and Huang (2000) said: "Corporate reputation is highly connected with behavioral relationships because reputation essentially consists of the corporate behaviors that publics remember" (p. 35). Recently, J. Grunig and Hung (2002) theorized that reputation is a direct product of organization-public relationships, so reputation can be managed indirectly by relationships.

Based on the results of the Excellence study, L. Grunig, J. Grunig, and Dozier (2002) suggested:

1. The quality of relationships determines reputation.

2. Quality relationships and reputation result more from the behavior of organizations than from messages disseminated.

3. The value of relationships includes the value of reputation.

From the perspective of crisis management, Coombs (2000) and Coombs and Holliday (2001) have studied the link between organization-public relationships and organizational reputation. Coombs (2000) said that organizational reputation is damaged by crises, which often resulted from negative stakeholder-organization relationships. For example, Coombs (2000) satiated as follows:

An unfavorable reputation results from ignoring or abusing the stakeholder-organization relationship. Ignoring customer complaints, lack of community involvement, and disregard for employee safety are actions that can contribute to an unfavorable reputation. (p. 81)

Coombs and Holladay (2001), in an experimental study, found that a negative relationship history produced a negative effect on organizational reputations and crisis responsibility. They conceptualized that performance history (including relationship history and crisis history) affects both organizational reputation and crisis responsibility.

Hagan (2003) studied the effect of organization-public relationships on reputation of an automotive manufacturer in its handing of vehicle recalls (i.e., Audi 5000 recalls). Hagan (2003) found that both experiential and mediated (second-hand) relationships strongly affected corporate and brand reputations.

Yang (Yang, 2004; Yang & J. Grunig, 2005; Yang & Mallabo, 2003; S. K. Yang & S. U. Yang, 2003) has studied the effect of organization-public relationships on organizational reputation extensively. In a qualitative study of the relationships between a South Korean environmental activist organization and its publics, including strategic publics (e.g., the news media, corporate donors, individual donors) and members of the general population, Yang and Mallabo (2003) found supporting results for J. Grunig and Hung's (2002) theory. They found that research participants with first-hand experience and high levels of familiarity and involvement tended to estimate reputation of the case organization based on his or her subjective perceptions of relationships, which resulted from behaviors of the case organization. However, research participants, who lacked first-hand experience, familiarity, and involvement, tended to speculate about relationships with the case organization based on hearsay, mostly from the mass media. S. K. Yang and S. U. Yang (2003) investigated the interaction effect between perceptions of organization-public relationships and involvement in predicting reputations of the five organizations studied. They found a positive and strong interaction effect between perceptions of a *communal* relationship and involvement in predicting reputations.

Recently, Yang and J. Grunig (2005) proposed and tested a model in which they posited causal relations among the quality of organization-public relationship outcomes, organizational reputation, and overall evaluation of organizational performance with such external factors as behaviors of search for information (information seeking and processing) and familiarity. They found that the model had tenable data-model fits across the five different organizations they studied. More specifically, they found that the effect of organization-public relationship outcomes is positive and strong on organizational reputation as well as on overall evaluation of organizational performance.

The Effects of Relationships on Reputation from the Perspective of Psychology

From the perspective of social psychology, many scholars have suggested interpersonal relationship status, or "relational schemas," affects personal reputation. Planalp (1987) first suggested the concept of "relationship schemas" or "relational schemas" in referring to cognitive working models of how interpersonal relationships operate. Likewise, a number of social psychology scholars (e.g., Baldwin, 1997, 1999; Collins & Read, 1990) also have studied relational schemas. In particular, Collins and Read (1990) studied adult attachment and found that dimensions of attachment style were strongly related with relational schema (i.e., how each partner perceives the relationship). Conley and Collins (2002) investigated how relationship status can affect how others perceive that person (i.e., reputation) and found supportive results.

The Effects of Relationships on Reputation from the Perspective of Business

Business scholars have emphasized the critical role of quality relationships between a corporation and its strategic constituents in the corporation's obtaining favorable reputation (e.g., Fombrun, 1996; Fombrun & Rindova, 2000; Fombrun & Van

Riel, 2003; Knox, Maklan, & Thompson, 2000; Rindova & Kotha, 2002; Schultz, Hatch, & Larsen, 2000). For example, Fombrun (1996) emphasized the role of organization-public relationships as an important precursor of corporate reputations: "To acquire a reputation that is positive, enduring, and resilient requires managers to invest heavily in building and maintaining good relationships with their company's constituents" (p. 57). For reputations of corporations to be maintained properly, Knox et al. (2000) and Schultz et al. (2000) suggested that corporations should manage good long-term relationships with their strategic constituents.

Rindova and Kotha (2001) investigated how strategic actions, or behaviors, of new firms affect corporate reputation. They found that relational actions (i.e., corporate actions to establish stakeholder-corporation relationships) influence corporate reputation over time. Most recently, Fombrun and Van Riel (2003) explained that, in terms of "corporate citizenship" (p. 118), socially responsible behaviors of organizations is the primary factor in forming favorable organizational reputation.

Summing up the above discussion and review of the literature, I suggest the following hypothesis:

Hypothesis 1: The better the quality of organization-public relationship outcomes, the more favorable the reputation of an organization.

Additionally, Hon and J. Grunig (1999) and L. Grunig et al. (2002) suggested that *communal* organization-public relationships produce more quality organization-public relationship outcomes than *exchange* organization-public relationships. Also, business scholars have suggested the effects of socially responsible behaviors of corporations on corporate reputation (e.g., Fombrun, 1996; Fombrun & Van Riel, 2003). Since I consider theories (regarding the effects of organization-public relationship types on organization-public relationship outcomes and organizational reputation) have not been solid yet, I suggested a research question instead of positing a hypothesis ground in theories.

Research Question: How do organization-public relationship types (communal and exchange relationships) affect the quality of organization-public relationship outcomes and organizational reputation in the proposed model?

Antecedents of Relationships and Reputation

Broom, Casey, and Ritchey (2000) described about antecedents of organization-public relationships as follows: "Antecedents to relationships include the perceptions, motives, needs, behaviors, and so forth, posited as contingencies or as causes in the formation of relationships" (p. 16). In this study, after reviewing the literature from different perspectives such as public relations, business, and psychology, I posited the following variables as antecedents of organization-public relationships and organizational reputation: 1) communication behaviors of publics, 2) familiarity with an organization, and 3) personal experience.

Communication Behaviors of Publics

Hon and J. Grunig (1999) and J. Grunig and Huang (2000) explained why publics form relationships with organizations. According to them, when publics and an organization have consequences on the other, publics begin to form a relationship with an organization (J. Grunig & Hunt, 1984). Because of such consequences, organizations also need to build relationships with strategic publics (J. Grunig & Huang, 2000).

In public relations research, scholars have suggested active communication behavior of publics as a key predictor of the quality of relationships between organizations and publics (e.g., Bruning & Ledingham, 1999; Ferguson, 1984; J. Grunig & Huang, 2000; J. Grunig & Hung, 2002; Youngmeyer, 2002). To identify publics who have active communication behaviors, scholars have widely used the situational theory of publics (e.g., Heath, Bradshaw, & Lee, 2002; Major, 1993, 1998; Youngmeyer, 2002). In particular, level of involvement that publics perceive with an organization has been suggested as a significant variable that decides positive estimation of relationship outcomes such as trust and commitment (Anderson & Narus, 1990; Stewart et al., 2002). Youngmeyer (2002) used the level of involvement measure in the situational theory to predict the quality of department-student relationships. About the theoretical reason behind this, Youngmeyer suggested that publics with high involvement with an organization (in this case, the department) have the potential to develop more quality relationships.[25]

Citing Millar and Rogers (1976, p. 87), from a symbolic interaction perspective, Broom, Casey, and Ritchey (2000) also viewed communication behaviors of publics as a critical component in the formation of organization-public relationships: "These relationships, whether primarily interpersonal or role specific, are bestowed, sustained, and transformed through communicative behaviors" (p. 7).

---

[25] Youngmeyer (2002) explained in detail as follows: "The nature and quality of such relationships would be expected to vary as a function of the degree to which an individual felt connected to the organization. A high level of involvement would tend to relate to stronger, more positive attitudes about the relationship, since the individuals have more invested in the relationship. Individuals who feel relatively involved with an organization would be expected to identify with it more strongly and hence rate their relationship more positively. Individuals with a weaker connection to an organization, however, would be expected to identify with it less and their attitudes about the relationship would be correspondingly weaker" (p. 10).

Summing up the above discussion and review of the literature, I suggest the following hypothesis:

Hypothesis 2: The more active the communication behaviors of publics, the better the quality of organization-public relationship outcomes.

Familiarity

Familiarity is commonly referred to as the extent to which an entity has knowledge about another entity, which is often acquired by direct or indirect experience (Bromley, 2000). Sources of individual familiarity with an organization can be direct experience with an organization as well as indirect experience mediated throughout the mass media (Rindova & Kotha, 1998) and other social networks (Bromley, 1993).

J. Grunig and Hung (2002) theorized that active communication behaviors, familiarity, and personal experience are correlated causes that affect the quality of organization-public relationships. J. Grunig and Hung (2002) coined a term "reputational" relationships (i.e., secondary relationships) to describe organization-public relationships that are not based on first-hand experience, differentiating them from "experiential" relationships that have been built from direct experience and high level of familiarity with an organization (p. 20). Then, J. Grunig and Hung (2002) proposed active communication behaviors of publics and familiarity, embedded in experiential organization-public relationships, result in quality of organization-public relationships and in turn organizational reputation.

More specifically about the effect of familiarity on organizational reputation, business scholars often claim that familiarity of organizations to their multiple constituents is one of the strongest variables that predict favorable corporate reputation (e.g., Deephouse, 2000; Fombrun & Van Riel, 2003; Pollack & Rindova, 2002). For example, Fombrun and Van Riel (2003) said as follows: "The evidence we've gathered from the RQ project [the Reputation Quotient project] to date is very much that reputations are built on a foundation of high top-of-mind awareness. *Simply put, the more familiar you are to the public, the better the public rates you*" (p. 104). From the perspective of social psychology, Zajonc (1968) hypothesized that mere exposure to a repeated stimulus results in favorable attitude formation driven by that stimulus.

Thus, summing up the above discussion and review of the literature, I suggest the following hypotheses:

Hypothesis 3: The more familiar a public is with an organization, the better the quality of organization-public relationships.

Hypothesis 4: The more familiar a public is with an organization, the more favorable the reputation of an organization.

Predictor Variables of Active Communication Behaviors

As I previously noted, J. Grunig and Hunt (1984) suggested high involvement, high problem recognition, and low constraint recognition as situational predictors of active communication behaviors of publics. Therefore, I adopted the following hypotheses from the situational theory of publics:

Hypothesis 5: The higher the problem recognition, the more active the communication behaviors of publics.

Hypothesis 6: The lower the constraint recognition, the more active the communication behaviors of publics.

Hypothesis 7: The higher the self involvement, the more active the communication behaviors of publics.

Hypothesis 8: The higher the community involvement, the more active the communication behaviors of publics.

Personal Experience

J. Grunig and Hung (2002) and Bromley (1993) suggested that personal experience is one of the strong predictors of familiarity with an organization, and that direct (or first-hand) experience will result in higher familiarity with an organization than indirect (or second-hand) experience. Therefore, I posited personal experience functions as a predictor of familiarity with organizations. However, I did not impose personal experience of publics to affect the quality of organization-public relationships or reputation directly. This was because I consider that the existence of personal (first-hand or second-hand) experience may not be a direct predictor of organization-public relationship outcomes and organizational reputation. Rather, the degree of personal experience can influence perceptions of organization-public relationship outcomes and organizational reputation through the mediation of familiarity. Thus, I suggested the following hypothesis to study:

Hypothesis 9: The more direct experience a public has with an organization, the more familiar it will be with the organization.

Summary of Hypotheses and Research Question

The purpose of this study was to investigate the effects of organization-public relationships and organizational reputation from the perspective of publics. To this end, I suggested the following hypotheses and research question to study.

Hypothesis 1: The better the quality of organization-public relationship outcomes, the more favorable the reputation of an organization.

Hypothesis 2: The more active the communication behaviors of publics, the better the quality of organization-public relationship outcomes.

Hypothesis 3: The more familiar a public is with an organization, the better the quality of organization-public relationships.

Hypothesis 4: The more familiar a public is with an organization, the more favorable the reputation of an organization.

Hypothesis 5: The higher the problem recognition, the more active the communication behaviors of publics.

Hypothesis 6: The lower the constraint recognition, the more active the communication behaviors of publics.

Hypothesis 7: The higher the self involvement, the more active the communication behaviors of publics.

Hypothesis 8: The higher the community involvement, the more active the communication behaviors of publics.

Hypothesis 9: The more direct experience a public has with an organization, the more familiar it will be with the organization.

Research Question: How do organization-public relationship types (communal and exchange relationships) affect the quality of organization-public relationship outcomes and organizational reputation in the proposed model?

Next, now that I have explained hypotheses and research question to study, I will present the hypothesized structural equation model where each of the causal paths represented each of the hypotheses and research question.

The Hypothesized Model

Overview of the Model

I proposed a causal model in which the quality of organization-public relationship outcomes, perceived types of organization-public relationships (communal and exchange relationships), and familiarity affect organizational reputation. Also, based on theoretical reasons, I also identified some of the external influencers to such predictors of organizational reputation. For example, first, I proposed that four independent variables (problem recognition, constraint recognition, self involvement, and community involvement) affect active communication behaviors of publics and, in turn, that active communication behaviors affect evaluations of the quality of organization-public relationship outcomes. Secondly, I posited that the degree of personal experience affects familiarity and, in turn, that familiarity affects evaluations of the quality of organization-public relationship outcomes and organizational reputation. Last, I imposed the effects of organization-public relationships (communal and exchange relationships) on organization-public relationships outcomes and organizational reputation.

I will explain each part of the model in detail. First, as variables that affect active communication behaviors of publics, I used the three independent variables of the situational theory of publics (J. Grunig & Hunt, 1984). Also, I added community involvement, which is operationally defined as the degree of the perceived connection between one's community and an organization. In the model, I hypothesized that those four variables 1) influence active communication behaviors of publics directly, 2) affect the quality of organization-public relationship outcomes indirectly through the mediation of active communication behaviors, and 3) predict organizational reputation through the mediations of active communication behaviors and the quality of organization-public relationship outcomes. Finally, the four predictor variables of communication behaviors are correlated with personal experience and the two types of organization-public relationships (communal and exchange relationships) in the model. Therefore, there are additional "indirect" influences from personal experience and the two types of organization-public relationships in the links descried the above.

Secondly, another important external influencer is personal experience. In the proposed model, I hypothesized that the degree of direct experience 1) affects familiarity directly, 2) influences the quality of organization-public relationship outcomes indirectly through the mediation of familiarity, and 3) predict organizational reputation through the mediations of familiarity and the quality of organization-public relationship outcomes. Personal experience is correlated with the four predictor variables of communication behaviors and the two types of organization-public relationships (communal and exchange relationships) in the model. Therefore, there are additional "indirect" influences from the four predictor variables of communication behaviors and the two types of organization-public relationships in the links descried the above.

Last, the model proposed that the two types of organization-public relationships (communal and exchange relationships) 1) affect the quality of organization-public relationship outcomes and organizational reputation directly and 2) influence organizational reputation through the mediation of the quality of organization-public relationship outcomes. As explained previously, the correlations among independent variables also indicate additional indirect influences from the four predictor variables of communication behaviors and personal experience in the links described the above.

In summary, I proposed that the quality of organization-public relationship outcomes affect organizational reputation, considering the correlated effects from independent variables (i.e., the four predictor variables of communication behaviors, personal experience, and the two types of organization-public relationships), and additional causal inputs from active communication behaviors and familiarity (Figure II).

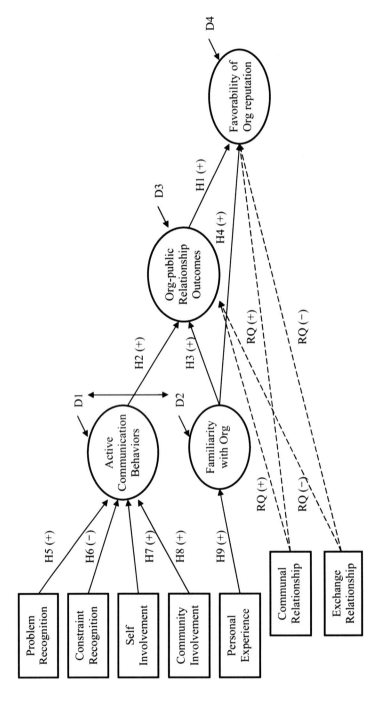

Figure 11. The proposed structural equation model with hypothesis/research question notation. For the sake of brevity, I omitted covariances among exogenous variables, and error terms for indicators of latent variables from the figure. Latent variables are shown in ellipses, and observed variables are shown in rectangles.

CHAPTER III: Methodology

The purpose of this study was to investigate the causal effects of organization-public relationships on organizational reputation, taking into account the external influence of such variables as communication behaviors of publics, familiarity, and personal experience with the organizations studied. To this end, I suggested 9 specific hypotheses and one research question to examine causal links theoretically imposed in the model.

In this chapter, I will discuss methodology to be used to answer those hypotheses and research question. First, I will discuss relevance of survey as the primary method in this study. I will review different types of research designs such as experimental, quasi-experimental, and survey designs and explain why I considered that a survey is most relevant for the purpose of this study.

Then, in the section of research design, I will elaborate on data collection, the population and sample of a survey, sampling method, criteria used for the selection of the organizations studied, and finally the results of two pretests and a preliminary survey. After I give details about measurement instruments, I will explain data collection procedures, data reduction, and data analysis. More specifically about data analysis, I will explain statistical procedures for data analysis. Also, I will discuss the criteria used to evaluate statistical results. Finally, I will describe ethics of research that I abided by in this study.

Survey as Research Method

Relevance of the Quantitative Method

A researcher should select a research method based on the purpose of the proposed study (Nardi, 2003). As I discussed previously, the purpose of this study was to explain causal links between organization-public relationships and organizational reputation. Also, the major goal of a research question and specific hypotheses was to analyze associations between variables of interest in the proposed model.

In this study, I did not intend to understand socially constructed realities contingent on a given context and based on the diverse viewpoints brought by research participants (Denzin & Lincoln, 1998; Guba, 1990). Rather, I aimed to predict outcomes of participants' perceptions or opinions and analyze hypothesized associations between variables of interest based on such outcomes, or numerical descriptions (Judd, Smith, & Kidder, 1991; Nardi, 2003). Therefore, I considered that the quantitative method is more appropriate for this study than the qualitative method. In the following section, I will explain different types of research designs to discuss why I selected survey method as the primary method of this study.

Different Types of Research Designs

Scholars often suggest that experimental, quasi-experimental, and survey designs are common research designs in social science (e.g., Judd, Smith, & Kidder, 1991). First, in experimental designs, the independent variable is manipulated; participants are randomly assigned to the control group or different levels of the independent variables (Campbell & Stanley, 1963; Shadish, Cook, Campbell, 2002). By doing so, experimental designs are most relevant in "universalistic" research where the primary purpose of research is to explain causation of interesting constructs (Kruglanski, 1975).

Secondly, when manipulation of the independent variable or randomization is not feasible, scholars suggest using quasi-experimental research designs (e.g., Campbell & Stanley, 1963; Shadish, Cook, Campbell, 2002). However, a relative disadvantage of those designs over experimental designs includes that quasi-experimental designs are subject to a variety of validity threats, such as selection, history, maturation, testing, and regression to the mean (Campbell & Stanley, 1963; Shadish, Cook, Campbell, 2002). For the sake of brevity, I will skip explanations of those validity threats.

Last, survey research is one of most popular methods available to social scientists (Babbie, 2001). Like quasi-experimental designs, a researcher can use survey designs when the manipulation of the independent variables or randomization is not possible or desirable (Judd, Smith, & Kidder, 1991). In contrast to experimental designs, survey designs are most relevant in "particularistic" research where a researcher's primary goal is to generalize the findings of research to a particular group of elements (i.e., a sample) in the population (Kruglanski, 1975).

Babbie (2001) defined a survey research as "the administration of questionnaires to a sample of respondents selected from a population" (p. 282). Fowler (2002) described characteristics of surveys as follows:

1. The purpose of a survey is to produce statistics—that is, quantitative or numerical descriptions about some aspects of the study population.

2. The main way of collecting information is by asking people questions; their answers constitute the data to be analyzed.

3. Generally, information is collected about only a fraction of the population (i.e., a sample) rather than every member of the population. (pp. 1-2)

In summary, experimental research designs are most appropriate in research where a researcher seeks to maximize internal validity by randomization at the cost of external validity (Campbell & Stanley, 1963; Shadish, Cook, Campbell, 2002). However, a trade-off of experimental designs is the limited external validity, since research is conducted in a laboratory setting with relatively selective samples of participants (Judd, Smith, & Kidder, 1991). On the other hand, survey research designs are most suitable in research where a researcher is interested in 1) documenting of the distribution of some variables of interest in some population, 2) establishing associations between variables of interest, and 3) ensuring external validity to generalize the findings beyond the immediate settings and samples studied (Judd, Smith, & Kidder, 1991). Next, I will discuss why I believe that survey research was relevant for this study.

Relevance of Survey Research

I considered that survey research was more suitable for this study than experimental and quasi-experimental research. This was largely because I did not intend to manipulate variables of interest in a laboratory setting although I aimed to examine causal links between interesting constructs, in particular the effect of organization-public relationships on organizational reputation.

I argue that I can enhance the construct validity of such key constructs in this study more in a nonexperimental setting than in experimental setting. To measure *organization-public relationships* and *organizational reputation* in a valid manner, I consider that those concepts should be assessed based on an uncontrolled setting where research participants' past intersections, experience, and relationship history were embedded. Also, in a practical sense, survey research is ideal to study the perceptions or opinions of a large number of participants (Fowler, 2002). For this reason, surveys have

been the major method used to measure the concept of organizational reputation (e.g.,

Bromley, 1993; Fombrun & Gardberg, 2000).

Babbie (1990, 2001) said that a researcher can use surveys for descriptive,

explanatory, and exploratory purposes. Also, a researcher can use survey research to

examine causal relationships between variables of interest. Weisberg, Krosnick, and

Bowen (1996) said: "… survey research is especially suitable for testing causal

propositions [using structural equation modeling]" (p. 94). Structural equation modeling

makes it possible to test causal links between variables of interest using nonexperimental

data (Byrne, 1994; Kline, 1998; Hancock & Mueller, 2004). To sum up, because of the

reasons I discussed the above, I considered that survey research was most appropriate for

the purpose of this study and to deal with hypotheses and research question proposed in

this study. Next, I will discuss specific elements of survey research design such as data

collection, the population and a sample, and sampling method as well as the results of

pretests and a preliminary survey.

Research Design

Sampling Method

I used *quota sampling* to collect data for this study. Random sampling is ideal for

data collection because a researcher can establish external validity to generalize the

findings of a survey (Fowler, 2002; Nardi, 2003; Judd, Smith, & Kidder, 1991).

However, I chose quota sampling for data collection for convenience and economy of

sampling. As I noted previously, in this study, I did not seek to generalize the findings

beyond the immediate sample that I studied. Also, quota sampling can be relevant to analyze theory-derived links between variables in the proposed model. Judd, Smith, and

Kidder (1991) explained the logic of sampling as follows:

> Some research aims at testing theoretically hypothesized relationships, with no
>
> specific population or setting as the focus of interest ... In such cases, the ability
>
> to extend the research results from the sample to some population is of no interest.
>
> Instead, the applicability of the *theory itself* outside the research context is the
>
> central question... (p. 130)

Judd et al. (1991) described quota sampling: "Quota sampling adds provisions to

guarantee the inclusion of diverse elements of the population and to make sure that they

are taken account of in the proportions in which they occur in the population" (p. 135). In

other words, quota sampling makes it possible to ensure representation of sampling

elements of interest in the final sample although it is still nonprobability sampling (Nardi,

2003).

Population and Sample

The population of the survey consisted of residents in a South Korean

metropolitan city, Gwangju city. To facilitate data collection, I chose residents of one city

as the population. Also, by doing so, I attempted to ensure homogeneity of the sample,

following Bromley's (1993) suggestions on the selection of homogenous elements to

measure organizational reputation.

For quota sampling, I selected participants between the ages of 20 and 49 years; I

replicated the proportions of sex and age from the population. From the Korean National

Statistical Office, a governmental bureau in charge of statistical information, I obtained

the most recent South Korean census data and planned to "replicate" the quota of my choice in a final sample. I found that the data of this study had almost the same proportions of sex and age with the population. I chose this quota (i.e., sex and age in the ages of 20 and 49 years) because I considered that participants within this age range were most likely to have prior experience with the organizations studied and hence were able to answer questions in the questionnaire, in particular the open-end measure of organizational reputation.

Selection of Organizations to Study

The goal of organization selection was to diversify types of organizations, which made it possible to validate the proposed model across different types of organizations. I considered practical conditions for data collection and chose the following four organizations after two pretests and a preliminary survey: a domestic corporation (Samsung Electronics), a multinational corporation (Sony Korea), a nonprofit sports association (the Korea Football Association), and a nonprofit social service organization (the Korean National Red Cross).

Pretests and a Preliminary Survey

I conducted two pretests and a preliminary survey before the survey of this study. First, a bilingual (i.e., a native Korean American) translated a questionnaire, written in English by J. Grunig and Hung (2002), to Korean. After the initial translation, another bilingual compared the Korean-version questionnaire with the original questionnaire and revised some wordings in the questionnaire.

Then, I conducted the first pretest on 20 participants of the population in the summer of 2002. I collected feedback from each of the participants. Participants of the pretest suggested minor revisions in wordings of some questions and pointed out the difficulty of using 9-point scales. For example, I changed wordings in an item to measure communal organization-public relationships ("I think that this organization succeeds by stepping on other people; a reversed item): from "stepping on other people" to "ignoring other people's interests."

From October 8 to November 8, 2002, for the duration of one month, I conducted a preliminary survey about five South Korean-based organizations (Samsung Electronics, SK Telecom, the KFA, the KNRC, and IBM Korea); I collected about 320 analyzable questionnaires. After completing the questionnaire, some of survey respondents suggested the following revisions in the questionnaire: 1) the difficulty of using 9-point scales, and 2) lengthy questionnaire with many numbers of questions to answer and organizations to answer about. Also, I found some additional issues in analyzing the data: 1) Many participants were not familiar enough with IBM Korea to answer the open-end question of cognitive representations, and 2) sometimes there were multiple thoughts listed in the open-end question, which made coding of the answer difficult and subject to bias.

Based on the above discussion, I made the following changes in the questionnaire: 1) I changed the scale to 5-point scales, 2) I reduced the number of organizations studied to four organizations, 3) I replaced IBM Korea with Sony Korea for higher visibility and in turn higher response rate for the open-end question, and 4) I revised the open-end question on cognitive representations to allow multiple thoughts listed. In the revised measure of cognitive representations, participants were encouraged to list up to four different thoughts and later to go back to their thoughts to report the valence of each thought listed as well as overall ratings of the entire thoughts listed.

After I made such revisions in the questionnaire, I conducted a pretest of 50 participants in the population in April 2003. At this time, participants did not suggest changes in the questionnaire, except for clarifying instructions in the measure of personal experience with the organization studied. I polished wordings in the instruction and changed the format of questions to a contingent type based on different types of experience.

Data Collection Processes

After conducting a pretest in April 2003, I conducted a survey from May 12 to June 13, 2003, for the duration of about a month, to collect the data used for this study. My brother, a professor in a South Korean university, initially recruited 20 college students as research assistants to help me with the research project. Among them, four students ended their participation during two training meetings. Therefore, 16 students contributed to data collection. These students volunteered to collect the data for their experience in research. Each student was paid about $45 (i.e., 50,000 won in Korean currency) for transportation expenses. There was no other apparent reward for their help such as extra credit or monetary reward.

Before data collection, two training meetings were held, in which research assistants were instructed to avoid 1) asking their own friends or acquaintances to be participants and 2) concentrating on areas, such as shopping malls and theaters, where large numbers of people are available to be recruited. Also, they got full information about the research so as not to mislead participants. To ensure that the research assistants followed such instructions, my brother asked them to write their names on the questionnaire they collected and to give contact information of participants and brief descriptions of the locations where they collected data. Each questionnaire was numbered; hence, it was clear who collected the data from whom and where. My brother informed research assistants that he would check such information. And participants were randomly called back to verify participation.

Based on the quota of interest (i.e., sex and the age range of 20 to 49 years), chosen from the most recent census data, each of the research assistants was assigned a specific quota to collect the data in the field. Each of the research assistants was expected to collect 20 questionnaires from the assigned quota. Response rate was about 45 percent: 684 potential participants were contacted; 305 questionnaires were finally collected. Among them, I excluded 11 questionnaires because the consent form was not signed by the participant.

When participants agreed to participate in the survey, research assistants gave the information about the research (e.g., the purpose of the survey, the researchers, participation conditions, and the consent form). Depending on the participant's choice, some participants answered the questionnaire on the spot; others had a week or so to return the completed questionnaire to assigned research helpers. In the latter case, researcher assistants were responsible for collecting the data by mail, fax, or by visiting a place of the participant's choice. Participants were offered a gift for their participation, which cost around two US dollars (i.e., 2,500 won in Korean currency).

Instrumentation

In the hypothesized model (see Figure II), I aimed to investigate the causal relationships between organization-public relationship outcomes, a latent variable with four indicators (control mutuality, trust, satisfaction, and commitment), organizational reputation, a latent variable with three indicators (net positive representations, overall personal rating, and perceived media rating), communication behaviors of publics, a latent variable with two indicators (information seeking and information processing), and familiarity, a latent variable with two indicators (overall personal familiarity and familiarity with media reports). Also, included in the analysis were measured exogenous variables of problem recognition, constraint recognition, self involvement, perceived community involvement, experience, and organization-public relationship types (communal and exchange relationships).

The first series of questions measured indicators of communication behaviors and familiarity and four predictor variables of such communication behaviors. The second series consisted of the open-end question to measure cognitive representations as organizational reputation. I asked participants to list each thought up to four thoughts in separate boxes. The third series measured indicators of the quality of organization-public relationship outcomes and the two types of organization-public relationships. In the fourth series of questions, I asked participants to go back to their answers on the open-end question of cognitive representations and to report the valence of each thought listed (i.e., neutral, negative, and positive) as well as overall rating of the entire thoughts listed. Additionally, an item was used to measure perceived media reputation of organizations. The fifth series measured prior experience with each of the organizations studied: Whether each participant had direct or indirect experiences and, if so, what was the dominant source of experience. Finally, the sixth series measured demographic information on sex, age, and education levels.

I used questions, written by J. Grunig and Hung (2002), for scales of such constructs as communication behaviors of publics, familiarity, organization-public relationship outcomes, and organization-public relationship types. I modified their open-end measure of cognitive representations slightly to make participants list multiple thoughts and report valence of the thoughts they listed. In addition to J. Grunig and Hung's (2002) measurement items, I added scales to measure personal experience, one item used to measure familiarity (i.e., familiarity with the media coverage of the organization), one item measuring level of involvement (i.e., community involvement), and one item measuring perceived media reputation.

Scales used for the closed-end questions were Likert-type scales with five-categories ranging from "strongly agree" to "strongly disagree" or other labeling of response categories, such as "very unlikely" to "very likely" or "not at all" to "very much." To help participants answer questions, I labeled response categories clearly in each scale used. Next, I will introduce measurement questions used in the questionnaire.

Organization-public Relationship Outcomes

Huang (1997) initially developed a measurement instrument for organization-public relationship outcomes in her dissertation: 1) control mutuality (Stafford & Canary, 1991), 2) trust (Morgan & Hunt, 1994), 3) commitment (Morgan & Hunt, 1994; Mowdays et al., 1979; Stafford & Canary, 1991), and 4) relational satisfaction (Hendrick, 1988). J. Grunig and Hung (2002) modified Huang's (1997) measurement instrument; J. Grunig and Hung's (2002) scales of organization-public relationship outcomes were first reported in Hon and J. Grunig (1999). The questions related to the quality of organization-public relationship outcomes were:

Control Mutuality

1. This organization and people like me are attentive to what each other say.

2. This organization believes the opinions of people like me are legitimate.

3. In dealing with people like me, this organization has a tendency to throw its weight around. (Reversed)

4. This organization really listens to what people like me have to say.

Trust

1. This organization treats people like me fairly and justly. (Integrity)

2. Whenever this organization makes an important decision, I know it will be concerned about people like me. (Integrity)

3. This organization can be relied on to keep its promises. (Dependability)

4. I believe that this organization takes the opinions of people like me into account when making decisions. (Dependability)

5. I feel very confident about this organization's skills. (Competence)

6. This organization has the ability to accomplish what it says it will do. (Competence)

Commitment

1. I feel that this organization is trying to maintain a long-term commitment to people like me.

2. I can see that this organization wants to maintain a relationship with people like me.

3. There is a long-lasting bond between this organization and people like me.

4. Compared to other organizations, I value my relationship with this organization more.

Relational Satisfaction

1. I am happy with this organization.

2. Both the organization and people like me benefit from the relationship.

3. Most people like me are happy in their interactions with this organization.

4. Generally speaking, I am pleased with the relationship this organization has established with people like me.

Organization-public Relationship Types

J. Grunig and Hung (2002) developed instrument to measure organization-public relationship types, which were based on the concepts of communal and exchange relationships developed by Clark and Mills (Clark, 1984; Clark & Mills, 1993; Clark & Mills, 1993; Mills & Clark, 1982, 1994). Like the questions measuring the quality of organization-public relationship outcomes, J. Grunig and Hung's (2002) measure was first reported in Hon and J. Grunig (1999). First, the questions inquiring into communal relationships were:

1. This organization does not especially enjoy giving others aid. (Reversed)

2. This organization is very concerned about the welfare of people like me.

3. I feel that this organization takes advantage of people who are vulnerable. (Reversed)

4. I think that this organization succeeds by ignoring other people's interests. (Reversed)

Secondly, the questions inquiring into exchange relationships were:

1. Whenever this organization gives or offers something to people like me, it generally expects something in return.

2. Even though people like me have had a relationship with this organization for a long time, it still expects something in return whenever it offers us a favor.

3. This organization will compromise with people like me when it knows that it will gain nothing.

4. This organization takes care of people who are likely to reward the organization.

Organizational Reputation

This study used J. Grunig and Hung's (2002) open-end measure of cognitive representations, which reads: "In a few phrase, please tell me what comes to mind when you think of the following organization." According to J. Grunig and Hung (2002), this is essentially the same as Bromley's (1993) method of measuring reputations. To lessen bias in coding answers, I instructed each participant to list up to four different thoughts when they thought of each of the four organizations studied. Later, I asked participants to go back to their answers and to report valence of each thought listed (as non-evaluative, negative, or positive) as well as overall rating of the entire thoughts listed. I considered that participants' overall rating of representations was necessary because the importance of each thought listed might have been different, so the unweighted summation may not represent cognitive representations correctly. To study individual representations, as opposed to overall personal rating, I produced the value of "net positive representations" in given open-end responses by calculating the number of positive representations less the number of negative representations.

Finally, as Bromley (1993) and Rindova and Kotha (2002) suggested, the media play a critical role in reputation formation, especially those publics who lack of direct experience with an organization. For those publics, perceptions of media reputation (i.e., perceptions of how media rate organizational performance) can serve as an important indicator to measure organizational reputation. For this study, I used the following items to measure perception of media reputation: "Please indicate how you think the mass media, in general, rate each of these organizations these days."

Communication Behaviors of Publics

J. Grunig and Hung (2002) developed a measure of communication behaviors of publics. This measure is grounded in J. Grunig's situational theory of publics (e.g., J. Grunig, 1997; J. Grunig & Hunt, 1984), which suggests problem recognition, constraint recognition, and level of involvement as the variables predicting communication behaviors. For the observed variables of communication behaviors, I used the items of information seeking and information processing in J. Grunig and Hung's (2002) questionnaire.

Additionally, I developed an item of community involvement because I considered community involvement as one of important precursors of organization-public relationships and organizational reputation. Ledingham and Bruning (1998, 2000) also emphasized community involvement in measuring organization-public relationships and used it as one of indicators of organization-public relationships. The question items measuring communication behaviors of publics were:

1. Information seeking: There are all kinds of information available on the Internet today. Please circle a number that indicates how likely you would be to search for the web pages described below.

2. Information processing: The following are opening lines from stories you might hear on a television new program. Please choose a number from 1 to 5 that suggests how much attention you would pay to each of these stories.

3. Problem recognition: Now consider how often you stop to think about each of the following organizations.

4. Constraint recognition: Please think about the following organizations and circle a number to indicate the extent to which you could do anything personally that would make a difference in the way these organizations do their business. (Reversed)

5. Self involvement: Please circle a number that indicates the degree to which you see a connection between yourself, personally, and each of these organizations. There would be a connection if you believe the organizations has affected or could affect you or someone close to you personally.

6. Community involvement: Please circle a number that indicates the degree to which you see a connection between your community and each of these organizations. There would be a connection if you believe the organizations has affected or could affect the community that you belong to.

Familiarity

To measure familiarity, first, I used a question to measure overall personal familiarity in J. Grunig and Hung's (2002) instrument. Additionally, as suggested by

Saxton (1998) and Fombrun and Van Riel (2003), the degree of exposure to the media coverage of an organization may be a critical indicator of familiarity. The indicators included in familiarity were:

1. Familiarity with the media coverage: Please indicate how much you think you, personally, have been exposed to media reports about each of the following organizations these days.

2. Overall personal familiarity: On a scale from 1 to 5, please indicate, overall, how familiar you are with each of these organizations.

Personal Experience

I measured personal experience of participants in self-reported contingent questions. First, I instructed participants to indicate whether they had direct, indirect only, or non-experience with each of the organizations studied. Then, based on their answers, I asked them to specify a type of the dominant source of their experience among various categories, such as "from the mess media," "from acquaintances," "as a customer," "as a donor," and so forth.

Data Reduction and Data Analysis

Statistical Procedures for Data Analysis

In this study, I used structural equation modeling (SEM) as the primary statistical method to analyze hypothesized causal links imposed in the proposed model (see Figure II). Additionally, I analyzed the answers of the open-end measure of cognitive representations by means of content analysis.

Structural Equation Modeling

To analyze the data using structural equation modeling, I conducted a two-step process of latent path modeling (Hancock & Mueller, 2004). First, in the measurement phase, I conducted initial confirmatory factor analysis (CFA) by imposing a model where all factors were allowed to covary. Because the initial measurement model fitted satisfactorily, I did not revise the model with model respecification methods.

Secondly, in the structural phase, I compared the final confirmatory model with the proposed structural model. I compared data-model fits statistically in nested models, between the final confirmatory model and the initial structural model. Also, to answer the research questions, I compared two structural models in a hierarchical relation: a model with structural paths from the two types of organization-public relationships and another model without such paths. Since I found the structural model with causal paths from organization-public relationship types had good data-model fits based on multiple fit indexes, I did not make model respecifications.

Before analyzing data in structural equation modeling, I screened the data to check if there were any obvious univariate outliers, and if the univariate distribution of data looked reasonably symmetric (Hancock & Mueller, 2004). I used maximum likelihood (ML) estimation method to lessen the effect of non-normal distribution of data.

Rubin (1976) and Little and Rubin (1987) explained three major patterns of missing data (cited in Byrne, 2001):

1. MCAR (Missing Completely at Random): The missingness is independent of both the unobserved values and the observed values of all other variables in the data.

2. MAR (Missing at Random): The missingness is independent only of the missing values and not of the observed values of other variables in the data.

3. NMAR (Nonignorable): The least restrictive condition and refers to the missingness is nonrandom, or of a systematic nature. (p. 288)

To handle missing data, I used the method used in AMOS, a direct approach based on maximum likelihood (ML) estimation[26] (Arbuckle, 1996; Byrne, 2001). According to Byrne (2001), the AMOS approach (i.e., its ML estimation) to handle incomplete data is theoretically based and "will exhibit the least bias" compared with the other options, such as listwise deletion, pairwise deletion, and imputation (p. 292).

I did not the method of pair-wise deletion of cases, since pairwise deletion can result in nonpositive definite covariance matrices that cause estimation with a computer fail (Kline, 1998; Byrne, 2001). Citing Arbuckle (1996; Arbuckle & Wothke, 1999), Byrne (2001) summarized the extent to which ML estimation in AMOS offers important advantages over deletion approaches in dealing with incomplete data:

1. Where the unobserved values are MCAR, listwise and pairwise are consistent, but not efficient (in the statistical sense); ML estimates are both consistent and efficient.

2. Where the unobserved values are only MAR, both listwise and pairwise estimates can be biased; ML estimates are asymptotically unbiased.

3. Pairwise estimation, in contrast to ML estimation, is unable to yield standard error estimates or to provide a method for testing hypotheses.

---

[26] According to Hancock and Mueller (2004), "Maximum-Likelihood (ML) estimation is an estimation procedure selecting parameter estimates so as to maximize the likelihood of the observed sample data" ("Structural Equation Modeling: Modern Path Analysis," p. 18).

4. When missing values are NMAR, all procedures can yield biased results; ML estimates will exhibit the least bias. (p. 292)

Another popular way to deal with missing data is data imputation, such as mean-substitution or regression-based substitution (Hancock, 2004; Kline, 1998; Tabachnick & Fidell, 2001). Also, as in the deletion methods, data imputation methods have some drawbacks. For example, the method of data imputation would bias the covariance to under-represent the true population covariance (Bentler, 1985; Byrne, 2001; Hancock, 2004).

After the process of data screening, I reversed the scores of negatively worded items (i.e., control mutuality item 3, constraint recognition item, and communal relationship item 1, 2, and 4).

There were multiple items to measure each indicator of the quality of organization-public relationship outcomes and organization-public relationship types. For each of these indicators, I constructed a single composite indicator to reduce a model size. Rather than summing all indicators, I conducted principal component analyses (PCA) to form a composite indicator. This was because the principal component scores can generate a closer representation of latent factors than unweighted summation of observed variables. Also, to eliminate possible bias, I computed the principal component scores consistently within each of the four organizations studied.

Finally, there were three indicators of cognitive representations in this study: 1) self-reported overall rating and 2) net positive representations of organizations. As I discussed previously, I instructed each participant to 1) list up to four different thoughts in their minds when they thought of each of the four organizations studied and 2) report valence of each thought listed (as non-evaluative, negative, or positive) as well as the

overall rating of the entire thoughts listed. I computed net positive representations of

organizations by "the number of positive representations less the number of negative

representations" in each answer. Scores was first coded negative (-1), non-evaluative (0),

and positive (+1); therefore, the sum of the total scores could be ranged from -4 to +4 in

each answer. Then, to differentiate a non-evaluative answer from non-response data,[27] I

rescaled the scores to scores ranged from +1 to +9, with switching -4 to +1, 0 to +5, and

+4 to +9 respectively.

Content Analysis

In addition to data analysis using structural equation modeling, I conducted

content analysis of answers in the open-end question of cognitive representations. I used

the following existing categories in coding answers. First, I used J. Grunig and Hung's

(2002) taxonomy of cognitive representations about organizations (i.e., object-object,

object-attribute, behavior, and evaluative versus non-evaluative representations) to

categorize each answer into broad dimensions of cognitive representations. Additionally,

to categorize answers into specific types of responses, I used Bromley's (2000)

attribution categories in free description of organizations.

Bromley's (2000) attribution categories included: 1) physical plant, products and

services, and production methods; 2) human resources and management style; 3)

finances, markets, and market status; 4) history, current situation, and future prospect, 5)

critical events and circumstances; 6) institutional status, aims, and business strategies; 7)

code of conduct, corporate identity, and corporate reputation; 8) presentation style (e.g.,

---

[27] I will treat the following categories of answers as non-response data: 1) missing values,
2) "don't know/not familiar," and 3) "not interested."

advertising, livery, public relations); 9) competitors, allies, and successfulness; 10) scope

(e.g., local, national, multinational, governmental); 11) public or private, commercial or

charitable; and 12) legal status and features.

Also, I generated categories based on naturally occurring patterns of respondents'

answers. As Bromley (1993, 2000) explained, I tried to come up with effective categories

that were mutually exclusive and were as exhaustive as possible. There was the category

of "other" to include any miscellaneous answers that did not fit to existing categories; I

merged some of categories into a broader category to make the coding scheme simpler.

Since there were 1,391 responses in total to be coded, it was difficult to assess

intercoder reliability in all responses. As the primary coder, I coded 1,391 thoughts listed

by participants, using J. Grunig and Hung's (2002) taxonomy of cognitive representations

and Bromley's (2000) attribution categories in addition to categories driven from data.

Then, a fellow graduate student independently coded a SPSS-generated random 10% of

all coding unit (140 thoughts out of 1,391) based on the coding categories.

Criteria for Evaluating Statistical Results

I used the following standards suggested by scholars as criteria for evaluating

statistical results. First, to assess data-model fit, I used multiple data-model fit indexes,

such as CFI (Comparative Fit Index; an incremental fit index), RMSEA (Root Mean

Square Error of Approximation; a parsimonious fit index), χ^2/df (a parsimonious fit

index), and AIC (Akaike Information Criterion; a parsimonious fit index). Hu and Bentler

(1999) called for using multiple fit indexes and suggested joint-cut off criteria. This is

partly because of assessment of data-model fit in a structural equation model has been

controversial. Loehlin (1992) described this controversy of data-model fit as follows:

"This area is in a state of flux. There have been numerous articles in the past few years criticizing existing indices and proposing new ones. The only strong recommendation that seems justified at present is to treat the indications of any one such index with caution" (p. 71).

Recently, Hu and Bentler (1999) developed joint-cutoff criteria for fit indexes in structural equation model (SEM), which can be useful to test tenable data-model fit. According to them, a SEM model with "CFI (i.e., Comparative Fit Index) $\geq$ .96 and SRMR (i.e., Standardized Root Mean Square Residual) $\leq$ 1.0" or "RMSEA (i.e., Root Mean Square Error of Approximation) $\leq$ .06 and SRMR $\leq$ .10" can be suggested that the fit between the data and the proposed model is tenable. However, since AMOS program does not offer SMRM index, I used multiple indexes such as CFI (Comparative Fit Index; an incremental fit index), RMSEA (Root Mean Square Error of Approximation; a parsimonious fit index), χ^2/df (a parsimonious fit index), and AIC (Akaike Information Criterion; a parsimonious fit index). According to Byrne (1994, 2001), Hu and Bentler (1999), and Kline (1998), a structural equation model can be valid when 1) the value of χ^2/df is less than 3, 2) the value of CFI is equal to or greater than .95, and 3) the value of RMSEA is less than .08.

Secondly, following Broom and Dozier's (1990) suggestion, I used Holsti's formula[28] in computing intercoder reliability in the open-end measure of cognitive representations. Kaid and Wadsworth (1989) said that a desirable level of Holsti's

---

[28] Intercoder reliability is 2M/(N1 + N2) where M is the number of cases in which the two coders agree in their classification, N1 is the number of cases coded by coder 1, and N2 is the number of cases coded by coder 2 (Broom & Dozier, 1990, p. 142).

intercoder reliability is often equal to or greater than .85. If the intercoder reliability is lower than .80, coding becomes unacceptable according to Kaid and Wadsworth (1989).

Ethics of the Research

Fowler (2002) explained the basic principles of ethical issues in survey research: 1) informing respondents, 2) protecting respondents, and 3) explaining benefits to respondents. Before beginning to collect the data in the summer of 2003, I submitted the proposed protocol to the University of Maryland Institutional Review Board (IRB) which approved it. Also, the University of Maryland IRB officially approved my using the data for this study.

Through the research process, I was attentive to the ethical manner. First, each participant was informed of the following information in the cover letter of the questionnaire: 1) the name of the investigators and the organization carrying out the research; 2) the sponsorship; 3) an accurate, though brief, description of the purposes of the research; 4) an accurate statement of the extent to which answers are protected with respect to confidentiality; 5) assurance that cooperation is voluntary; and 6) assurance that respondents can skip any questions they do not want to answer.

Secondly, to protect participants, participants' responses will be anonymous. The questionnaires did not ask for any specific identifying information about the participants, except basic demographic information such as age, sex, and education level. I have kept the completed research materials in my locked office; five years after any publication resulting from the research, I will shred the completed research materials to prevent any misuse of the data.

Third, I did not overstate the benefits of the participation. After debriefing, participants were encouraged to contact me about the result of the study, if they are interested.

In addition to abiding by these ethical issues, I also fulfilled ethical responsibilities to research assistants (Fowler, 2002). I made sure that research assistants had full and accurate information to give about the research and to not put them in a position of being deceptive, misleading, or inaccurate. Also, I cared about research assistants' safety in recruiting participants. Research assistants was told explicitly that they were not required to go to somewhere under circumstances that they feel are unsafe.

CHAPTER IV: Results

Descriptions of Sample and Variables

Descriptions of Sample

The purpose of this study was to investigate the link between organization-public relationships and organizational reputations. In particular, I aimed to examine how organization-public relationships affect organizational reputations in a causal model. For this purpose, I conducted a survey to collect data for this study. In this section, to describe a sample of the survey, I will explain 1) sampling method, 2) marital status and education level of participants, and 3) experience that participants reported for the organizations studied.

Sampling Method

By using *quota sampling*, I tried to ensure the representation of participants in which I was interested (i.e., sex and age from 20 to 49 years) in a sample from the population of this survey, residents in a South Korean metropolitan city. I designed a within-participants questionnaire to encourage comparison of different organizations. I asked each of the participants to answer questions about four South Korean-based organizations: Samsung Electronics, Sony Korea, Korea Football Association (the KFA), and Korean National Red Cross (the KNRC).

I initially planned to collect around 300 questionnaires. According to Kline (1998), common descriptive guidelines about sample size for structural equation modeling (SEM) are small if $N < 100$, moderate if $N < 200$, and large if $N > 200$. Sixteen research assistants (after four assistants dropped) gathered questionnaires from participants following the assigned segments of the quota. Returned questionnaires totaled 305 with a 45 percent response rate: 684 potential participants were contacted; 305 questionnaires were finally collected. The original sample of 305 was reduced to 294 ($N = 294$) by 11 participants who did not sign the consent form in the returned questionnaires.

From the Korean National Statistical Office, a governmental bureau in charge of statistical information, I obtained most recent South Korean census data and planned to "replicate" the quota of my choice in a final sample. Table IV.1 summarizes sex and age of participants compared to the corresponding proportion in the population of this survey.

Table IV.1

Age of Participants ($N_1 = 294$; $N_2 = 684,553$)

Age at time of survey (years)	Sample (N₁)	%	Population (N₂)	%
Male				
20-29	57	19.4	129,864	19.0
30-39	52	17.7	118,587	17.3
40-49	41	13.9	93,896	13.7
Male total	150	51	342,347	50
Female				
20-29	54	18.4	129,529	18.9
30-39	50	17.0	117,684	17.2
40-49	40	13.6	94,993	13.9
Female total	144	49	342,206	50
Total	294	100	684,553	100

Note. N_1 = the sample of the survey; N_2 = the population of the survey (Korea National Statistical Office, 2002).

Although the proportion of sex and age in the sample is slightly different from the proportion in the population, Table IV.1 indicates that the interested quota was overall successfully filled for the sample of this study. Participants were about 51 percent male ($n = 150$) and 49 percent female ($n = 144$). The age of participants, ranged from 20 to 49 years old, distributed as follows: 20s ($n = 111$; about 37.8 percent), 30s ($n = 102$; about 34.7 percent), and 40s ($n = 81$; about 27.5 percent).

Marital Status and Education Level

In addition to sex and age, I also asked about the marital status and education level of participants (Table IV.2).

Table IV.2

Demographic Characteristics of Participants (N= 294)

Age at time of survey (years)	*n*	%
Highest education level completed		
Lower than or equal to high school	46	15.6
Currently enrolled in college	100	34.0
Undergraduate school	124	42.2
Graduate school	17	5.8
Did not specify education level	7	2.4
Marital status		
Married	170	57.8
Unmarried	123	41.8
Did not specify marital status	1	.3
Total	294	100

Experience of Participants with the Organizations Studied

Most of the participants reported that they had either direct or indirect experience with all of the four organizations studied (see Table IV.3).

Table IV.3

Types of Experience (N = 294)

Experience type	Samsung	Sony	KFA	KNRC	Total
Direct experience					
Customer	177	104			281
Investor	1	1			2
Employee	2	1	1	1	5
Member			5	19	24
Donor				151	151
Other		1	1		2
Total (direct experience)	180	106	7	171	464
Indirect experience only					
Mass media	42	52	169	47	310
Ad/PR	63	68	79	53	263
Interpersonal	4	15	7	14	40
Other		1		2	3
Total (indirect experience only)	109	136	255	116	616
No experience	3	48	28	3	82
Did not specify experience	2	4	4	3	
Total	294	294	294	294	

Note. Samsung = Samsung Electronics; Sony = Sony Korea; KFA = Korea Football Association; KNRC = Korean National Red Cross.

Additionally, except for the KFA, most of the participants reported that they had *direct* experience with the organizations studied, including Samsung Electronics, Sony Korea, and the KNRC. For this reason, I consider that the survey participants, in general, had "experiential" relationships (i.e., relationships based on first-hand experience) with the organizations studied rather than "reputational" relationships (i.e., relationships based on second-hand experience), using J. Grunig and Hung's (2002) terms. Sony Korea was the organization for which the most participants (n = 48; 16.3%) reported "no experience," whereas Samsung Electronics and the KNRC were those organizations for which the fewest participants (n = 3; 1%) reported no experience. Most of the participants reported that they *only* had indirect experience with the KFA, in particular through the mass media.

More specifically, first, about *direct* experience, Table IV.3 shows that the fewest participants (n = 7; 2.4%) reported direct experience with the KFA, whereas the most participants (n = 180; 61.2%) reported direct experience with Samsung Electronics, in particular as customers (n = 177; 60.2%). Secondly, about *indirect* experience, the most participants (n = 255; 86.7%) reported indirect experience with the KFA, such as indirect experience through the mass media (57.5%) or exposure to advertisements or public relations materials (26.9%). Exposure to advertisements or public relations materials, across all organizations studied, turned out to be the dominant source of indirect experiences, except for the KFA.

Descriptive Statistics

In this section, I will explain the descriptive data analysis. I posited causal links between the following four groups of variables in the hypothesized structural equation model: 1) communication behaviors of publics, 2) familiarity and experience, 3) organization-public relationships (including organization-public relationship outcomes and organization-public relationship types), and 4) organizational reputation.

Communication Behaviors of Publics

To measure the latent variable, "communication behaviors of publics," I used the concepts of information *seeking* and information *processing* following the situational theory of publics (e.g., J. Grunig, 1997; J. Grunig & Hunt, 1984). Also, for the independent variables of such communication behaviors, I used problem recognition, constraint recognition, and two types of involvement (self involvement and community involvement) as the situational theory of publics also explains (e.g., J. Grunig, 1997; J. Grunig & Hunt, 1984).

First, for the indicator variables of communication behaviors, Table IV.4 reveals that the participants reported relatively higher information processing for the KNRC (M = 3.45, SD = .97) and Samsung Electronics (M = 3.41, SD = 1.02) than for Sony Korea and the KFA.

Table IV.4

Means and Standard Deviations of Communication Behavior Variables

Variables	Samsung ($N = 290$)		Sony ($N = 286$)		KFA ($N = 285$)		KNRC ($N = 289$)	
	M	*SD*	*M*	*SD*	*M*	*SD*	*M*	*SD*
Independent variables								
Problem recognition	3.45	.98	2.52	1.04	2.69	1.05	3.11	1.04
Self involvement	3.26	1.07	2.63	.99	2.59	1.08	3.04	1.10
Community involvement	3.41	.98	2.72	1.01	2.90	.98	3.15	.99
Constraint recognition	3.09	1.19	3.65	1.06	3.56	1.16	3.08	1.18
Communication behaviors								
Information processing	3.41	1.02	3.24	1.08	2.81	1.18	3.45	.97
Information seeking	3.16	1.10	2.92	1.10	2.53	1.15	2.80	1.08

Note. N = listwise of the group of variables in each organization.

Samsung = Samsung Electronics; Sony = Sony Korea; KFA = Korea Football Association; KNRC = Korean National Red Cross.

For information seeking, participants reported, relatively, higher values for the profit organizations studied, Samsung Electronics ($M = 3.16$, $SD = 1.10$) and Sony Korea ($M = 2.92$, $SD = 1.10$), than for the nonprofit organizations studied, the KNRC ($M = 2.80$, $SD = 1.08$) and the KFA ($M = 2.53$, $SD = 1.15$). This may be because the participants in general tended to seek more information about products or services of those profit organizations studied, Samsung Electronics and Sony Korea, than the nonprofit organizations studied, since products or services of profit organizations are often personally more relevant than programs or activities of nonprofit organizations.

To sum up, the participants reported the most active communication behaviors for Samsung Electronics and the least active communication behaviors for the KFA when the data analysis is limited to descriptive statistics of information seeking and information processing.

Secondly, for the independent variables of communication behaviors, participants reported the highest values for problem recognition ($M = 3.45$, $SD = .98$), self involvement ($M = 3.26$, $SD = 1.07$), community involvement ($M = 3.41$, $SD = .98$), and the second lowest value for constraint recognition ($M = 3.09$, $SD = 1.19$) for Samsung Electronics among the four organizations studied. On the other hand, Sony Korea, another profit organization studied, had the highest value for constraint recognition ($M = 3.65$, $SD = 1.06$) and the lowest value for problem recognition ($M = 2.52$, $SD = 1.04$) and community involvement ($M = 2.72$, $SD = 1.01$).

I found a similar pattern for IBM Korea, a multinational corporation, in a previous survey (Yang & J. Grunig, 2005). In particular, across two different surveys, participants consistently reported relatively *low* values for community involvement and *high* values for constraint recognition for the multinational companies studied, Sony Korea and IBM Korea. In a later section of this chapter, I will discuss more about negative cognitive representations of Sony Korea's "lack of social contribution," which I had also found for IBM Korea in a previous survey.

In summary, descriptive statistics indicates that there existed "strong" associations between the two indicators of communication behaviors (information seeking and processing) and the four independent variables, as the situational theory of publics predicts (e.g., J. Grunig, 1997; J. Grunig & Hunt, 1984). Specifically, the participants consistently reported, for Samsung Electronics and the KNRC, relatively *high* values for communication behaviors, problem recognition, the two types of involvement (self involvement and community involvement), and *low* value for constraint recognition. On the other hand, participants reported the "opposite" patterns consistently for Sony Korea and the KFA.

Familiarity and Experience

Next, for the indicator variables of the latent variable, familiarity, descriptive statistics indicates that *overall personal familiarity* and *familiarity with media coverage of the organization* were markedly "similar" across all organizations studied as follows (Table IV.5): overall personal familiarity ($M = 3.44$, $SD = 1.07$) and familiarity with media coverage of the organization ($M = 3.88$, $SD = 1.04$) for Samsung Electronics, overall personal familiarity ($M = 2.53$, $SD = 1.03$) and familiarity with media coverage of the organization ($M = 2.45$, $SD = 1.08$) for Sony Korea, overall personal familiarity ($M = 2.77$, $SD = 1.07$) and familiarity with media coverage of the organization ($M = 2.71$, $SD = 1.03$) for the KFA, and overall personal familiarity ($M = 3.05$, $SD = 1.09$) and familiarity with media coverage of the organization ($M = 2.88$, $SD = .99$) for the KNRC.

Table IV.5

Means and Standard Deviations of Experience and Familiarity Variables

	Samsung (N = 292)		Sony (N = 290)		KFA (N = 290)		KNRC (N = 291)	
Variables	M	SD	M	SD	M	SD	M	SD
Experience								
Personal experience[a]	1.60	.51	1.21	.70	.93	.34	1.58	.51
Familiarity								
Overall personal familiarity	3.44	1.07	2.53	1.03	2.77	1.07	3.05	1.09
Familiarity with media coverage of the org	3.88	1.04	2.45	1.08	2.71	1.03	2.88	.99

Note. N = listwise of the group of variables in each organization.

Samsung = Samsung Electronics; Sony = Sony Korea; KFA = Korea Football Association; KNRC = Korean National Red Cross. [a]Personal experience: direct experience = 2; indirect experience only = 1; none experience = 0

This suggests that the extent to which a participant felt personally familiar with an organization was highly linked with individual perceptions of organizational visibility in the mass media.

In summary, comparing the indicator variables of familiarity across all organizations studied, I found that participants reported relatively high values for familiarity with Samsung Electronics and the KNRC, whereas they reported low values for familiarity with Sony Korea and the KFA across the two indicator variables of familiarity.

This pattern in the indicator variables of familiarity is consistent with the patterns in communication behaviors of publics and the four independent variables of communication behaviors, suggesting that the latent variables of communication behaviors and familiarity are closely linked. J. Grunig and Hung (2002) and Yang and J. Grunig (2005) suggested that, in particular when a member of a public has "experiential" relationships with an organization, communication behaviors of publics and familiarity can function as strong, correlated predictors for such constructs as organization-public relationship outcomes and organizational reputation. Bivariate correlations between indicators of such latent variables were mostly significant by a non-chance amount (at least at the .05 level), across all organizations studied.

Also, Table IV.5 shows that experience was highly associated with familiarity. Participants also reported that they had more *direct* experience with Samsung Electronics and the KNRC than the other two organizations studied, Sony Korea and the KFA. This may support a common assumption that the more *direct* experience a member of a public has with an organization, in general, the more *familiar* the person will be with the organization. And such combined conditions might be a necessary precursor of "experiential" relationships, rather than reputational relationships, as J. Grunig and Hung (2002) explained.

Quality of Organization-public Relationships Outcomes and Organization-public Relationship Types

Organization-public relationship types. Now that I have explained the results of descriptive statistics for the communication behaviors of publics and for familiarity, I will explain descriptive results of organization-public relationships. First, for types of organization-public relationships, Table IV.6 shows that the participants in general reported higher values for communal relationships for both nonprofit organizations studied, the KNRC ($M = 3.51$, $SD = .69$) and the KFA ($M =$

2.90, *SD* = .62) than they did for the two profit organizations studied, Samsung

Electronics (*M* = 2.88, *SD* = .65) and Sony Korea (*M* = 2.90, *SD* = .62).

Table IV.6

Means and Standard Deviations of Organization-public Relationship Quality and

Relationship Type

Variables	Samsung (N = 281)		Sony (N = 273)		KFA (N = 276)		KNRC (N = 277)	
	M	*SD*	*M*	*SD*	*M*	*SD*	*M*	*SD*
Org-public relationship outcomes								
Control mutuality (4 items[a])	3.12	.67	2.82	1.04	2.76	.64	3.22	.67
Trust (6 items)	3.30	.59	3.02	.99	2.87	.62	3.30	.61
Satisfaction (4 items)	3.28	.66	2.88	1.01	2.85	.65	3.35	.71
Commitment (4 items)	3.47	.71	2.95	1.06	2.90	.73	3.46	.74
Org-public relationship types								
Communal relationships (4 items)	2.88	.65	2.72	1.08	2.90	.62	3.51	.69
Exchange relationships (4 items)	3.47	.67	3.58	1.10	3.33	.66	2.76	.76

Note. *N* = listwise of the group of variables in each organization. Samsung = Samsung

Electronics; Sony = Sony Korea; KFA = Korea Football Association; KNRC =

Korean National Red Cross. [a]The number of items used for means.

Additionally, Table IV.6 shows that the participants reported relatively lower values

forexchange relationships for the two nonprofit organizations, the KNRC (*M* = 2.76,

SD = .76) and the KFA (*M* = 3.33, *SD* = .66) than they did for the two profit

organizations studied, Samsung Electronics (*M* = 3.47, *SD* = .67) and Sony Korea (*M*

= 3.58, *SD* = .66).

As compared to other organizations studied, the participants reported markedly more organization-public relationship types for the KNRC: the highest value for communal relationships and the lowest value for exchange relationships among all organizations studied. However, even though the KFA is a nonprofit organization like the KNRC, participants reported almost similar organization-public relationship types for the KFA as for the two profit organizations. This suggested that participants did not take automatically assign desirable organization-public relationship types to nonprofit organizations.

As noted previously, the participants reported the highest value for constraint recognition and the lowest value for community involvement for Sony Korea among the four organizations studied. At the same time, the participants assigned the highest value for exchange relationships and the lowest value for communal relationships to Sony Korea among the four organizations studied. This showed that communication behaviors of the participants and evaluations of organization-public relationship types were highly linked in the data.

Quality of organization-public relationship outcomes. As for organization-public relationship outcomes, Table IV.6 shows that the participants reported highly desirable values for the KNRC across the four indicators of the latent variable, organization-public relationship outcomes: control mutuality ($M = 3.22$, $SD = .67$), trust ($M = 3.30$, $SD = .61$), satisfaction ($M = 3.35$, $SD = .71$), and commitment ($M = 3.46$, $SD = .74$). Except for commitment, participants assigned the highest quality relationship outcomes to the KNRC.

Other noticeable patterns in the data also were, first, that the participants reported the poorest quality relationship outcomes for the KFA across the four indicators. Secondly, despite the unattractive types of organization-public relationships for Samsung Electronics relative to the KNRC, the participants reported desirable organization-public relationship outcomes for Samsung Electronics compared to the KNRC: trust ($M = 3.30$, $SD = .59$) the same mean as the KNRC; the highest value for commitment ($M = 3.47$, $SD = .71$); and a similar value for control mutuality ($M = 3.12$, $SD = .62$) and satisfaction ($M = 3.28$, $SD = .66$).

When compared with previous results for communication behaviors and familiarity, the descriptive results for organization-public relationship outcomes indicate that the three latent variables in the hypothesized model are highly interconnected. Across the three latent variables, I consistently found the most desirable status for Samsung Electronics and the KNRC and an unattractive standing for the KFA. The descriptive data analysis, therefore, suggests, that latent variables, such as communication behaviors and familiarity, may serve as critical predictors of the quality of organization-public relationship outcomes, as previous research has found (e.g., J. Grunig & Hung, 2002; Yang & J. Grunig, 2005).

In addition, the data suggest that, regardless of the quality of organization-public relationship outcomes, the participants generally tended to evaluate organization-public relationship types for the nonprofit organizations studied more positively than for the profit organizations. However, the participants did discriminate between organizations of the same type. They assigned more favorable types of organization-public relationships and evaluations of organization-public relationship outcomes to: 1) the KNRC over the KFA for nonprofit organizations and 2) Samsung Electronics over Sony Korea for profit organizations. This also suggested that organization-public relationship types can be considered to be one of critical predictors for the quality of organization-public relationship outcomes, as Hon and J. Grunig (1999) and L. Grunig, J. Grunig, and Dozier (2002) suggested.

Organizational Reputation

   Valence of cognitive representations. I measured the latent variable,

organizational reputation using three indicator variables: 1) overall personal rating of

representations, 2) net positive representations, and 3) perceived media rating.[29] For

all three indicator variables, the participants reported the highest values for Samsung

Electronics and similarly high values for the KNRC, whereas they reported the lowest

overall personal rating for the KFA (M = 2.93, SD = 1.03) and the lowest net positive

representations (M = 3.16, SD = 2.68) and perceived media rating (M = 3.11, SD =

.77) for Sony Korea (Table IV.7).

---

[29] In the survey questionnaire, participants first were asked to list up to four different
thoughts that "come to their minds when they think of each of the organizations
studied." Later, participants were asked to go back to their open-end responses. After
reading through all responses, participants reported valence (negative, positive, or
neutral) for each the idea listed. Then, participants provided on overall rating of all
thoughts listed and a perceived media rating for each organization studied.

Table IV.7

Means and Standard Deviations of Organizational Reputation Variables

	Samsung		Sony		KFA		KNRC	
	(N = 281)		(N = 274)		(N = 276)		(N = 275)	
Variables	M	SD	M	SD	M	SD	M	SD
Overall personal rating	3.77	.91	3.21	.84	2.93	1.03	3.68	.95
Net positive representations[a]	5.16	1.82	3.16	2.68	3.20	2.53	4.10	2.56
Perceived media rating	3.88	.91	3.11	.77	3.35	.96	3.82	.86

Note. N = listwise of the group of variables in each organization.

Samsung = Samsung Electronics; Sony = Sony Korea; KFA = Korea Football

Association; KNRC = Korean National Red Cross. [a]Net positive representations = the

number of positive representations less the number of negative representations in each

open-end measure.

First, the descriptive results indicate that the participants reported their

perceptions of media rating *congruently* with their cognitive representations (i.e.,

"how and what they think of each of the organizations"). In other words, I found that

participants' individual representations of the organizations studied were highly

associated with individual perceptions of the *valence* in media coverage of those

organizations.

Secondly, the descriptive statistics for organizational reputation also suggested

that, consistently throughout the four organizations studied, the four latent variables in

the hypothesized model (i.e., communication behaviors of publics, familiarity,

organization-public relationship outcomes, and organizational reputation) were highly

correlated in this study. For example, participants reported favorable organizational reputation for Samsung Electronics and the KNRC relative to Sony Korea and the KFA in the same pattern as they did for indicators of other latent variables.

Distribution of cognitive representations. J. Grunig and Hung (2002) defined organizational reputation as the distribution of cognitive representations shared by members of a public about an organization. I focused on the *valence* of cognitive representations which I could use in structural equation modeling (SEM) of this study.

However, for "descriptive" and "exploratory" purposes, I investigated the distribution of cognitive representations to look for critical information to analyze organizational reputations. This is because organizational reputation should be conceptualized at the *collective* level as opposed to personal impressions at the individual level. To put it another way, the distribution of cognitive representations is a useful way to interpret how personal impressions of an organization at the individual level were shared at the collective level (Bromley, 1993; 2000; J. Grunig & Hung, 2002).

Cognitive representations[30] of the profit organizations studied were highly shared about "the quality of products and services" (see Table IV.8 and Figure IV.5 for Samsung Electronics and Table IV.9 and Figure IV.6 for Sony Korea): Samsung Electronics (246 representations out of 398 total representation; about 61.8%) and Sony Korea (192 representations out of 375 total representations; about 51.2%), for

---

[30] Participants reported valence of cognitive representations by themselves in the questionnaire. On the other hand, for the distribution of cognitive representations, two independent coders coded data into categories. As the primary coder, I coded 1,391 thoughts listed by participants, using J. Grunig and Hung's (2002) taxonomy of cognitive representations and Bromley's (2000) attribution categories in addition to categories driven from data. Then, a fellow graduate student independently coded an SPSS-generated random 10% of the entire coding unit (140 thoughts out of 1,391) based on the coding descriptions/definitions. The initial intercoder reliability between coders was moderate with Holsti intercoder reliability of .79. After revision in some coding categories, intercoder reliability in the second-wave improved to an acceptable level: Holsti intercoder reliability of .83 in the randomly selected 10 percent of the coding units.

both *positive* and *negative* cognitive representations. This may be because most of participants had direct experience with those organizations as "customers" (see Table IV.3): Samsung ($n = 177$; 60.6%) and Sony Korea ($n = 104$; 35.9%).

Table IV.8

Distribution of Cognitive Representations about Samsung Electronics (N = 398)

Representations	P1[a]	P2	P3	P4	P-Total	N1	N2	N3	N-Total	M-Total	Total
Object-Object											
Org scope	1 (.4)[a]	1 (2.9)			2 (.7)					1 (14.3)	3 (.8)
Object-Attribute											
Quality of products/services	176 (71.8)	11 (32.4)	2 (66.7)		189 (66.8)	54 (53.5)	1 (16.7)		55 (50.9)	2 (28.6)	246 (61.8)
Quality of employees, working environment etc.	5 (2.0)	1 (2.9)			6 (2.1)	5 (5.0)	1 (16.7)		6 (5.6)	--	12 (3)
Current situations, future prospectus etc.	3 (1.2)	2 (5.9)			5 (1.8)		1 (16.7)		1 (.9)	--	6 (1.5)
Org presentation style	3 (1.2)	1 (2.9)			4 (1.4)	1 (1.0)			1 (.9)	--	5 (1.3)
Market/field leadership	12 (4.9)	1 (2.9)			13 (4.6)	1 (1.0)			1 (.9)	--	14 (3.5)
Relational attributes	12 (4.9)	1 (2.9)			13 (4.6)				--		13 (3.3)
Emotional attributes	9 (3.7)	4 (11.8)			13 (4.6)	3 (3.0)			3 (2.8)	--	16 (4.8)
Identity, image, brand etc.	8 (3.3)	8 (23.5)			16 (5.7)	2 (2.0)			2 (1.9)	--	18 (4.5)
Financial strength	4 (1.6)				4 (1.4)	1 (1.0)			1 (.9)	--	5 (1.3)

(Table IV.8 continues)

(Table IV.8 continues)

Representations	P1[a]	P2	P3	P4	P-Total	N1	N2	N3	N-Total	M-Total	Total
Personal interest	1 (.4)				1 (.4)	1 (1.0)			1 (.9)	--	2 (.5)
Familiarity/popularity	1 (.4)				1 (.4)				--	--	1 (.3)
Personal interest	1 (.4)				1 (.4)	1 (1.0)			1 (.9)	--	2 (.5)
Supportive behavior/intention	1 (.4)				1 (.4)				--	--	1 (.3)
Competent/productive management					--	4 (4.0)			4 (3.7)	--	4 (1.0)
Behavior											
Contribution to society	8 (3.3)	4 (11.8)			13 (4.6)	5 (5.0)		1 (100)	6 (5.6)	--	19 (4.8)
Public/customer focus	1 (.4)			1 (100)	2 (.7)	1 (1.0)	1 (16.7)		2 (1.9)	--	4 (1.0)
Ethical/transparent management			1 (33.3)		--	18 (17.8)	1 (16.7)		19 (17.6)	--	19 (4.8)
Not interested					--					3 (42.9)	3 (.8)
Don't know					--					1 (14.3)	1 (.3)
Total	245 (100)	34 (100)	3 (100)	1 (100)	283 (100)	101 (100)	6 (100)	1 (100)	108 (100)	7 (100)	398 (100)

Note. [a]P1 = positive representation 1; P2 = positive representation 2; P3 = positive representation 3; P4 = positive representation 4; P-total = the total number of positive representations in each category; N1 = negative representation 1; N2 = negative representation 2; N3 = negative representation 3; N-total = the total number of negative representations in each category; M-total = the total number of neutral representations in each category; Total = sum of the total number of representations in each row or column of categories. [b]Percentage of frequency in each column.

Table IV.9

Distribution of Cognitive Representations about Sony Korea (N = 375)

Representations	P1[a]	P2	P-Total	N1	N2	N3	N-Total	M-Total	Total
Object-Object									
Org scope			--	1 (1.1)	1 (9.1)		2 (1.9)	6 (6.1)	8 (2.1)
Object-Attribute									
Quality of products/services	120 (74.5)[b]	7 (70.0)	127 (74.3)	53 (57)	6 (54.5)	1 (100)	60 (57.1)	5 (5.1)	192 (51.2)
Org missions/functions etc.			--				--	2 (2.0)	2 (.5)
Current situations, future prospectus etc.	1 (.6)		1 (.6)				--	--	1 (.3)
Org type			--				--	1 (1.0)	1 (.3)
Org presentation style	2 (1.2)		2 (1.2)	1 (1.1)			1 (1.0)	--	3 (.8)
Market/field leadership	5 (3.1)		5 (2.9)	6 (6.5)	2 (18.2)		8 (7.6)	--	13 (3.5)
Relational attributes	5 (3.1)	1 (10.0)	6 (3.5)				--	--	6 (1.6)
Emotional attributes	3 (1.9)		3 (1.8)	9 (9.7)			9 (8.6)	--	12 (3.2)
Identity, image, brand etc.	14 (8.7)	1 (10.0)	15 (8.8)	7 (7.5)	1 (9.1)		8 (7.6)	1 (1.0)	24 (6.4)

(Table IV.9 continues)

(Table IV.9 continues)

Representations	P1[a]	P2	P-Total	N1	N2	N3	N-Total	M-Total	Total
Financial strength	3 (1.9)	1 (10.0)	4 (2.3)				--	--	4 (1.1)
Familiarity/popularity	2 (1.2)		2 (1.2)	3 (3.2)			3 (2.9)	--	5 (1.3)
Competent/productive management			--	3 (3.2)			3 (2.9)	--	3 (.8)
Behavior									
Contribution to society	3 (1.9)		3 (1.8)	4 (4.3)	1 (9.1)		5 (4.8)	--	8 (2.1)
Public/customer focus	2 (1.2)		2 (1.2)	3 (3.2)			3 (2.9)	--	5 (1.3)
Ethical/transparent management	1 (.6)		1 (.6)	3 (3.2)			3 (2.9)	--	4 (1.1)
Not interested			--				--	12 (12.1)	12 (3.2)
Don't know			--				--	72 (72.7)	72 (19.2)
Total	161 (100)	10 (100)	171 (100)	93 (100)	11 (100)	1 (100)	105 (100)	99 (100)	375 (100)

Note. [a]P1 = positive representations 1; P2 = positive representation 2; P-total = the total number of positive representations in each category; N1 = negative representation 1; N2 = negative representation 2; N3 = negative representation 3; N-total = the total number of negative representations in each category; M-total = the total number of neutral representations in each category; Total = sum of the total number of representations in each row or column of categories. [b]Percentage of frequency in each column.

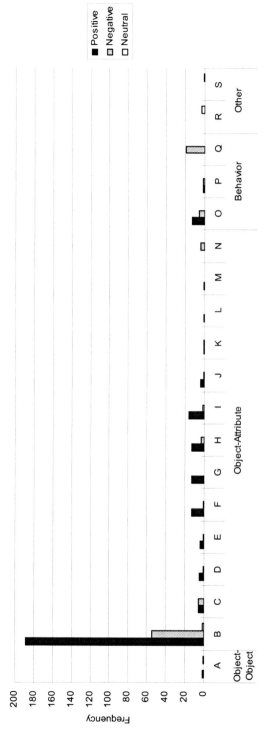

Figure IV.1. Distribution of cognitive representations about Samsung Electronics ($N = 398$). A = org scope; B = quality of products/services; C = quality of employees, working environment etc; D = current situations, future prospectus etc; E = org presentation style; F = market/field leadership; G = relational attributes; H = emotional attributes; I = identity, image, brand etc; J = financial strength; K = personal interest; L = familiarity/popularity; M = supportive behavior/intention; N = competent/productive management; O = contribution to society; P = public/customer focus; Q = ethical/transparent management; R = not interested; S = don't know.

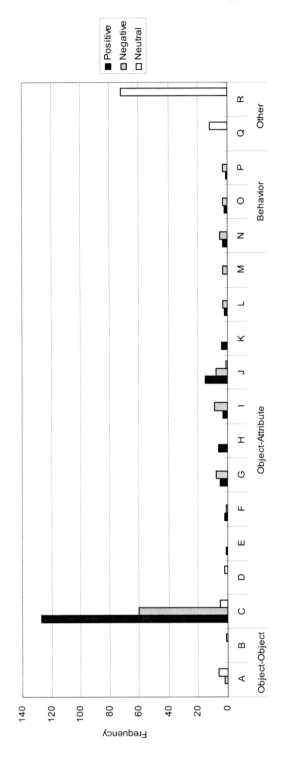

Figure IV.2. Distribution of cognitive representations about Sony Korea (*N* = 375). A = org scope; B = org type; C = quality of products/services; D = org missions/functions etc; E = current situations, future prospectus etc; F = org presentations style; G = market status/leadership; H = relational attributes; I = emotional attributes; J = identity, image, brand etc; K = financial strength; L = familiarity/popularity; M = competent/productive management; N = contribution to society; O = public/customer focus; P = ethical/transparent management; Q = not interested; R = don't know.

Interestingly, the participants shared *both* positive and negative representations about the "quality of products and services," which suggests that the participants held cognitive representations that were based on highly *individual* experience. For Samsung Electronics, the participants had 66.8% ($n = 189$) of their positive representations and 50.9% ($n = 55$) of their negative representations in the category of "the quality of products and services." Secondly, for Sony Korea, the participants shared 74.3 % ($n = 177$) of their positive representations and 57.1% ($n = 60$) of their negative representations in the category.

For *behavioral* representations (i.e., "what participants remembered about behaviors of the organization studied"), participants held *negative* representations of those two profit organizations, in particular about "ethical and transparent management." In addition, unlike for Samsung Electronics, participants shared negative representations of "(lack of) social contribution" for Sony Korea.

Unlike the profit organizations studied, the nonprofit organizations studied, the KFA and the KNRC, had *behavioral* representations as the dominant category of cognitive representations (see Table IV.10 and Figure IV.7 for the KFA and Table IV.11 and Figure IV.8 for the KNRC).

Table IV.10

Distribution of Cognitive Representations about Korea Football Association (N = 300)

Representations	P1[a]	P2	P-Total	N1	N2	N3	N-Total	M-Total	Total
Object-Object									
Soccer	--		--				--	8 (9.4)	8 (2.7)
Object-Attribute									
Quality of employees, working environment etc.			--	2 (2.0)		1 (33.3)	3 (2.6)	--	3 (1.0)
Org missions/functions etc.	2 (1.9)[b]		2 (1.9)				--	5 (5.9)	7 (2.3)
Current situations, future prospectus etc.	4 (3.8)		6 (5.6)	10 (9.9)			10 (8.8)	--	16 (5.3)
CEO/president			--	1 (1.0)			1 (.9)		2 (.7)
Special events/circumstances	5 (4.8)		5 (4.6)				--	4 (4.7)	9 (3.0)
Org presentation style	1 (1.0)		1 (.9)				--	1 (1.2)	2 (.7)
Market/field leadership	1 (1.0)		1 (.9)	1 (1.0)			1 (.9)	--	2 (.7)
Relational attributes	7 (6.7)		7 (6.5)	5 (5.0)			5 (4.4)	--	12 (4.0)
Emotional attributes			--	10 (9.9)	2 (20.0)		12 (10.5)	--	12 (4.0)

(Table IV.10 continues)

(Table IV.10 continues)

Representations	P1[a]	P2	P-Total	N1	N2	N3	N-Total	M-Total	Total
Identity, image, brand etc.	5 (4.8)	1 (25.0)	6 (5.6)	4 (4.0)	1 (10.0)		5 (4.4)	--	11 (3.7)
Familiarity/popularity	8 (7.7)		8 (7.4)				--	--	8 (2.7)
Personal interest	9 (8.7)		9 (8.3)	1 (1.0)			1 (.9)	--	10 (3.3)
Supportive behavior/intention			--	3 (3.0)			3 (2.6)	1 (1.2)	4 (1.3)
Competent/productive management	1 (1.0)		1 (.9)	22 (21.8)	2 (20.0)		24 (21.1)	--	25 (8.3)
Behavior									
Contribution to society	47 (45.2)	2 (50.0)	49 (45.4)	3 (3.0)	2 (20.0)	1 (33.3)	6 (5.3)	7 (8.2)	62 (20.7)
Public/customer focus	7 (6.7)	1 (25.0)	8 (7.4)	1 (1.0)			1 (.9)	--	10 (3.3)
Ethical/transparent management			--	26 (25.7)	3 (30.0)	1 (33.3)	30 (26.3)	--	30 (10.0)
Not interested							--	30 (35.3)	30 (10.0)
Don't know			--				--	29 (34.1)	29 (9.7)
Total	104 (100)	4 (100)	108 (100)	101 (100)	10 (100)	3 (100)	114 (100)	85 (100)	300 (100)

Note. [a]P1 = positive representations 1; P2 = positive representation 2; P-total = the total number of positive representations in each category; N1 = negative representation 1; N2 = negative representation 2; N3 = negative representation 3; M-total = the total number of neutral representations in each category; N-total = the total number of negative representations in each category; Total = sum of the total number of representations in each row or column of categories. [b]Percentage of frequency in each column.

Table IV.11

Distribution of Cognitive Representations about Korean National Red Cross (N = 318)

Representations	P1[a]	P2	P3	P-Total	N1	N2	N-Total	M-Total	Total
Object-Object									
North Korea				--			--	3 (5.3)	3 (.9)
Org type				--			--	2 (3.5)	2 (.6)
Object-Attribute									
Quality of services	2 (1.1)[b]			2 (1.0)			--	1 (1.8)	3 (.9)
Org missions/functions etc.	24 (13.1)	1 (11.1)		25 (13.0)			--	12 (21.1)	37 (11.6)
Current situations, future prospectus etc.	1 (.5)			1 (.5)	2 (3.2)	1 (20.0)	3 (4.4)	--	4 (1.3)
Org presentation style				--	7 (11.1)		7 (10.3)	--	7 (2.2)
Market/field leadership	1 (.5)			1 (.5)			--	--	1 (.3)
Relational attributes	10 (5.5)			10 (5.2)	1 (1.6)		1 (1.5)	--	11 (3.5)
Financial strength		1 (11.1)		1 (.5)	1 (1.6)		1 (1.5)	--	2 (.6)
Emotional attributes	18 (9.8)	1 (11.1)		19 (9.8)	2 (3.2)		2 (2.9)	1 (1.8)	22 (6.9)

(Table IV.11 continues)

(Table IV.11 continues)

Representations	P1[a]	P2	P3	P-Total	N1	N2	N-Total	M-Total	Total
Identity, image, brand etc.		2 (22.2)		2 (1.0)		1 (20.0)	1 (1.5)	--	3 (.9)
Familiarity/popularity	6 (3.3)			6 (3.1)	6 (9.5)		6 (8.8)	--	12 (3.8)
Personal interest	5 (2.7)	1 (11.1)		6 (3.1)	3 (4.8)		3 (4.4)	--	9 (2.8)
Supportive behavior/intention				--	2 (3.2)		2 (2.9)	5 (8.8)	7 (2.2)
Competent/productive management	2 (1.1)			2 (1.0)	21 (33.3)	1 (20.0)	22 (32.4)	1 (1.8)	25 (7.9)
Behavior									
Contribution to society	77 (42.1)	2 (22.2)	1 (100)	80 (41.5)	1 (1.6)		1 (1.5)	3 (5.3)	84 (26.4)
Public/customer focus	27 (14.8)			27 (14.0)	2 (3.2)		2 (2.9)	2 (3.5)	31 (9.7)
Ethical/transparent management	1 (.5)	1 (11.1)		2 (1.0)	15 (23.8)	2 (40.0)	17 (25.0)	3 (5.3)	22 (6.9)
Not interested				--			--	9 (15.8)	9 (2.8)
Don't know				--			--	13 (22.8)	13 (4.1)
Total	183 (100)	9 (100)	1 (100)	193 (100)	63 (100)	5 (100)	68 (100)	57 (100)	318 (100)

Note. [a]P1 = positive representation 1; P2 = positive representation 2; P3 = positive representation 3; P-total = the total number of positive representations in each category; N1 = negative representation 1; N2 = negative representation 2; N-total = the total number of negative representations in each category; M-total = the total number of neutral representations in each category; Total = sum of the total number of representations in each row or column of categories. [b]Percentage of frequency in each column.

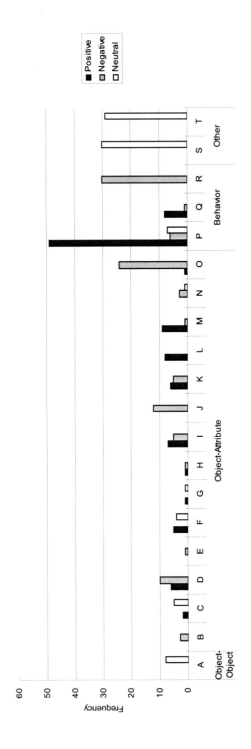

Figure IV.3. Distribution of cognitive representations about Korea Football Association (*N* = 300). A = soccer; B = quality of employees, working environment etc; C = org missions/functions etc; D = current situations, future prospectus etc; E = CEO/president; F = special events/circumstances; G = org presentation style; H = market/field leadership; I = relational attributes; J = emotional attributes; K = identity, image, brand etc; L = familiarity/popularity; M = personal interest; N = supportive behavior/intention; O = competent/productive management; P = contribution to society; Q = public/customer focus; R = ethical/transparent management; S = not interested; T = don't know.

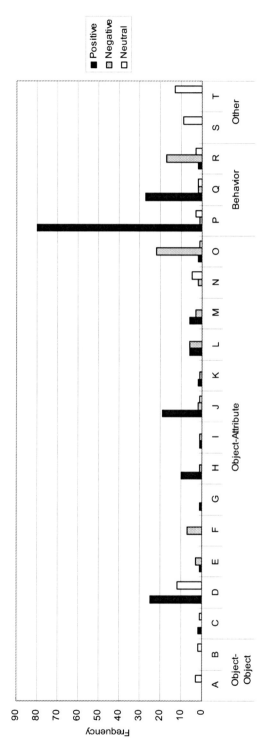

Figure IV.4. Distribution of cognitive representations about Korean National Red Cross (*N* = 318). A = North Korea; B = org type; C = quality of services; D = org missions/functions etc; E = current situations, future prospectus etc; F = org presentation style; G = market/field leadership; H = relational attributes; I = financial strength; J = emotional attributes; K = identity, image, brand etc; L = familiarity/popularity; M = personal interest; N = supportive behavior/intention; O = competent/productive management; P = contribution to society; Q = public/customer focus; R = ethical/transparent management; S = not interested; T = don't know.

This may be because organizational behaviors were more salient for the nonprofit organizations studied in light of organizational goals and missions perceived by participants, than for the profit organizations studied. For example, for the KFA, 34% of all representations ($n = 300$) were behavioral representations. Among them, "contribution to society" was the most frequent positive representation (45.4%; $n = 49$). On the other hand, "ethical and transparent management" was the most frequent negative representation (26.4%; $n = 30$)—in particular, "discord between the leaders of the organization" and "deceiving use of donations and funds."

Additionally, the participants mostly shared *positive* behavioral representations of the KNRC (43% of 318 representations) unlike for the KFA. "Contribution to society," above all, was the most frequent positive representation (41.5%; $n = 80$) and "public focus" (14%; $n = 27$) was next. On the other hand, ethical and transparent management was the dominant negative representation (25%, $n = 17$) for the KNRC—in particular, "deceiving use of the donations."

To sum up, cognitive representations of the two profit organizations studied were more *undistributed*, or shared, than they were for two nonprofit organizations— in particular, because of the prevalence of "the quality of products and services" in cognitive representations. Even within the same category of representations, participants had *both* positive and negative representations based on individual experience and relationship history. Cognitive representations of the nonprofit organizations centered more on *behavioral* representations than for the profit organizations studied—in particular, contribution to society and use of donations. Additionally, the participants reported, in general, more positive behavioral representations about the KNRC than the KFA.

Finally, according to Table IV.10 and Table IV.11, many participants reported "Not interested" or "Don't know" about Sony Korea and the KFA, which supports the earlier findings about low degrees of familiarity and active communication behaviors for those organizations. In other words, the participants were not familiar with and did not communicate actively with Sony Korea and the KFA. On the other hand, Table IV.8 and Table IV.9 indicate that the participants were more familiar with and communicated more actively with Samsung Electronics and the KNRC.

Table IV.12

Coding Categories of Cognitive Representations

Taxonomy of Representations	Categories	Descriptions
Object-Object	Org scope	The scope of the organization: local, national, multinational, governmental etc.
	Org type	The type of the organization: public or private, commercial or charitable etc.
	Competitors, allies	The competitors or allies of the organization
	Soccer	(For Korea Football Association): soccer games
	North Korea	(For Korean National Red Cross): North Korea, North Korean etc.
Object-Attribute	Quality of products/services	Quality or reliability of products/services, product/technology development, price compared with quality etc.
	Special events/circumstances	Special events/circumstances of the organization at time of survey
	Current situations, future prospectus	Current situations or future prospectus of the organization at time of survey
	Org missions/functions etc.	(For Korean National Red Cross): Red Cross programs
	Quality of employees, working environment etc.	Human resource management, quality of employees/working conditions, employee-org relationships etc.
	Org presentation style	PR, Advertisement, livery etc.
	CEO, president	CEO or President of the organization
	Identity, image, brand etc.	Identity, image, brand, logo, symbol of the organization

(Table IV.12 continues)

(Table IV.12 continues)

Taxonomy of Representations	Categories	Descriptions
	Market/field leadership	Leadership status of the organization in the organizational field or market
	Relational attributes	Satisfied, trustworthy, faithful/responsible, hardworking etc.
	Financial strength	Financial strength of the organization
	Emotional attributes	Feeling good in general, kind, humanitarian, altruistic etc.
	Personal interest	Personal interest in the organization or the performance of the organization
	Familiarity, popularity	Familiarity of the organization and the performance of the organization, popularity of the organization or its products/services to publics etc.
	Competent/productive management	Management style: challenging, active, capable etc.
	Supportive behavior/intention	Public support, customer loyalty etc.
Behaviors	Contribution to society	Social services, importance to society, development of Korean soccer etc.
	Public focus	Customer focus, public interest/welfare, public health etc.
	Ethical/transparent management	Fair management, transparent use of donations, harmony in org leadership etc.
Other	Don't know	Don't know about the organization
	Not interested	Personally not interested in the organization

Structural Equation Modeling (SEM) Analysis

Data Reduction & Results of Confirmatory Factor Analysis

Now that I have explained characteristics of the sample and descriptive

statistics of the variables in the hypothesized structural equation modeling analysis,

this chapter turns to the results of the structural equation analysis. Using the statistical

program AMOS 4.0, the causal relationships were examined between 1) organization-

public relationship outcomes, a latent variable with four indicators (control mutuality,

trust, satisfaction, and commitment), 2) organizational reputation, a latent variable

with three indicators (net positive representations, overall personal rating, and

perceived media rating), 3) communication behaviors of publics, a latent variable with

two indicators (information seeking and information processing), and 4) familiarity, a

latent variable with two indicators (overall personal familiarity and familiarity with

the media coverage of the organization). Also, the analysis included exogenous

indicators of problem recognition, constraint recognition, self involvement, perceived

community involvement, personal experience, and types of organization-public

relationships (communal and exchange relationships).[31]

In this section, I will report the results of the data reduction and confirmatory

factor analysis:

1. Data reduction: composite variables using principal component analysis.

2. Results of confirmatory factor analysis: construct reliability and validity

   of the measurement items.

Data Reduction

---

[31] The hypothesized model is presented in Figure II (p. 121). Circles represent latent
variables, rectangles represent measured variables. Absence of a line connecting
variables implies lack of a hypothesized direct effect.

I measured some of the indicator variables with multiple items. To measure the quality of organization-public relationship outcomes, for example, I used 18 items: 6 items for trust, 4 items for control mutuality, 4 items for commitment, and 4 items for relational satisfaction. Also, for measures of organization-public relationship types, I used 4 items for communal relationships and also 4 items for exchange relationships.

To make the hypothesized model parsimonious, I decided to use composite variables for those indicator variables measured with multiple items. I used principal component (PC) scores rather than mean scores to create composite variables. Instead of *unweighted* summation of the observed variables in mean scores, principal components are linear combinations[32] of the original observed variables. Consequently, the extracted components summarize variance in the observed variables more effectively than mean scores when the construct has a single dimension.

Applying Kaiser's rule (Tabachnick and Fidell, 2001), I retained any component with an eigenvalue greater than or equal to one to see whether each indicator variable had a unidimensional structure. I found, throughout all cases, that there existed only one dominant component satisfying the criteria. Therefore, I created the *composite* variables with the dominant component using principal component analysis (PCA), assuming that such variables had a single dimension.

One of my goals in building the composite variables was to determine whether factor loadings of the extracted dominant component were "equivalent" across the

---

[32]By linear combinations, I mean: 1) each component accounts for the maximum amount of variation in the original data under the restriction that the preceding component explains more variation than the subsequent component; 2) each component is orthogonal to all other components (Tabachnick & Fidell, 2001).

four organizations studied. If factor loadings were markedly variant across the different organizations studied, the way of building the composite variables could influence subsequent analyses of hypothesis. The results indicated that this was not the case in this study.

Composites for organization-public relationship outcomes. First, for the indicators of organization-public relationship outcomes, Table IV.13 indicates that, overall, factor loadings of the observed variables were similar across all organizations studied.

Table IV.13

Factor Loadings of Organization-public Relationship Outcomes from Principal Component Analysis: Eigenvalues and Percentages of

Variances Explained

Item[a]	Control mutuality				Trust				Commitment				Satisfaction			
	S1[c]	S2	S3	S4	S1	S2	S3	S4	S1	S2	S3	S4	S1	S2	S3	S4
CM1	.74	.65	.70	.68												
CM2	.77	.74	.74	.81												
CM3 (R[b])	.76	.71	.75	.73												
CM4	.79	.76	.75	.79												
TR1					.73	.71	.61	.64								
TR2					.63	.65	.67	.59								
TR3					.74	.72	.73	.77								
TR4					.64	.62	.77	.75								
TR5					.69	.61	.72	.69								
TR6					.59	.54	.65	.57								

(Table IV.13 continues)

(Table IV.13 continues)

Item	Control mutuality				Trust				Commitment				Satisfaction			
	S1[c]	S2	S3	S4	S1	S2	S3	S4	S1	S2	S3	S4	S1	S2	S3	S4
CT1									.74	.71	.77	.71				
CT2									.76	.71	.77	.78				
CT3									.77	.82	.77	.78				
CT4									.77	.74	.76	.74				
RS1													.71	.63	.73	.72
RS2													.80	.74	.80	.79
RS3													.79	.70	.72	.74
RS4													.81	.79	.81	.83
Eigenvalues	2.33	2.05	2.16	2.28	2.72	2.48	2.88	2.71	2.27	2.24	2.34	2.27	2.44	2.07	2.34	2.36
% of variance	58.24	51.30	54.09	56.89	45.29	41.36	48.02	45.10	56.66	55.95	58.58	56.74	60.93	51.66	58.38	58.98

Note. [a]CM1 = control mutuality item 1; CM2 = control mutuality item 2; CM3 = control mutuality item 3; CM4 = control mutuality item 4; TR1 = integrity item 1; TR2 = integrity item 2; TR3 = dependability item 1; TR4 = dependability item 2; TR5 = competence item 1; TR6 = competence item 2; CT1 = commitment item 1; CT2 = commitment item 2; CT3 = commitment item 3; CT4 = commitment item 4; RS1 = satisfaction item 1; RS2 = satisfaction item 2; RS3 = satisfaction item 3; RS4 = satisfaction item 4. [b]Reversed item. [c]S1 = Samsung Electronics; S2 = Sony Korea; S3 = Korea Football Association; S4 = Korean National Red Cross.

For example, factor loadings of the observed variables for trust indicator were consistent as follows: the highest loadings were found in the items three[33] (i.e., dependability 1: "This organization can be relied on to keep its promise") in the range from .72 to .77; the lowest loadings were found for item six (i.e., competence 2: "This organization has the ability to accomplish what it says it will do") in the range from .54 to .65. Also, in terms of eigenvalues and explained variance, Table IV. 13 shows that more than 40% of the variance was consistently accounted for by the extracted principal component, with eigenvalues, ranged from 2.48 to 2.72.

Composites for organization-public relationship types. Second, factor loadings of items measuring types of organization-public relationships also were consistent for all organizations studied. For communal relationships, across all organizations studied, the highest loadings were found for item two (i.e., "This organization is very concerned about the welfare of people like me") with the range from .78 to .81. The lowest loading, except for the KFA with .55 for item four (i.e., reversed item: "I think that this organization succeeds by stepping on other people"), the lowest loadings were consistently found for item one (reversed item: "This organization does not especially enjoy giving others aid"), with the loadings ranging from .55 to .60 (Table IV.14).

---

[33]See the instrumentation section in the Chapter 3.

Table IV.14

Factor Loadings of Organization-public Relationship Types from Principal

Component Analysis: Eigenvalues and Percentages of Variances Explained

Item[a]	Communal relationships				Exchange relationships			
	Samsung[c]	Sony	KFA	KNRC	Samsung	Sony	KFA	KNRC
CR1 (R[b])	.55	.60	.63	.56				
CR2	.78	.80	.79	.81				
CR3 (R)	.69	.67	.68	.65				
CR4 (R)	.67	.63	.55	.72				
ER1					.76	.73	.79	.78
ER2					.76	.77	.77	.75
ER3					.80	.74	.78	.78
ER4					.44	.44	.40	.54
Eigenvalues	1.84	1.84	1.79	1.91	1.98	1.87	1.97	2.07
% of variances	45.96	46.11	44.84	47.77	49.49	46.81	49.34	51.72

Note. [a]CR 1 = communal relationships item1; CR2 = communal relationships item2; CR3 = communal relationships item3; CR4 = communal relationships item4; ER1 = exchange relationships item1; ER2 = exchange relationships item2; ER3 = exchange relationships item3; ER4 = exchange relationships item4. [b]Reversed item. [c]Samsung = Samsung Electronics; Sony = Sony Korea; KFA = Korea Football Association; KNRC = Korean National Red Cross.

Table IV.14 shows that the loadings for the exchange relationship items were similar for the first three items, which ranged from .73 to .80; the lowest loadings were found for item four (i.e., "This organization takes care of people who are likely to reward the organization"), with loadings ranging from .40 to .54. The extracted

components accounted for more than 40% of the variation in the observed variables

for both concepts, communal and exchange relationships: the amount of explained

variances ranged from 44.84% to 47.77% for the items for communal relationships

and from 46.81% to 51.72% for exchange relationships.

Reliability and Validity of Measurement: Results of Confirmatory Factor Analysis

(CFA)

Now that I have described data reduction by principal component analysis, I

will explain the results of confirmatory factor analysis to report construct reliability

and validity of the measurement model.

Introduction of alpha, coefficient H, & extracted variance. I conducted

confirmatory factor analysis (CFA) to check reliability and validity of the

measurement model. I used Coefficient H to assess *reliability* of the measurement

model and the amount of *extracted variance* (i.e., average squared standardized

loading; $\sum_{i=1}^{n_v} l_i^2 / n_v$ where l is the loading of each indicator with n_v as the number of

indicators for a given factor) to assess *construct validity*. Also, I checked data-model

fit indexes to see whether the hypothesized model in the measurement phase can be

retained as a valid model.

$$\text{Coefficient } H \left(= \cfrac{1}{1 + \cfrac{1}{\cfrac{l_1^2}{(1-l_1^2)} + \ldots + \cfrac{l_p^2}{(1-l_p^2)}}} \right. \text{ where } l \text{ is the loading of each}$$

indicator for a given factor) was used to assess "the 'stability' of a construct as

reflected in the data on the chosen indicator" (Hancock & Muller, 2004, p. 23).

Although researchers often use Cronbach's alpha as a coefficient to check the reliability of indicators, the utility of alpha is limited in assessing the reliability of "composite" scales (Hancock & Mueller, 2001). For Cronbach's alpha to be high, data should have a unidimensional structure because Cronbach's alpha is a "function of the number of test items and the average inter-correlation among the items" ("SPSS FAQ: What does Cronbach's alpha mean?" n.d.).

Therefore, instead of Cronbach's alpha, I used a measure of construct reliability suitable for latent variable systems. I chose *Coefficient H*, rather than Fornell and Larcker's *Construct Reliability* (RC), because of the following advantages of Coefficient H over construct reliability: "1) Coefficient H is not affected by loading's sign, 2) Coefficient H is never decreased by additional indicators, and 3) Coefficient H can't be smaller than the reliability of the best indicator" (Hancock & Muller, 2004, p. 23).

Factor loadings in CFA. The magnitude of the factor loadings, shown in Table IV.15, was greater than .30 for every standardized solution, which suggested that all indicators in the measurement model had at least moderate correlations with corresponding factors. All factor loadings in standardized solutions were statistically significant at $p < .001$.

Table IV.15

Standardized Solutions by Confirmatory Factor Analysis (CFA) for the Measurement Model

Item[a]	Communication Behaviors				Familiarity				Organization-public Relationship Outcomes				Organizational reputation			
	S1[b]	S2	S3	S4	S1	S2	S3	S4	S1	S2	S3	S4	S1	S2	S3	S4
ISK	.56	.64	.80	.61												
IPR	.34	.61	.55	.67												
FM1					.45	.67	.50	.51								
FM2					.64	.69	.64	.64								
RS									.85	.86	.87	.87				
CT									.85	.84	.86	.88				
TR									.86	.86	.84	.86				
CM									.82	.80	.87	.85				

(Table IV.15 continues)

(Table IV.15 continues)

Item[a]	Communication Behaviors				Familiarity				Organization-public Relationship Outcomes				Organizational reputation			
	S1[b]	S2	S3	S4	S1	S2	S3	S4	S1	S2	S3	S4	S1	S2	S3	S4
NRP													.32	.37	.34	.32
ORP													.62	.56	.59	.62
PMR													.50	.57	.64	.50
Construct Reliability[c]																
H[c]	.37	.56	.69	.58	.49	.63	.52	.51	.91	.91	.92	.92	.52	.52	.58	.52
Construct Validity																
VE[d]	.22	.39	.47	.41	.31	.46	.33	.34	.71	.71	.74	.75	.25	.26	.29	.25

(Table IV.15 continues)

(Table IV.15 continues)

Item[a]	Communication Behaviors				Familiarity				Organization-public Relationship Outcomes				Organizational reputation			
	S1[b]	S2	S3	S4	S1	S2	S3	S4	S1	S2	S3	S4	S1	S2	S3	S4
Correlations between latent variables																
Communication[c]	1	1	1	1	.34	.24	.48	.34	.37	.34	.59	.41	.24	.42	.51	.33
Familiarity	.34	.24	.48	.34	1	1	1	1	.44	.33	.39	.42	.35	.64	.44	.35
Relationships	.37	.34	.59	.41	.44	.33	.39	.42	1	1	1	1	.38	.68	.56	.48
Reputation	.24	.42	.51	.33	.35	.64	.44	.35	.38	.68	.56	.48	1	1	1	1

Note. [a]ISK = information seeking; IPR = information processing; FM1 = familiarity with media coverage; FM2 = overall familiarity; RS = relational satisfaction; CT = commitment; TR = trust; CM = control mutuality; NRP = net positive representations; ORP = overall personal rating; PMR = perceived media rating. [b]S1 = Samsung Electronics; S2 = Sony Korea; S3 = Korea Football Association; S4 = Korean National Red Cross. [c]*H* = "Coefficient *H*" (Hancock & Mueller, 2001). [d]*VE* = variance extracted (i.e., average squared standardized loadings). [e]Communication = communication behaviors; Familiarity = familiarity; Relationships = organization-public relationship outcomes; Reputation = organizational reputation.
All standardized solutions (i.e., factor loadings) are significant at $p < .001$; all latent variable correlations are significant at $p \leq .001$.
See data-Model fit indices for this confirmatory factor analyses in the next table (Table IV.16). In terms of CFI, for example, models for all studied organizations retained good data-model fits (e.g., Hu & Bentler, 1999): CFI = .989 for Samsung Electronics, CFI = .993 for Sony Korea, CFI = .992 for the KFA, and CFI = .990 for the KNRC.

First, "communication behaviors of publics" had stronger loadings with the "information seeking" indicator than the information processing indicator, except for the KNRC: .56 versus .34 for Samsung Electronics, .64 versus .61 for Sony Korea, .80 versus .55 for the KFA, and .61 versus .67 for the KNRC. The situational theory of publics suggested stronger effects on information seeking from the three independent variables of communication behaviors (level of involvement, problem recognition, and constraint recognition), than on information processing.

Secondly, across all organizations studied, factor loadings of the "overall personal familiarity" indictor were greater with the familiarity factor than the indicator of familiarity with media coverage: .64 versus .45 for Samsung Electronics, .69 versus .67 for Sony Korea, .64 versus .50 for the KFA, and .64 versus .51 for the KNRC.

Third, the indicators of the "organization-public relationship outcomes" factor had the largest loadings, across all organizations studied, among all indicators used in the hypothesized CFA model. All of standardized loadings were equal to or greater than .80, which suggested that the measure of organization-public relationship outcomes had good construct reliability and validity.

Finally, for the indicators of organizational reputation, the overall personal rating generally had the largest loadings among the three indicators; on the other hand, the indicator of net positive representations had the smallest loadings across all organizations studied. For example, standardized loadings of the overall personal rating were .62 for Samsung Electronics, .56 for Sony Korea, .59 for the KFA, and .62 for the KNRC.

Construct validity. I assessed construct validity of the CFA model based on the average amount of variance in indicator variables accounted for by each factor in the CFA model. A desirable level of Construct validity is for the variance extracted to exceed .50 (Hancock & Muller, 2004). The factor of organization-public relationship outcomes had this level of construct validity for all organizations studied.

The extracted variance in the latent variable of "organization-public relationship outcomes" was greater than .70 for all organizations studied: .71 for Samsung Electronics, .71 for Sony Korea, .74 for the KFA, and .75 for the KNRC. Construct validity of the rest of latent variables in the model was moderate: .22 to .47 in the latent variable of "communication behaviors," .31 to .46 in the latent variable of "familiarity," and .25 to .29 in the latent variable of "organizational reputation." Although other latent variables did not satisfy the cut-off point of .50, in terms of sign and magnitude of loadings, I consider the measurement of the investigated latent variables was generally acceptable: most of the loadings were greater than .5 except for the loading for the net positive representations measuring organizational reputation, with cohesive sign of loadings between indicators.

Construct reliability. I used Hancock and Mueller's (2002) coefficient H to assess construct reliability of the CFA model. Table IV.15 indicates that, as in construct validity, the latent variable of "organization-public relationship outcomes" had a desirable level of construct reliability across all organizations studied: Coefficient H of .91 for Samsung Electronics, Coefficient H of .91 for Sony Korea, Coefficient H of .92 for the KFA, Coefficient H of .92 for the KNRC.

For latent variables other than organization-public relationship outcomes, construct reliability in terms of Coefficient H was moderate or around .50. I consider that moderate or low construct reliability, perhaps, might have been resulted from a limited number of indicator variables to measure the latent variables—in particular "communication behaviors" and "familiarity."

Correlations between latent variables. Finally, the correlations between latent variables showed that all correlations between latent variables in the hypothesized CFA model were significant at least at the .001 level. In particular, correlations between "organization-public relationship outcomes" and "organizational reputation" were highly significant across all organizations studied: $\gamma = .38$ for Samsung Electronics, $\gamma = .68$ for Sony Korea, $\gamma = .56$ for the KFA, and $\gamma = .48$ for the KNRC. The direction of all correlations between latent variables were positive across all organization studied (Table IV.15).

Model estimation of CFA. Since the data-model indexes at the measurement phase indicate that the initial measurement model fits satisfactorily (Table IV.16), I did not make respecifications in the model (as post hoc theory dictates). Therefore, the initial confirmatory model was to equivalent for the final measurement model in this study.

Table IV.16

Model Comparisons: Chi-square Differences and Goodness-of-Fit Indices of the Proposed Model (N = 294)

Model	df	χ^2	χ^2/df	CFI	AIC	RMSEA	Δdf	$\Delta\chi^2$	p
		Organization: Samsung Electronics							
Model 1: CFA model	87	202.61***	2.33	.989	406.61	.067	--	--	--
Model 2: Structural model (Full model)	107	299.97***	2.83	.981	463.96	.078	--	--	--
Model 3: Structural model (No org-public relationship type)	122	560.711***	4.60	.958	694.71	.111	--	--	--
Model comparison: model 2 with model 3							15	260.74	$p < .001$
Model comparison: model 1 with model 2							20	97.36	$p < .001$

(Table IV.16 continues)

(Table IV.16 continues)

Model	df	χ^2	χ^2/df	CFI	AIC	RMSEA	Δdf	$\Delta\chi^2$	p
Organization: Sony Korea									
Model 1: CFA model	87	146.97***	1.69	.993	350.97	.049	--	--	--
Model 2: Structural model (Full model)	106	297.25***	2.80	.979	463.25	.078	--	--	--
Model 3: Structural model (No org-public relationship type)	121	552.997***	4.57	.952	489.00	.110			
Model comparison: model 2 with model 3							15	255.75	$p < .001$
Model comparison: model 1 with model 2							19	152.28	$p < .001$

(Table IV.16 continues)

(Table IV.16 continues)

Model	df	χ^2	χ^2/df	CFI	AIC	RMSEA	Δdf	$\Delta \chi^2$	p
Organizations: Korea Football Association									
Model 1: CFA model	87	160.10***	1.84	.992	364.10	.054	--	--	--
Model 2: Structural model (Full model)	107	356.91***	3.34	.973	520.91	.089	--	--	--
Model 3: Structural model (No org-public relationship type)	122	723.27***	5.93	.935	857.27	.130	--	--	--
Model comparison: model 2 with model 3							15	366.36	$p < .001$
Model comparison: model 1 with model 2							20	196.81	$p < .001$

(Table IV.16 continues)

(Table IV.16 continues)

Model	df	χ^2	χ^2/df	CFI	AIC	RMSEA	Δdf	$\Delta\chi^2$	p
Organization: Korean National Red Cross									
Model 1: CFA model	87	187.52***	2.16	.990	391.52	.063	--	--	--
Model 2: Structural model (Full model)	107	370.78***	3.47	.974	534.78	.092	--	--	--
Model 3: Structural model (No org-public relationship type)	122	747.81***	6.13	.938	881.81	.132	--	--	--
Model comparison: model 2 with model 3							15	377.03	$p < .001$
Model comparison: model 1 with model 2							20	183.26	$p < .001$

Note. CFI = comparative fit index; AIC = Akaike information criterion; RMSEA = root mean square error of approximation.

***$p < .001$.

For example, the Comparative Fit Index (CFI) for all organizations studied indicated good data-model fits: CFI = .989 for Samsung Electronics, CFI = .993 for Sony Korea, CFI = .992 for the KFA, and CFI = .990 for the KNRC. According to Hu and Bentler (1999), a model with CFI value equal to or higher than .95 can be retained as a valid model.

Also, the Root Mean Square Error of Approximation (RMSEA) for all organizations studied showed that the measurement model can be retained as an acceptable model: RMSEA = .067 for Samsung Electronics, RMSEA = .049 for Sony Korea, RMSEA = .054 for the KFA, and RMSEA = .063 for the KNRC. According to Byrne (2001) and Kline (1998), a RMSEA value less than or equal to .08 indicates an acceptable data-model fit of a structural equation model.

Research Question and Hypothesis Testing in SEM Analysis

Now that I have explained the results of the CFA model, I will explain the results of the structural model in this section. By doing so, I will answer the proposed research question and test the nine research hypotheses. More specifically, I will report the following information in this section:

1. Correlations between variables in the hypothesized structural model.

2. Research question: model comparisons of hierarchically related structural models.

3. Hypothesis testing: direct effects of parameter estimates.

4. Indirect effects of parameter estimates.

5. Additional analyses of structural equation modeling: measurement indicator loadings, and correlations between exogenous variables, disturbances, and indicator errors.

Correlations in the Hypothesized Structural Model

Exogenous variables of communication behaviors. Table IV.17 to Table IV.20
show the results of the descriptive analysis for the variables analyzed in the
hypothesized structural equation model.

First, the four exogenous variables of communication behaviors (problem
recognition, constraint recognition, self involvement, and community involvement)
had higher correlations with *information seeking* than information processing across
all organizations studied, except for Sony Korea. In the case of Sony Korea, according
to Table IV.18, information processing had slightly higher Pearson product-moment
correlations with problem recognition ($\gamma_{11.3} = .25 > \gamma_{10.3} = .24$) and with constraint
recognition ($\gamma_{11.4} = -.27 > \gamma_{10.4} = -.24$).

Table IV.17

Descriptive Statistics and Zero-Order Correlations for Indicator Variables for Samsung Electronics

Variable	1	2	3	4	5	6	7	8	9	10	11	12	13	14	15	16	17	18
1. Involvement 1	1																	
2. Involvement 2	.37	1																
3. Problem recognition	.38	.21	1															
4. Constraint recognition	-.57	-.16	-.31	1														
5. Personal experience	.07	.10	.10	-.03	1													
6. Communal relationships	.18	.11	.19	-.12	-.04	1												
7. Exchange relationships	-.23	-.13	-.09	.23	.01	-.62	1											
8. Familiarity with media coverage	.17	.20	.24	-.12	.16	.02	-.05	1										
9. Overall familiarity	.42	.23	.26	-.34	.09	.20	-.17	.29	1									
10. Information seeking	.26	.17	.28	-.24	.02	.17	-.10	.18	.33	1								
11. Information processing	.16	-.09	.09	-.14	.01	.20	-.07	.12	.11	.18	1							

(Table IV.17 continues)

(Table IV.17 continues)

Variable	1	2	3	4	5	6	7	8	9	10	11	12	13	14	15	16	17	18
12. Control mutuality	.34	.19	.29	-.34	-.00	.46	-.53	.23	.38	.28	.14	1						
13. Trust	.33	.29	.28	-.31	.10	.47	-.46	.35	.42	.37	.21	.73	1					
14. Commitment	.42	.28	.34	-.34	.10	.41	-.40	.31	.44	.34	.16	.72	.72	1				
15. Relational satisfaction	.37	.25	.33	-.27	.04	.50	-.44	.27	.40	.36	.28	.65	.73	.79	1			
16. Overall personal rating	.31	.19	.20	-.20	.08	.29	-.27	.12	.36	.30	.06	.39	.45	.43	.41	1		
17. Net positive representations	.08	.04	.12	-.05	.12	.11	.02	.07	.10	.09	.02	.17	.26	.17	.17	.29	1	
18. Perceived media rating	.22	.19	.12	-.14	.09	.15	-.09	.34	.31	.19	.11	.24	.40	.34	.34	.28	.18	1
M	3.26	3.41	3.47	3.09	1.60	1.00	1.00	3.93	3.45	3.21	3.39	.01	.03	.01	.00	3.79	5.36	3.91
SD	1.06	1.00	.96	1.20	.51	1.00	1.00	1.02	1.06	1.06	1.00	1.02	1.00	1.02	1.02	.92	1.55	.88

Note. *N* = 269. Correlations greater than .13 are significant at *p* < .05.

Table IV.18

Descriptive Statistics and Zero-Order Correlations for Indicator Variables for Sony Korea

Variable	1	2	3	4	5	6	7	8	9	10	11	12	13	14	15	16	17	18
1. Involvement 1	1																	
2. Involvement 2	.47	1																
3. Problem recognition	.36	.20	1															
4. Constraint recognition	-.56	-.38	-.30	1														
5. Personal experience	.31	.13	.37	-.22	1													
6. Communal relationships	.22	.30	.14	-.11	.00	1												
7. Exchange relationships	-.23	-.33	-.16	.21	.02	-.59	1											
8. Familiarity with media coverage	.41	.32	.36	-.38	.26	.20	-.25	1										
9. Overall familiarity	.43	.32	.46	-.39	.30	.17	-.16	.41	1									
10. Information seeking	.28	.13	.24	-.24	.11	.18	-.11	.17	.22	1								
11. Information processing	.27	.13	.25	-.27	.26	.15	-.08	.11	.19	.40	1							

(Table IV.18 continues)

(Table IV.18 continues)

Variable	1	2	3	4	5	6	7	8	9	10	11	12	13	14	15	16	17	18
12. Control mutuality	.37	.29	.22	-.37	.03	.46	-.47	.21	.23	.27	.28	1						
13. Trust	.39	.27	.24	-.32	.20	.45	-.37	.31	.30	.36	.33	.69	1					
14. Commitment	.38	.32	.29	-.34	.13	.42	-.40	.30	.27	.29	.29	.71	.72	1				
15. Relational satisfaction	.37	.27	.30	-.32	.15	.48	-.40	.28	.27	.34	.25	.65	.75	.79	1			
16. Overall personal rating	.24	.19	.33	-.26	.22	.21	-.23	.34	.26	.27	.23	.29	.43	.43	.48	1		
17. Net positive representations	.10	-.03	.22	-.14	.23	-.08	.04	.17	.19	.16	.18	.10	.23	.17	.23	.32	1	
18. Perceived media rating	.39	.30	.24	-.32	.25	.28	-.21	.42	.34	.18	.17	.35	.46	.34	.46	.26	.20	1
M	2.68	2.76	2.56	3.68	1.24	.97	-.00	2.47	2.57	2.96	3.26	.04	.04	.03	.03	3.21	3.38	3.12
SD	.99	1.00	1.03	1.05	.68	.97	.97	1.07	1.00	1.08	1.06	1.00	1.00	.99	.99	.85	2.65	.74

Note. $N = 254$. Correlations greater than .12 are significant at $p < .05$.

Table IV.19

Descriptive Statistics and Zero-Order Correlations for Indicator Variables for the Korea Football Association

Variable	1	2	3	4	5	6	7	8	9	10	11	12	13	14	15	16	17	18
1. Involvement 1	1																	
2. Involvement 2	.46	1																
3. Problem recognition	.36	.23	1															
4. Constraint recognition	-.57	-.41	-.36	1														
5. Personal experience	.03	.03	.24	-.05	1													
6. Communal relationships	.28	.29	.19	-.22	.07	1												
7. Exchange relationships	-.19	-.26	-.14	.25	-.09	-.59	1											
8. Familiarity with media coverage	.33	.35	.25	-.24	.15	.19	-.09	1										
9. Overall familiarity	.40	.42	.40	-.41	.15	.25	-.18	.28	1									
10. Information seeking	.31	.27	.35	-.32	.10	.38	-.31	.25	.41	1								
11. Information processing	.23	.25	.19	-.17	.08	.27	-.19	.16	.26	.45	1							

(Table IV.19 continues)

(Table IV.19 continues)

Variable	1	2	3	4	5	6	7	8	9	10	11	12	13	14	15	16	17	18
12. Control mutuality	.39	.40	.26	-.39	.00	.65	-.62	.25	.31	.44	.32	1						
13. Trust	.38	.41	.19	-.33	.02	.67	-.58	.18	.29	.48	.31	.76	1					
14. Commitment	.40	.41	.33	-.35	.13	.64	-.51	.28	.37	.52	.38	.73	.71	1				
15. Relational satisfaction	.40	.43	.37	-.37	.08	.64	-.50	.25	.36	.54	.35	.74	.72	.78	1			
16. Overall personal rating	.33	.32	.21	-.30	.06	.36	-.34	.13	.24	.40	.21	.42	.54	.43	.40	1		
17. Net positive representations	.21	.22	.16	-.17	.18	.14	-.14	.25	.17	.10	.05	.11	.18	.13	.11	.33	1	
18. Perceived media rating	.33	.42	.25	-.26	.17	.40	-.33	.31	.29	.31	.20	.36	.47	.42	.42	.34	.25	1
M	2.53	2.89	2.70	3.58	.93	-.04	.02	2.68	2.75	2.53	2.78	1.00	-.03	-.05	-.03	2.91	3.31	3.31
SD	1.08	.98	1.05	1.15	.33	1.01	.99	1.01	1.07	1.14	1.20	.98	.98	.98	.98	1.04	2.51	.92

Note. N = 257. Correlations greater than .12 are significant at *p* < .05.

Table IV.20

Descriptive Statistics and Zero-Order Correlations for Indicator Variables for the Korean National Red Cross

Variable	1	2	3	4	5	6	7	8	9	10	11	12	13	14	15	16	17	18
1. Involvement 1	1																	
2. Involvement 2	.46	1																
3. Problem recognition	.35	.29	1															
4. Constraint recognition	-.51	-.38	-.37	1														
5. Personal experience	.14	.10	.31	-.10	1													
6. Communal relationships	.11	.13	.16	-.13	.06	1												
7. Exchange relationships	-.13	-.16	-.12	.12	-.02	-.66	1											
8. Familiarity with media coverage	.28	.39	.15	-.19	.14	.11	-.12	1										
9. Overall familiarity	.38	.36	.38	-.48	.18	.25	-.16	.29	1									
10. Information seeking	.19	.23	.25	-.21	.03	.24	-.25	.30	.25	1								
11. Information processing	.11	.20	.20	-.20	.05	.34	-.29	.22	.28	.44	1							

(Table IV.20 continues)

Not applicable

(Table IV.20 continues)

Variable	1	2	3	4	5	6	7	8	9	10	11	12	13	14	15	16	17	18
12. Control mutuality	.26	.27	.28	-.35	.12	.57	-.64	.23	.33	.33	.37	1						
13. Trust	.24	.30	.16	-.29	.04	.62	-.60	.30	.33	.33	.45	.76	1					
14. Commitment	.32	.31	.28	-.34	.10	.61	-.60	.28	.37	.37	.37	.71	.72	1				
15. Relational satisfaction	.31	.28	.27	-.31	.07	.61	-.63	.29	.36	.38	.39	.70	.73	.81	1			
16. Overall personal rating	.17	.23	.16	-.11	-.01	.37	-.49	.22	.23	.29	.37	.42	.49	.44	.45	1		
17. Net positive representations	.07	.17	.05	-.05	-.01	.26	-.26	.18	.07	.09	.15	.20	.31	.22	.22	.40	1	
18. Perceived media rating	.21	.27	.23	-.18	.06	.40	-.35	.39	.31	.17	.24	.31	.35	.44	.48	.24	.19	1
M	3.01	3.15	3.11	3.07	1.58	.01	-.01	2.83	3.04	2.82	3.47	1.00	.98	-.01	.03	3.67	4.19	3.83
SD	1.08	.98	1.05	1.15	.33	1.01	.99	1.01	1.07	1.14	1.20	.98	.98	.98	.98	1.04	2.51	.92

Note. N = 257. Correlations greater than .12 are significant at p < .05.

All correlations were statistically significant across all organizations studied except for the correlations between community involvement and information processing (γ = -.09) and between problem recognition and information processing (γ = .09) for Samsung Electronics (Table IV.17), and the correlation between self involvement and information processing (γ = .11) for the KNRC (Table IV.20).

Secondly, throughout the four organizations studied, I found the strongest Pearson product-moment correlations, among the four exogenous variables of communication behaviors, consistently in the relationship between *problem recognition* and *self involvement*: γ = -.57 for Samsung Electronics, γ = -.56 for Sony Korea, γ = -.57 for the KFA, and γ = -.51 for the KNRC. Therefore, there did not seem to be a multicollinearity problem among those variables in the hypothesized structural equation model.

Third, I found a systematic pattern in the data regarding the four exogenous variables that predict communication behaviors: constraint recognition was negatively associated with every variable in data, except for exchange relationships across all organizations studied. The other variables (problem recognition and the two types of level of involvement) were "positively" associated with all variables of interest in this study. This may indicate that all sets of variables, suggested in the hypothesized model, were systematically linked to the four exogenous variables that predict communication behaviors. The relationships between constraint recognition and exchange relationships were positively significant ($p < .05$) across all organizations studied: γ = .23 for Samsung Electronics, γ = .21 for Sony Korea, γ = .25 for the KFA, and γ = .12 for the KNRC.

Communication behaviors of publics. First, the correlation between information seeking and information processing were positively significant ($p < .05$)

across all organizations studied: $\gamma = .18$ for Samsung Electronics, $\gamma = .40$ for Sony Korea, $\gamma = .45$ for the KFA, and $\gamma = .44$ for the KNRC. In most case, except for the KNRC, *information seeking* was more strongly associated with all variables of interest in this study than was information processing. For example, for the KFA, the degree of association with information seeking with "all" of the variables was greater than with information processing.

Secondly, for types of organization-public relationships, communal relationships were positively associated with both information seeking and information processing behaviors of publics in a significant manner across all organizations studied: respectively for information seeking and information processing, $\gamma = .17$ and $\gamma = .20$ for Samsung Electronics; $\gamma = .18$ and $\gamma = .15$ for Sony Korea; $\gamma = .38$ and $\gamma = .27$ for the KFA, and $\gamma = .24$ and $\gamma = .34$ for the KNRC. All correlations were significant ($p < .05$).

On the other hand, the correlations between the two types of communication behaviors and exchange relationships were "negative" across all organizations studied. Only for the "nonprofit" organizations, however, were the associations between communication behaviors and exchange relationships significant ($p < .05$): respectively for information seeking and information processing, $\gamma = -.31$ and $\gamma = -.19$ for the KFA; and $\gamma = -.25$ and $\gamma = -.29$ for the KNRC. This may suggest that communication behaviors of participants were "more inhibited by exchange relationships" with the nonprofit organizations than with the profit organizations.

Familiarity. For overall personal familiarity and familiarity with media coverage about the organization, the associations with all variables were consistently positive for all organizations studied except for *constraint recognition* and *exchange relationships.* In general, the associations between overall personal familiarity and the exogenous variables of "communication behaviors" and the "organization-public

relationship outcome" variables were stronger than were association with familiarity

with media coverage of the organization.

Organization-public relationship types. The two types of "organization-public

relationships" were strongly associated with the "organization-public relationship

outcomes" variables (control mutuality, trust, commitment, and satisfaction) and with

the "organizational reputation" variables. In particular, both of the organization-public

relationship types were the most significantly associated with the organization-public

relationship outcome variables, among all latent variables in the model, across all

organizations studied.

For "communal" relationships, all correlations with the organization-public

relationship outcome indicators were positively significant: 1) for Samsung

Electronics, $\gamma = .46$ with control mutuality, $\gamma = .47$ with trust, $\gamma = .41$ with

commitment, and $\gamma = .50$ with satisfaction; 2) for Sony Korea, $\gamma = .46$ with control

mutuality, $\gamma = .45$ with trust, $\gamma = .42$ with commitment, and $\gamma = .48$ with satisfaction;

3) for the KFA, $\gamma = .65$ with control mutuality, $\gamma = .67$ with trust, $\gamma = .64$ with

commitment, and $\gamma = .64$ with satisfaction; and 4) for the KNRC, $\gamma = .57$ with control

mutuality, $\gamma = .62$ with trust, $\gamma = .61$ with commitment, and $\gamma = .61$ with satisfaction.

In summary, the correlations between communal relationships and the organization-

public relationship outcome variables were stronger for the *nonprofit* organizations

studied than for the profit organizations studied.

Likewise, exchange relationships had stronger "negative" correlations with

the organization-public relationship outcome variables for the *nonprofit* organizations

studied than for the profit organizations studied. Correlations coefficients were: 1) for

Samsung Electronics, $\gamma = -.53$ with control mutuality, $\gamma = -.46$ with trust, $\gamma = -.40$ with commitment, and γ = -.44 with satisfaction; 2) for Sony Korea, γ = -.47 with control

mutuality, γ = -.37 with trust, γ = -.40 with commitment, and γ = -.40 with

satisfaction; 3) for the KFA, γ = -.62 with control mutuality, γ = -.58 with trust, γ = -

.51 with commitment, and γ = -.50 with satisfaction; and 4) for the KNRC, γ = -.64

with control mutuality, γ = -.60 with trust, γ = -.60 with commitment, and γ = -.63

with satisfaction.

Thus, based on the stronger association between the types of organization-

public relationships and the organization-public relationship outcomes, the results

suggested that organization-public relationship types affect the quality of

organization-public relationship outcomes more for the nonprofit organizations than

the profit organizations.

Additionally, the correlations with the organizational reputation variables also

showed differential effects of organization-public relationship types between the

profit and nonprofit organizations studied. However, the *direction* of some

correlations for the profit organizations studied was not consistent and the opposite as

I theoretically expected, despite insignificant correlations. For example, 1) for

Samsung Electronics, the correlation between exchange relationships and net positive

representations was positive (γ = .02); and 2) for Sony Korea, the correlation between

communal relationships and net positive representations was negative (γ = -.08) and

the correlation between exchange relationships and net positive representations was

positive (γ = .04).

Nonetheless, unlike for the profit organizations studied, the correlations

between the two types of organization-public relationships and the organizational

reputation variables were consistent and in the same direction, as I theoretically

expected, for the nonprofit organizations studied.

First, the correlation coefficients between *communal* relationships and the organizational reputation variables were (with all coefficients positively significant at $p < .05$): 1) for the KFA, $\gamma = .36$ with overall personal rating, $\gamma = .14$ with net positive representations, and $\gamma = .40$ with perceived media rating; and 2) for the KNRC, $\gamma = .37$ with overall personal rating, $\gamma = .26$ with net positive representations, and $\gamma = .40$ with perceived media rating.

Secondly, the correlation coefficients between *exchange* relationships and the organizational reputation variables included (with all coefficients negatively significant at $p < .05$): 1) for the KFA, $\gamma = -.34$ with overall personal rating, $\gamma = -.14$ with net positive representations, and $\gamma = -.33$ with perceived media rating; and 2) for the KNRC, $\gamma = -.49$ with overall personal rating, $\gamma = -.26$ with net positive representations, and $\gamma = -.35$ with perceived media rating.

As described the above, the correlations between exchange relationships and the organizational reputation variables were significant and, across all of the three indicators, stronger consistently for the KNRC than for the KFA. In summary, the results suggested that the two types of organization-public relationships were more strongly associated with the organization-public relationship outcome variables and the reputation variables in the *nonprofit* organizations studied than in the profit organizations studied. *Exchange* relationships, in particular, had markedly different effects on the organizational reputation variables between the profit and nonprofit organizations studied: stronger and more negative impacts in the *nonprofit* organizations studied than in the profit organizations studied.

Quality of organization-public relationship outcomes. As previously noted, I found that, regarding communication behavior variables, constraint recognition was negatively and significantly associated ($p < .05$) with the organization-public relationship outcome variables, for all four indicators of the latent variable (control mutuality, trust, commitment, and satisfaction), across all organizations studied.

The results indicated strong associations among the indicator variables of organization-public relationship outcomes. First, for Samsung Electronics, the correlations among the four indicators ranged from .65 (between control mutuality and satisfaction) to .79 (between commitment and satisfaction). Second, for Sony Korea, again, the correlations ranged from 65 (between control mutuality and satisfaction) to .79 (between commitment and satisfaction). Third, for the KFA, the correlations ranged from .71 (between trust and commitment) to .78 (between commitment and satisfaction). Last, for the KNRC, the correlations ranged from .70 (between control mutuality and satisfaction) to .81 (between commitment and satisfaction). Therefore, the results of correlations suggested that the participants in the survey most strongly associated commitment and relational satisfaction in evaluating the quality of organization-public relationship outcomes with the four organizations studied; but all of the relationship indicators were strongly associated.

Organizational reputation. Three variables were used to measure the latent variable of organizational reputation: 1) "net positive representations" (i.e., the number of positive representation less the number of negative representation in a given set of representations answered by each participant), 2) "overall personal rating" (i.e., overall impression based on the entire representations listed by each participant), and 3) "perceived media rating." Among those two variables generated by cognitive presentations hold by participants, the variable of net positive representations constituted of *memory-based* representations based on individual experience, whereas the latter centered on *overall* impressions toward the organizations studied.

The results in Table IV.16 to Table IV.19 indicate that the variable of *overall personal rating*, in general, had the strongest correlations with the four indicators used to measure the quality of organization-public relationship outcomes. The correlations among the organizational reputation variables and the organization-public relationship outcome variables were "positively" significant in most cases for all organizations studied (at $p < .05$), which suggested that the latent variables of organization-public relationship outcomes and organizational reputation were strongly intertwined.

Research Question: "How do the two types of organization-public relationships (communal and exchange relationships) affect the quality of organization-public relationship outcomes and organizational reputation?"

This research question addressed the effects of organization-public relationship types on relationship outcomes and reputation. More specifically, theories and research in the literature of public relations suggested that the two types of organization-public relationships, *communal* and *exchange* relationships, are related to the quality of organization-public relationship outcomes and organizational reputation.

Nested models among (Final) CFA, SEM with relationship types, & SEM without relationship types. To investigate the research question described the above, the SEM approach makes it possible to compare data-model ifts among "nested" models—or "hierarchically related" models. The term "nested models" means a model's set of parameters to be estimated is a subset of another model's set of parameters to be estimated (Hancock & Mueller, 2004). In this case, a researcher can conduct a χ^2 difference test to test which model has a better fit.

More conceptually speaking, to answer the suggested research question, I compared the two nested models (Table IV.15): the SEM model "without" structural paths from the two types of organization-public relationships (labeled as "Model 3")

and the SEM model "with" structural paths from the two types of organization-public

relationships (labeled as "Model 2"). Model 3 is nested within Model 2 because

Model 3 is a special case of Model 2 when paths from the two organization-public

relationship types have no direct effects on, or null relations with other latent

variables (i.e., zero parameter estimates of direct effects). This analysis made it

possible to see whether addition of paths from the two types of organization-public

relationships (to the quality of organization-public relationship outcomes and

organizational reputation) significantly improved the data-model fits of the

hypothesized structural models across different organizations studied.

In addition, a *two-step* process of structural equation modeling has been

widely suggested to test the data-model fit of a hypothesized structural model (Byrne,

1994, 2001; Hancock & Mueller, 2004; Kline, 1998). Before advancing to test the

hypothesized latent path model in the *structural* phase, researchers need to

demonstrate a sound data-model fit of the CFA measurement model. Since the initial

CFA measurement model had good data-model fits across all organizations studied, I

did not make model respecifications in the measurement phase; thus, the *initial* CFA

measurement model became the *final* CFA measurement model. As I previously

noted, the CFA measurement model had good data-model fits on the basis of multiple

fit indexes: CFI values equal to or greater than .99 and, at the same time, RMSEA

values less than .08 across all organizations studied (Table IV.15). To compare

models, I labeled this final measurement model as "Model 1."

Thus, I conducted a χ^2 difference test to compare the data-model fits among

three nested models: the final CFA measurement model (Model 1), the structural

model "with" paths from the two types of organization-public relationships (Model 2), and the structural model "without" paths from the two types of organization-public

relationships (Model 3). I found the following nested relations among those models:

1. Model 3 is nested within Model 2.

2. Model 2 is nested within Model 1.

3. Model 3 is nested within Model 1.

4. Therefore, Model 3 is the most "parsimonious" model (i.e., the most

    degrees of freedom in the hypothesized model).

If models are in nested relations, a more parsimonious model should be chosen, as

long as the χ^2 difference test indicates a non-significant difference between nested

models. On the other hand, a significant χ^2 difference between nested models

suggests that addition of a path or some paths develops a significantly better fitting of

the model, so the path(s) should be included in the hypothesized model (Hancock &

Mueller, 2004).

The results of the χ^2 difference test between Model 2 and Model 3 indicated

that the hypothesized structural model was significantly improved by addition of the

paths from the two organization-public relationship types to the quality of

organization-public relationship outcomes and organizational reputation: $\chi^2_{d.ff}(15) =$

260.74, $p < .001$, for Samsung Electronics; $\chi^2_{d.ff}(15) = 255.75$, $p < .001$, for Sony

Korea; $\chi^2_{d.ff}(15) = 366.36$, $p < .001$, for the KFA; and $\chi^2_{d.ff}(15) = 377.03$, $p < .001$,

for the KNRC. Therefore, the results of the χ^2 difference tests for all organizations

studied indicated that there existed significant effects of organization-public

relationship types (communal and exchange relationships) on the quality of

organization-public relationship outcomes and organizational reputation in the

hypothesized structural model.

Results of multiple data-model fit indexes. In addition, according to multiple data-model fit indexes such as CFI, AIC, and RMSEA, I found that the structural model with the two types of organization-public relationships produced a better fit consistently across all organizations studied.

1. For Samsung Electronics: Model 2 (i.e., the *full* model) had CFI = .981, AIC = 463.96, and RMSEA = .078; Model 3 (i.e., the model *without* the effects of organization-public relationship types) had CFI = .958, AIC = 694.71, and RMSEA = .111.

2. For Sony Korea, Model 2 had CFI = .979, AIC = 463.25, and RMSEA = .078; Model 3 had CFI = .952, AIC = 489.00, and RMSEA = .110.

3. For the KFA, Model 2 had CFI = .973, AIC = 520.91, and RMSEA = .089; Model 3 had CFI = .935, AIC = 857.27, and RMSEA = .130.

4. For the KNRC, Model 2 had CFI = .974, AIC = 534.78, and RMSEA = .092; Model 3 had CFI = .938, AIC = 881.81, and RMSEA = .132.

Interestingly, the models for the *nonprofit* organizations studied had "unacceptable" data-model fits without structural paths from organization-public relationship types, which suggested that the participants in the survey cared about organization-public relationship types especially when the organization was a nonprofit organization. In this case, CFI was .935 for the KFA and .938 for the KNRC, which were less than the cutoff value of .95 (Hu & Bentler, 1999), whereas CFI was .958 for Samsung Electronics and .952 for Sony Korea. However, in terms of RMSEA, the models in those profit organizations still failed to have acceptable data-model fits: RMSEA = .111 for Samsung Electronics and .110 for Sony Korea, which were higher than the cutoff value of .08 (Byrne, 2002; Kline, 1998).

Based on such results, I summarize that the paths from the *organization-public relationship types* to the quality of organization-public relationship outcomes and organizational reputation should not be dropped for a sound data-model fit of the hypothesized structural equation model. Additionally, this full model (i.e., Model 2 with the effects of organization-public relationship types) had acceptable data-model fits on the basis of multiple fit indexes such as CFI and RMSEA across all organizations studied, so I did not make model respecifications and chose this model as the *final* structural model.

Finally, when comparing data-model fits between the final CFA measurement model and the final structural model, I found that the final CFA model had a significant χ^2 difference, suggesting that the structural model could be more improved by adding more paths: $\chi^2_{d.ff}(20) = 97.36, p < .001$, for Samsung Electronics; $\chi^2_{d.ff}(19) = 152.28, p < .001$, for Sony Korea; $\chi^2_{d.ff}(20) = 196.81, p < .001$, for the KFA; and $\chi^2_{d.ff}(20) = 183.26, p < .001$, for the KNRC. Since the structural model had good data model-fits across all organizations studied—for example, CFI values higher than .97 throughout the four organizations studied (Table IV.15), it was not necessary to make model respecifications. Making model respecifications is suggested only when "post hoc theory dictates" and in turn is limited in theoretical model testing (Hancock & Mueller, 2004, "Latent Variable Path Modeling," p. 9).

Model Estimation of the Hypothesized Structural Model

Maximum likelihood (ML) estimation was employed to estimate all models. The independence model that tested the hypothesis that all variables are uncorrelated could be rejected: $\chi^2(171, N = 294) = 10589.939, \chi^2/df = 61.919, p < .001$ for

Samsung Electronics; $\chi^2(171, N = 294) = 9239.586$, $\chi^2/df = 54.033$, $p < .001$ for Sony

Korea; $\chi^2(171, N = 294) = 9379.570$, $\chi^2/df = 54.851$, $p < .001$ for the KFA; and

$\chi^2(171, N = 294) = 10308.137$, $\chi^2/df = 60.282$, $p < .001$ for the KNRC.

As I noted previously, to test the data-model fits of the hypothesized latent

variable path model, I first tested the fit of the CFA measurement model. I did not

make model respecifications as the initial CFA model had good fits on the basis of

multiple fit indexes, such as χ^2/df (less than 3), CFI ($\geq .95$), and RMSEA ($\geq .08$), for

all organizations studied.

Overview of Hypothesis Testing

I proposed nine hypotheses, each of which represented a structural path in the

structural equation model. In addition, based on the results of comparing nested

models, I included types of organization-public relationships (communal and

exchange relationships) in the final structural model and analyzed significance of

related paths in the model. According to Table IV.21, the following paths were

significant consistently for all organizations studied: 1) the effect of organization-

public relationship outcomes on organizational reputation (*H1*, at least $p < .05$), 2) the

effect of communication behaviors on organization-public relationship outcomes (*H2*,

all $p < .001$), 3) the effect of familiarity on organizational reputation (*H4*, at least $p <$

.01), 4) the effect of problem recognition on communication behaviors (*H5*, at least p

$< .01$), and 5) the effect of personal experience on familiarity (*H9*, all at $p < .01$).

Table IV.21

Standardized Direct Effects in the (Final) Structural Equation Model (N = 294)

Independent factors		Dependent factors	H/R	Samsung	Sony	KFA	KNRC
Quality of org-public relationships	→	Favorability of org reputation	H1	.39*	.49***	.55**	.31*
Active communication behaviors	→	Quality of org-public relationships	H2	.52***	.46***	.60***	.40***
Familiarity with an org	→	Quality of org-public relationships	H3	.18	.12^	-.21*	.11
Familiarity with an org	→	Favorability of organizational reputation	H4	.54**	.57***	.37**	.51**
Problem recognition	→	Active communication behaviors	H5	.30**	.28***	.22**	.19**
Constraint recognition	→	Active communication behaviors	H6	-.24*	-.20*	-.07	-.23*
Self involvement	→	Active communication behaviors	H7	.04	.27**	.20**	-.04
Community involvement	→	Active communication behaviors	H8	.08	-.04	.21**	.14^
Experience	→	Familiarity	H9	.22**	.45**	.22**	.23**

(Table IV.21 continues)

228

(Table IV.21 continues)

Independent factors		Dependent factors	H/R	Samsung	Sony	KFA	KNRC
Communal relationships	→	Quality of org-public relationships	R	.28***	.32***	.43***	.28***
Communal relationships	→	Favorability of org reputation	R	.16	.01	.05	.13
Exchange relationships	→	Quality of org-public relationships	R	-.29***	-.23***	-.31***	-.48***
Exchange relationships	→	Favorability of org reputation	R	.09	.05	-.11	-.38**

Note. Samsung = Samsung Electronics; Sony = Sony Korea; KFA = Korea Football Association; KNRC = Korean National Red Cross.

$p^{\wedge} < .10$ $*p < .05$. $**p \leq .01$. $***p < .001$.

Also, the following paths were partially supported for some of the
organizations studied: 1) the effect of familiarity on communication behaviors (*H3*,
significant for the KFA at *p* < .05), 2) the effect of constraint recognition on
communication behaviors (*H6*, significant consistently except for the KFA *at* p < .05),
3) the effect of self involvement on communication behaviors (*H7*, significant for
Sony Korea and the KFA at *p* < .01), and 4) the effect of community involvement on
communication behaviors (*H8*, significant for the KFA at *p* < .01).

Overview of the Effects of Organization-public Relationship Types

Among the structural paths showing the effects of types of organization-
public relationships, there were significant effects of both communal and exchange
relationships on the quality of organization-public relationship outcomes (*all
significant at the .001 level*) for all organizations studied. However, the effects of
types of organization-public relationships on organizational reputation were almost
not supported except for the effect of exchange relationships on organizational
reputation for the KNRC (*p* < .01).

Results of Hypothesis Testing

*H1: The better the quality of organization-public relationship outcomes, the
more favorable the reputation of an organization.* Many public relations scholars have
suggested that the quality of organization-public relationship outcomes affects
organizational reputation (e.g., J. Grunig & Hung, 2002; L. Grunig, J. Grunig, &
Dozier, 2002; Yang & J. Grunig, 2005). However, there has been minimal empirical
research that directly tested the causal effect of organization-public relationship
outcomes on organizational reputation. Table IV.21 indicates that the effect of the
quality of organization-public relationship outcomes on organizational reputation was
highly significant for all organizations studied. The standardized parameter estimates

(i.e., standardized loadings or "β weights") were: .39 ($p < .05$) for Samsung

Electronics, .49 ($p < .001$) for Sony Korea, .55 ($p < .01$) for the KFA, and .31 ($p <$

.05) for the KNRC.

In terms of the absolute magnitude of the correlations, for example, the latent

variables of "organization-public relationship outcomes" and "organizational

reputation" shared 30.25% of their variance in common (i.e., $R^2 = .55^2$) for the KFA,

which is significant at the .001 level. The smallest variance explained by this path was

9.6% ($R^2 = .31^2$) for the KNRC.

According to Kline (1998, p. 118), Cohen (1988) suggested guidelines about

interpreting the effect size of correlations in the social sciences: 1) *small* effects:

standardized path coefficients with absolute values less than .10; 2) *medium* effects:

coefficient with absolute values around .30; and 3) *large* effects: coefficients with

absolute values of .50 or more. Following such criteria, the effects of the

organization-public relationship outcomes on organizational reputation, in this study,

were at least *medium* or *large* throughout all organizations studied. In addition, in

light of the direction of the structural relations, the results of this study consistently

showed *positive* effects of organization-public relationship outcomes on

organizational reputation for all organizations studied.

H2: the more active the communication behaviors of publics, the better the

quality of organization-public relationship outcomes. This structural path was one of

the strongest and most significant paths in the model for all organizations studied. The

literature of public relations, such as J. Grunig and Huang (2000), Hon and J. Grunig

(1999), J. Grunig and Hung (2002), Rhee (2004), and Yang and J. Grunig (2005), has

emphasized communication behaviors of publics as the key variable affecting the

quality of organization-public relationship outcomes. Individual members of a public who engage in active communication behaviors with an organization are more likely to initiate and cultivate a quality relationship with an organization (Rhee, 2004). In a reciprocal manner, an organization is more likely to care about members of a public who maintain active communication behaviors because of (potential) consequences on achieving organizational goals (J. Grunig & Huang, 2000).

The results of this study supported the second hypothesis about the effect of communication behaviors on the quality of organization-public relationship outcomes. The standardized parameter estimates were highly significant with "large" positive effect sizes of coefficients. All coefficients were significant at the .001 level across all organizations studied: .52 for Samsung Electronics, .46 for Sony Korea, .60 for the KFA, and .40 for the KNRC. Based on squared multiple correlations (R^2), the largest explained variance was 36% for the KFA ($R^2 = .60^2$) and the smallest explained variance was 16% for the KNRC ($R^2 = .40^2$).

In light of the strength of correlations, the results in Table IV.22 indicate that the effect size of correlations was at least *medium* or *large* for all organizations studied. Except for the KFA, the effect sizes of the coefficients in this path were large with values greater than .51. Also, as I hypothesized, the direction of the structural relation was consistently *positive* for all organizations studied.

H3: the more familiar a public is with an organization, the better the quality of organization-public relationship outcomes. I found that the results of this study did *not* support the hypothesis about the effect of familiarity on organization-public relationship outcomes. Only for the KFA was the structural path significant at the .05 level. However, the direction of the coefficient was the "opposite" as I theoretically proposed: $\gamma = -.21$ (p < .05) for the KFA.

Except for the KFA, the standardized parameter estimates had *positive* values across all organization: .18 (*ns*) for Samsung Electronics, .12 (*ns, p < .*10) for Sony Korea, and .11 (*ns*) for the KNRC. Therefore, unlike the strong and positive effect of communication behaviors on organization-public relationship outcomes, there were no significant effects of familiarity on the quality of organization-public relationship outcomes in this study.

Table IV.18 shows that bivariate correlations indicated that all of the bivariate correlations among the indicator variables of familiarity and the four indicator variables of organization-public relationship outcomes were *positive* and *significant* at least at the .05 level. However, when I controlled for the multivariate effects in the hypothesized structural equation model, there was a *negative* effect of familiarity on the quality of organization-public relationship outcomes for the KFA.

This may be because participants in the survey reported the lowest quality of organization-public relationship outcomes for the KFA, across the four indicator variables, among all organizations studied. Therefore, such results may suggest that the more the participants were familiar with the KFA, the lower they rated the quality of organization-public relationship outcomes with the KFA, when the effects of other factors (e.g., personal experience, organization-public relationship types, and communication behaviors) were considered in the model.

H4: the more familiar of a public is with an organization, the more favorable the reputation of an organization. Familiarity has been considered as the key variable affecting favorability of organizational reputation in the literature of business, as the importance of a "top-of-mind awareness" or salience of an organization in minds of stakeholders (Fombrun, 1996; Fombrun & Van Riel, 2003) and visibility in media reports (e.g., Deephouse, 2000; Rindova & Kotha, 2001). Indeed, as in the effect of communication behaviors on the quality of organization-public relationship outcomes, this path was one of the strongest and most significant paths for all organizations studied.

By imposing *experience* of participants as an exogenous variable of familiarity, along with covariations among *communication behaviors*, I assessed the effect of familiarity on organizational reputation from the perspective of (active) publics—those who had either direct or indirect experience and had active communication behaviors with the organizations studied. Still, I found the effect size of the standardized coefficients for the effect of familiarity on organizational reputation was generally "large" (significant at least $p < .01$). Standardized parameter estimates included: .54 ($p < .01$) for Samsung Electronics, .57 ($p < .001$) for Sony Korea, .37 ($p < .01$) for the KFA, and .51 ($p < .01$) for the KNRC. Based on squared multiple correlations (R^2), the largest explained variance was 32.49% for Sony Korea ($R^2 = .57^2$) and the smallest explained variance was 13.69% for the KFA ($R^2 = .37^2$). The direction of the structural relation was consistently *positive* for all organizations studied as I hypothesized.

H5: the higher the problem recognition, the more active the communication behaviors of publics. Among the four exogenous variables predicting communication behaviors of publics, the effect of problem recognition on communication behaviors was significant across all organizations studied at the .01 level. Standardized parameter estimates included: .30 for Samsung Electronics, .28 for Sony Korea, .22 for the KFA, and .19 for the KNRC. Therefore, the effect size of this path was mostly moderate. The problem recognition variable explained 9% of variance ($R^2 = .30^2$) in the latent variable of communication behaviors the most for Samsung Electronics and 3.61% of variance ($R^2 = .19^2$) the least for the KNRC. The direction of this path was *positive* consistently across all of the organizations studied as the situational theory of publics predicts (e.g., J. Grunig, 1997; J. Grunig & Hunt, 1984).

H6: the lower the constraint recognition, the more active the communication behaviors of publics. Except for the KFA, this hypothesis was supported in this study and was significant at the .05 level: -.24 ($p < .05$) for Samsung Electronics, -.20 ($p < .05$) for Sony Korea, -.07 (*ns*) for the KFA, and -.23 ($p < .05$) for the KNRC. Like the effect of problem recognition, the effect size of path coefficients was mostly moderate. The constraint recognition variable explained 5.76% of variance ($R^2 = .24^2$) in the latent variable of communication behaviors the most for Samsung Electronics and .49% of variance ($R^2 = .07^2$) the least for the KFA. For all organizations studied, the direction of this path was *negative* consistently as the situational theory of publics predicts.

H7: the higher the self involvement, the more active the communication behaviors of publics. This hypothesis was partially supported in this study. For Sony Korea and the KFA, path coefficients were significant at the .01 level: .27 for Sony Korea and .20 for the KFA. In other organizations studied, effect size of this structural path was minimal. Only for those organizations with significant coefficients, was the direction of the causal relation *positive* as the situational theory of publics predicts.

H8: the higher the community involvement, the more active the communication behaviors of publics. Like the previous hypothesis, this hypothesis was only partially supported for the KFA with a standardized parameter estimate of .21 (significant at the .01 level). Additionally, I found that the path was significant at the .10 level in the other nonprofit organizations studied, the KNRC, with a coefficient of .14. Therefore, the results of this hypothesis may suggest that participants in the survey considered *community* involvement to be more relevant for the nonprofit organizations studied than for the profit organizations studied. Along with the previous hypothesis about the effect of self involvement on communication behaviors, this structural path showed a *small* effect size of correlations with *positive* causal direction. In terms of squared multiple correlations, for example, those two types of involvement together explained about 8.41% of variance in communication behaviors of publics ($R^2 = .20^2 + .21^2$).

H9: the more direct personal experience a public has with an organization, the more it will be familiar with the organization. As noted previously, I attempted to reflect the perspective of (active) publics in the proposed SEM analysis by explaining the latent variable of "familiarity" directly by *experience* and indirectly by covariations with other exogenous variables, the communication behaviors.

To put it another way, unlike the common conceptualization of familiarity as a "top-of-mind awareness" in the literature of business (e.g., Fombrun & Van Riel, 2003), I made experience of the participants the key source of familiarity with an organization (Bromley, 1993; J. Grunig & Hung, 2002). Additionally, in terms of *experiential* organization-public relationship outcomes and organizational reputation (J. Grunig & Hung, 2002), I posited that *direct* experience would result in higher familiarity and, in turn, higher mediating effects of familiarity on the quality of organization-public relationship outcomes and organizational reputation (as *experiential* organization-public relationships and organizational reputation), than would indirect or no experience.

Table IV.21 shows that this hypothesis was supported at the .01 level across all organizations studied. Standardized parameter estimates were: .22 for Samsung Electronics, .45 for Sony Korea, .22 for the KFA, and .23 for the KNRC. In terms of squared multiple correlations (R^2), personal experience explained variance in the range of 4.8% ($R^2 = .22^2$) to 20.25% ($R^2 = .45^2$) of variance in familiarity. The direction of the structural path was *positive* throughout all organizations studied, as hypothesized.

Results of Structural Paths from Organization-public Relationship Types

After I demonstrated that types of organization-public relationships significantly improved the data-model fits of the hypothesized structural equation model across all organizations studied, I specifically analyzed the effects of structural paths from the exogenous variables shown in Table IV.21. The results of path coefficients indicated significant structural effects of organization-public relationship types on the quality of organization-public relationship outcomes, but not on the favorability of organizational reputation.

First, for the effect of *communal* relationships, standardized parameter estimates were: .28 ($p < .001$) for Samsung Electronics, .32 ($p < .001$) for Sony Korea, .43 ($p < .001$) for the KFA, and .28 ($p < .001$) for the KNRC. Effect size of coefficients was generally *medium*, ranging from .28 to .43. Additionally, the direction of the structural path was "positive" across all organizations studied, as posited earlier in Chapter II: the more communal the org-public relationships, the better quality of organization-public relationship outcomes.

Secondly, for predicting the quality organization-public relationship outcomes, the effect of exchange relationships was significantly "negative" across all organizations studied. Standardized parameter estimates were: -.29 ($p < .001$) for Samsung Electronics, -.23 ($p < .001$) for Sony Korea, -.31 ($p < .001$) for the KFA, and -.48 ($p < .001$) for the KNRC. Like the effect size of communal relationships, effect size of exchange relationship coefficients was medium. Overall, the effects of exchange relationships were slightly stronger in the nonprofit organizations studied than the profit organizations studied.

On the other hand, the effects of organization-public relationship types on organizational reputation was *not* significant. There were minimal effect size of path coefficients for all organizations studied, in particular the effect of *exchange* relationships on organizational reputation. The exception was the KNRC: -.38 ($p <$ .01) in the effect of exchange relationships on organizational reputation.

The direction of the structural path was "positive" for all organizations in the effect of communal relationships on organizational reputation, as conceptualized. However, the direction of exchange relationships on reputation was not consistent throughout all organizations studied: positive for the profit organizations studied and not positive for the nonprofit organizations studied. The effects of exchange relationships were not negative and were minimal in the profit organizations studied, but they were negative and generally stronger (-.11 for the KFA and -.39 for the KNRC) in the nonprofit organizations studied than the profit organizations studied (i.e., .09 for Samsung Electronics and .05 for Sony Korea). Hon and J. Grunig (1999), and L. Grunig, J. Grunig, and Dozier (2002) explained that types of organization-public relationships are particularly important to public relations management of nonprofit organizations since publics generally expect communal relationships with nonprofit organizations.

I conducted a subsequent analysis of the indirect (or mediating) effects of parameter estimates to analyze the differential *direct* effects of *exchange* relationships on organizational reputation between the profit and nonprofit organizations studied, particularly the positive effects of exchange relationships on organizational reputation in the profit organizations studied.

Indirect Effects of Parameter Estimates

According to Kline (1998), "Indirect effects involve one or more intervening variables that 'transmit' some of the causal effects of prior variables onto subsequent variables. (Intervening variables in indirect effects are also called *mediator variables*.)" (p. 52).

I used AMOS 4.0 to analyze the hypothesized structural equation model. Since AMOS 4.0 does not offer a method to conduct significance tests of indirect effects, I used the Sobel test to analyze indirect effects (Sobel, 1982; Preacher & Leonardelli, 2003). The Sobel test equation is as follows: z-value $= a \times b / \sqrt{(b^2 \times S_a^2 + a^2 \times S_b^2)}$, where a = unstandardized regression coefficient for the association between IV and mediator, b = raw coefficient for the association between the mediator and the DV (when the IV is also a predictor of the DV), S_a = standard error of a, and S_b = standard error of b. Using the interactive website created by Preacher and Leonardelli (2003), I conducted a Sobel test for indirect effects of parameter estimates in this structural equation model.

Table IV.22 reports the results of indirect effects in the hypothesized structural equation model.

Table IV.22

Standardized Indirect Effects in the Final Structural Equation Model (N = 294)

Mediated Paths	Samsung	Sony	KFA	KNRC
Problem recognition (→ Active communication behaviors of publics)[a] → Quality of organization-public relationship outcomes	.13* (.016[b])	.16** (.005)	.13** (.009)	.08
Problem recognition (→ Active communication behaviors of publics → Quality of organization-public relationship outcomes) → Favorability of organizational reputation	.06	.06	.07	.02
Constraint recognition (→ Active communication behaviors of publics) → Quality of organization-public relationship outcomes	-.09	-.13* (.030)	-.04	-.09
Constraint recognition (→ Active communication behaviors of publics → Quality of organization-public relationship outcomes) → Favorability of organizational reputation	-.05	-.05	-.02	-.03
Self involvement (→ Active communication behaviors of publics) → Quality of organization-public relationship outcomes	.12	.02	.12* (.019)	-.02

(Table IV.22 continues)

(Table IV.22 continues)

Mediated Paths	Samsung	Sony	KFA	KNRC
Self involvement (→ Active communication behaviors of publics) → Quality of organization-public relationship outcomes) → Favorability of organizational reputation	.06	.01	.07	-.01
Community involvement (→ Active communication behaviors of publics) → Quality of organization-public relationship outcomes	-.02	.04	.13* (.011)	.06
Community involvement (→ Active communication behaviors of publics → Quality of organization-public relationship outcomes)→ Favorability of organizational reputation	-.01	.02	.07	.02
Communal relationships (→ Quality of organization-public relationship outcomes) → Favorability of organizational reputation	.16^ (.063)	.11*** (.000)	.23*** (.001)	.09
Exchange relationships (→ Quality of organization-public relationship outcomes) → Favorability of organizational reputation	-.11^ (.062)	-.11*** (.001)	-.17** (.003)	-.15^ (.097)

(Table IV.22 continues)

(Table IV.22 continues)

Mediated Paths	Samsung	Sony	KFA	KNRC
Experience (→ Familiarity) → Quality of organization-public relationship outcomes	.05	.04	-.05	.03
Experience (→ Familiarity) → Favorability of organizational reputation	.12^ (.056)	.26*** (.000)	.08	.12^ (.053)
Experience (→ Familiarity → Quality of organization-public relationship outcomes) → Favorability of organizational reputation	.02	.03	-.03	.01
Active communication behaviors of publics (→ Quality of organization-public relationship outcomes) → Favorability of organizational reputation	.23^ (.073)	.20*** (.000)	.33** (.005)	.12
Familiarity (→ Quality of organization-public relationship outcomes) → Favorability of organizational reputation	.06	.07	-.12	.03

Note. Samsung = Samsung Electronics; Sony = Sony Korea; KFA = Korea Football Association; KNRC = Korean National Red Cross.
[a]Mediating path(s). [b]p value.

p^ $< .10$ *$p < .05$. **$p < .01$. ***$p \le .001$.

Among the listed mediating effects, I found the following mediating paths were significant:

1. The effect of communal relationships on organizational reputation, mediated by organization-public relationship outcomes.

2. The effect of exchange relationships on organizational reputation, mediated by organization-public relationship outcomes.

3. The effect of personal experience on organizational reputation, mediated by familiarity.

4. The effect of communication behaviors on organizational reputation, mediated by organization-public relationship outcomes.

The effect of "communal" relationships on organizational reputation, mediated by organization-public relationship outcomes. The indirect effects in these paths (Communal relationships → Organization-public relationship outcomes→ Organizational reputation) were generally significant except for the KNRC. Standardized parameter estimates of indirect effects were: .16 ($p = .063$) for Samsung Electronics, .11 ($p < .001$) for Sony, .23 ($p = .001$) for the KFA, and .09 (*ns*) for the KNRC. Therefore, in most organizations studied, the quality of organization-public relationship outcomes highly mediated the effect of communal relationships on organizational reputation. As in the direct effect, the direction of such mediating effects was "positive" across all organizations studied.

The effect of "exchange" relationships on organizational reputation, mediated by organization-public relationship outcomes. The mediating effects in these paths (Exchange relationships → Organization-public relationship outcomes → Organizational reputation) were overall significant. Standardized parameter estimates of indirect effects were: -.11 ($p = .062$) for Samsung Electronics, -.11 ($p = .001$) for

Sony, -.17 ($p < .01$) for the KFA, and -.15 ($p = .097$) for the KNRC. As I noted

previously, the direct effect of exchange relationships on organizational reputation

was positive in the profit organizations studied and negative in the nonprofit

organizations studied. However, I found that the mediating effects on such causal

paths were negative consistently across all organizations studied. In other words,

when organization-public relationship outcomes mediated such a causal relation (i.e.,

the effect of exchange relationship on organizational reputation), there were negative

effects of exchange relationships on organizational reputation even for the profit

organizations studied.

For example, for Samsung Electronics, the direct effect of exchange

relationships on organizational reputation had positive coefficient, $\gamma = .09$. To test

mediating effects, I included the following information in the equation of indirect

effects: the direct effect of exchange relationships on organization-public relationship

outcomes was $\gamma = -.29$, and the direct effect of organization-public relationship

outcomes on organizational reputation was $\gamma = .39$. Therefore, the direction of the

mediating effects (Exchange relationships → Organization-public relationship

outcomes → Organizational reputation) was *negative*, (-.29) x .39 = -.11 ($p = .062$).

Secondly, for Sony Korea, the direct effect of exchange relationships on

organizational reputation had positive coefficient, $\gamma = .05$. To test mediating effects, I

included the following information: the direct effect of exchange relationships on

organization-public relationship outcomes was $\gamma = -.23$, and the direct effect of

organization-public relationship outcomes on organizational reputation was $\gamma = .49$.

Therefore, the direction of the mediating effects (Exchange relationships →

Organization-public relationship outcomes → Organizational reputation) was

negative, (-.23) x .49 = -.11 ($p = .001$).

The effect of experience on organizational reputation, mediated by familiarity.
I would explain these mediating paths (Experience → Familiarity → Organizational
reputation) by saying "the more direct experience a public has with an organization,
the more favorable the reputation of the organization, when the influence from
familiarity on organizational reputation is considered." Table IV.22 indicates that
such mediating paths were generally significant. Standardized parameter estimates
were: .12 ($p = .56$) for Samsung Electronics, .26 ($p < .001$) for Sony Korea, .08 (*ns*)
for the KFA, and .12 ($p = .053$) for the KNRC.

The effect of communication behaviors on organizational reputation, mediated
by organization-public relationship outcomes. When the quality of organization-
public relationship outcomes was considered, what was the effect of communication
behaviors on organizational reputation? The mediating effects in these paths
(Communication behaviors → Organization-public relationship outcomes →
Organizational reputation) were significant overall, except for the KNRC.
Standardized parameter estimates of indirect effects were: .23 ($p = .073$) for Samsung
Electronics, .20 ($p < .001$) for Sony, .33 ($p < .01$) for the KFA, and .12 (*ns*) for the
KNRC. The direction of such mediating effects was positive across all organizations
studied as in the direct effect of communication behaviors on organizational
reputation.

Additional Analyses in Structural Equation Model: Measurement Indicator Loadings
& Correlations between Exogenous Variables, Disturbances, & Errors

Now that I have explained the direct and indirect effects of parameter
estimates, this section will explain 1) measurement indictor loadings and 2)
correlations between exogenous variables, disturbances, and error terms in the
hypothesized structural equation model. The information about measurement

indicator loadings is useful to see the relationships between a latent variable and the indicators used to measure the latent variable. Correlations between exogenous variables are also important in analyzing and interpreting the data. Finally, correlations between disturbances (errors for latent variables) and between errors for indicators need to be clearly explained based on theoretical and methodological reasons, since such model respecifications could affect data-model fits of a structural equation model.

Factor loadings of the indicator variables. Factor loadings of the indicator variables are reported in Table IV.23.

Table IV.23

Standardized Coefficient of Measurement Indicators in the Final Structural Equation Model (N = 294)

Latent variables		Indicator variables	Samsung	Sony	KFA	KNRC
Active communication behaviors of publics	→	Information seeking	.62	.47	.64	.56
Active communication behaviors of publics	→	Information processing	.59	.21	.48	.56
Familiarity	→	Overall familiarity	.63	.58	.59	.55
Familiarity	→	Familiarity with media coverage	.72	.51	.54	.64
Quality of org-public relationship outcomes	→	Satisfaction	.86	.84	.85	.86
Quality of org-public relationship outcomes	→	Control mutuality	.83	.83	.84	.86
Quality of org-public relationship outcomes	→	Trust	.85	.84	.83	.84
Quality of org-public relationship outcomes	→	Commitment	.79	.80	.85	.82
Favorability of organizational reputation	→	Overall personal rating	.69	.60	.57	.56
Favorability of organizational reputation	→	Net positive representations	.38	.33	.30	.23
Favorability of organizational reputation	→	Perceived media rating	.68	.48	.59	.47

Note. Samsung = Samsung Electronics; Sony = Sony Korea; KFA = Korea Football Association; KNRC = Korean National Red Cross.

All loadings were significant at *p* < .001.

All factor loadings in the hypothesized structural equation model were significant at the .001 level. For the loadings of communication behavior, information seeking was greater than information processing in the three organizations studied and was equal for the KNRC. Therefore, following the theoretical reasoning of the situational theory of publics, I named the factor as *"active" communication behaviors of publics* for better interpretations of the causal relations imposed in the model. Factor loadings of information seeking were: .62 for Samsung Electronics, .47 for Sony Korea, .64 for the KFA, and .56 for the KNRC. Additionally, factor loadings of information processing were: .59 for Samsung Electronics, .21 for Sony Korea, .48 for the KFA, and .56 for the KNRC.

Secondly, the loadings of familiarity were all greater than .50 across the two indicator variables for all organizations studied. Factor loadings of overall personal familiarity were: .63 for Samsung Electronics, .58 for Sony Korea, .59 for the KFA, and .55 for the KNRC. Additionally, factor loadings of familiarity with media coverage about the organization were: .72 for Samsung Electronics, .51 for Sony Korea, .54 for the KFA, and .64 for the KNRC.

Third, all loadings of organization-public relationship outcomes were greater than .75, across all four indicator variables, for all organizations studied. For the sake of brevity, I will not report factor loadings of organization-public relationship outcomes here (see Table IV.23).

Finally, for factor loadings of organizational reputation, the loadings for overall personal rating were generally the greatest, whereas the loading of net positive representations were the smallest. For example, the loadings for overall personal rating were: .69 for Samsung Electronics, .60 for Sony Korea, .57 for the KFA, and

.56 for the KNRC. The loadings for net positive representations were: .38 for

Samsung Electronics, .33 for Sony, .30 for the KFA, and .23 for the KNRC.

Correlations between exogenous variables, disturbances, & errors. Table

IV.24 reports correlations between exogenous variables, between disturbances, and

between errors for indicators. As noted previously, correlations between exogenous

variables show the associations between independent variables used in the SEM

analysis. Also, as ways of model respecifications, correlations between disturbances

and between indicator errors needs to be clearly explained based on theoretical and

methodological reasons.

Table IV.24

Correlations between Exogenous Variables, Disturbances, and Errors in the Final Structural Equation Model

Correlated Factors			Organizations[c]			
			Samsung	Sony	KFA	KNRC
Problem recognition	↔	Community involvement	.24***	.20**	.23***	.30***
Problem recognition	↔	Constraint recognition	-.29***	-.29***	-.35***	-.39***
Problem recognition	↔	Self involvement	.39***	.38***	.32***	.34***
Constraint recognition	↔	Self involvement	-.53***	-.51***	-.55***	-.53***
Constraint recognition	↔	Community involvement	-.15**	-.31***	-.41***	-.39***
Self involvement	↔	Community involvement	.38***	.47***	.48***	.48***
Community involvement	↔	Experience	.09	.13*	.02	.10^
Self involvement	↔	Experience	.09	.38***	.04	.17**
Constraint recognition	↔	Experience	-.03	-.25***	-.00	-.13*
Problem recognition	↔	Experience	.13*	.40***	.23***	.29***
Exchange relationships	↔	Experience	.02	-.01	-.08	-.05
Communal relationships	↔	Experience	-.02	.05	.06	.09
Exchange relationships	↔	Community involvement	-.11^	-.28***	-.32***	-.23***
Exchange relationships	↔	Self involvement	-.21***	-.28***	-.25***	-.17**

(Table IV.24 continues)

(Table IV.24 continues)

Correlated Factors		Organizations[c]			
		Samsung	Sony	KFA	KNRC
Exchange relationships	↔	Constraint recognition	.22***	.22***	.27***	.18**
Exchange relationships	↔	Problem recognition	-.07	-.17**	-.16**	-.14*
Communal relationships	↔	Community involvement	.09	.23***	.32***	.13*
Communal relationships	↔	Self involvement	.16**	.24***	.30***	.11^
Communal relationships	↔	Constraint recognition	-.12*	-.15*	-.23***	-.13*
Communal relationships	↔	Problem recognition	.13*	.16**	.19**	.16**
Communal relationships	↔	Exchange relationships	-.61***	-.60***	-.59***	-.63***
Disturbance1[a]	↔	Disturbance2	.82***	.03	.65***	.68***
Error9[b]	↔	Error11		-.50**		

Note. [a]Disturbance1 = residual of communication behaviors; Disturbance2 = residual of familiarity. [b]Error9 = overall personal rating;

Error11 = perceived media rating. [c]Samsung = Samsung Electronics; Sony = Sony Korea; KFA = Korea Football Association; KNRC =

Korean National Red Cross.

^$p < .10$. *$p < .05$. **$p < .01$. ***$p < .001$.

First, I found that a multicollinearity problem does not exist among the four exogenous variables predicting communication behaviors. The largest covariance among those variables was in the relation between *constraint recognition* and *self involvement* across all organizations studied: -.53 ($p < .001$) for Samsung Electronics, -.51 ($p < .001$) for Sony Korea, -.55 ($p < .001$) for the KFA, and -.53 ($p < .001$) for the KNRC. Across all organizations studied, every covariance among the four exogenous variables of communication behaviors (problem recognition, constraint recognition, self-involvement, and community involvement) was significant at least at the .01 level with a "medium" effect size of correlations. Regarding the direction of covariances among those variables, only *constraint recognition* had the opposite direction as the other three variables had as the situational theory of publics predicts.

Secondly, there were two interesting correlations between experience and other exogenous variables: 1) experience was significantly associated with other exogenous variables consistently especially for Sony Korea, and 2) the correlation between problem recognition and experience was significant across all organizations studied. For example, except for correlations between experience and organization-public relationship types, all correlations with exogenous variables were significant for Sony Korea (Table IV.24). Additionally, experience was highly associated with problem recognition: .13 ($p < .05$) for Samsung Electronics, .40 ($p < .001$) for Sony Korea, .23 ($p < .001$) for the KFA, and .29 ($p < .001$) for the KNRC. This suggested that research participants who had high problem recognition with an organization were more likely to have direct experience with the organization studied than those who had low problem recognition.

Third, with regard to correlations between organization-public relationship types and other exogenous variables, both types of organization-public relationships were significantly associated with *self involvement* and *constraint recognition* across

all organizations studied. Also, the correlations between communal and exchange

relationships were significant (all at the .001 level) and "negative" throughout all

organizations studied: -.61 for Samsung Electronics, -.60 for Sony Korea, -.59 for the

KFA, and -.63 for the KNRC. This suggested that the two types of organization-

public relationships generally were opposites of each other, as theories proposed (e.g.,

Hon & J. Grunig, 1999). However, they did not necessarily produce a single

dimension of structure in the data. For example, a correlation coefficient of -.60

means that about 64% of variance in those two types of organization-public

relationships is not shared—that is, $1 - (-.60)^2 = .64$.

Other than correlations among exogenous variables, I allowed correlations

between disturbance of communication behaviors (disturbance 1) and disturbance of

familiarity (disturbance 2) to examine the strength of the association between

communication behaviors and familiarity above and beyond the correlations between

the hypothesized indicators in the model. Interestingly, except for Sony Korea,

correlations between disturbance 1 and disturbance 2 were positively strong and

significant (all at the .001 level): .82 for Samsung Electronics, .65 for the KFA, and

.68 for the KNRC, suggesting that communication behaviors and familiarity were

highly associated in this study.[34]

In addition to correlations between disturbances, I also allowed error 9 (the

error term for overall personal rating) and error 11 (the error for perceived media

rating) to correlate for Sony Korea. Initially, squared multiple correlation (R^2) for

---

[34] The correlation for Sony Korea was only .03. This may be because of the following
reasons: 1) exogenous variables for those latent variables significantly covaried for
Sony Korea, and 2) both familiarity ($R^2 = .200$) and communication behaviors ($R^2 =
.319$) had the largest variance explained by corresponding exogenous variables for
Sony Korea.

organizational reputation was greater than 1, which should be normally equal to or less than 1 (Kline, 1998). I found, for Sony Korea, errors between error 9 and error 11 were significantly correlated ($\gamma = -.50$, $p < .01$). After I correlated errors between error 9 and error 11, as a means of model respecifications, I fixed the problem of anomalous squared multiple correlations for Sony Korea.

Summary of Structural Equation Models

Finally, now that I have answered the hypotheses and research question, this section will summarize the overall results of SEM analysis for all four organizations studied. By doing so, I introduce a conceptual framework of organizational reputation formation. For an effective summary of SEM analysis, first, the results for each of the four organizations studied are illustrated in Figure IV.9 to Figure IV.12. In addition, based on the results, a generalized causal model is illustrated in Figure IV.13. Circles represent latent variables, and rectangles represent measured variables. Absence of a line connecting variables implies lack of a hypothesized direct effect. For the sake of brevity, I omitted covariances between exogenous measured variables, indicators for latent variables, and errors for the indicators from the figure.

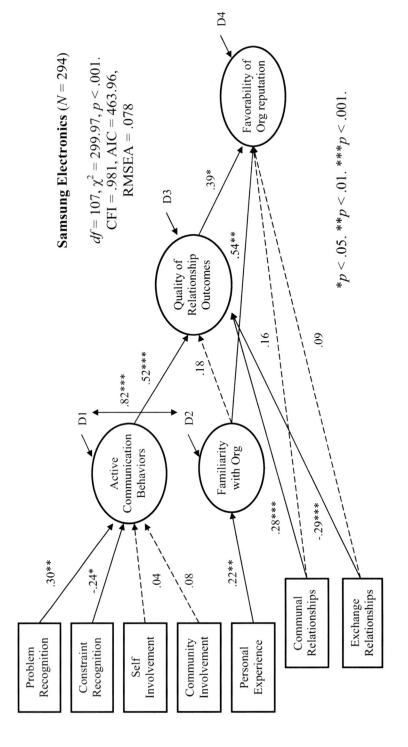

Samsung Electronics ($N = 294$)

$df = 107, \chi^2 = 299.97, p < .001.$
CFI $= .981$, AIC $= 463.96$,
RMSEA $= .078$

$*p < .05. **p < .01. ***p < .001.$

Figure IV.5. The results of structural equation model for Samsung Electronics. Note paths of *p* value stronger than .05 are in bold arrow.

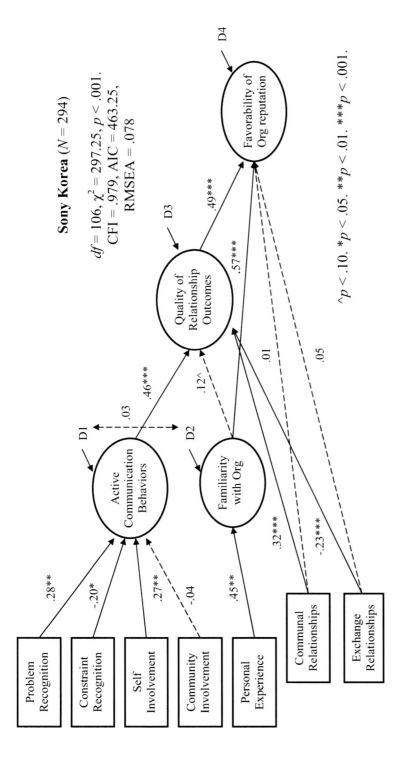

Figure IV.6. The results of structural equation model for Sony Korea. Note paths of *p* value stronger than .05 are in bold arrow.

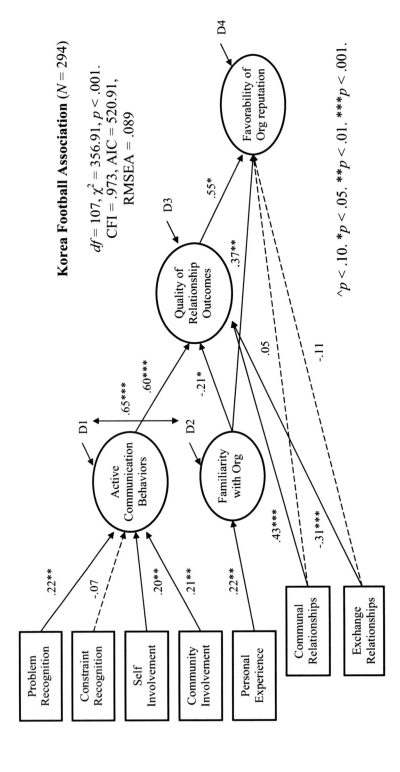

Korea Football Association (*N* = 294)

df = 107, χ^2 = 356.91, *p* < .001.
CFI = .973, AIC = 520.91,
RMSEA = .089

^*p* < .10. *p* < .05. **p* < .01. ***p* < .001.

Figure IV.7. The results of structural equation model for Korea Football Association. Note paths of *p* value stronger than .05 are in bold arrow.

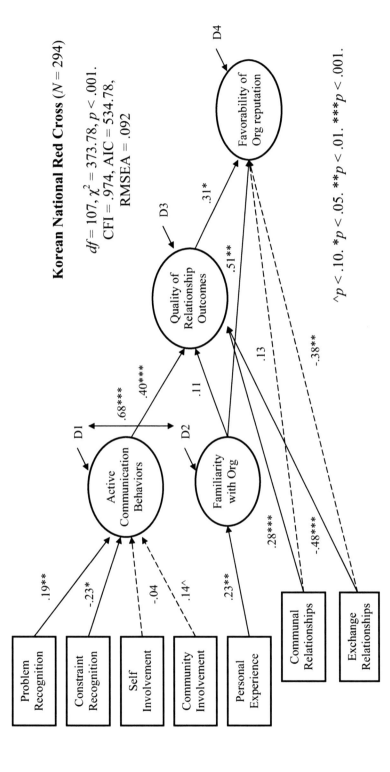

Figure IV.8. The results of structural equation model for Korean National Red Cross. Note paths of *p* value stronger than .05 are in bold arrow.

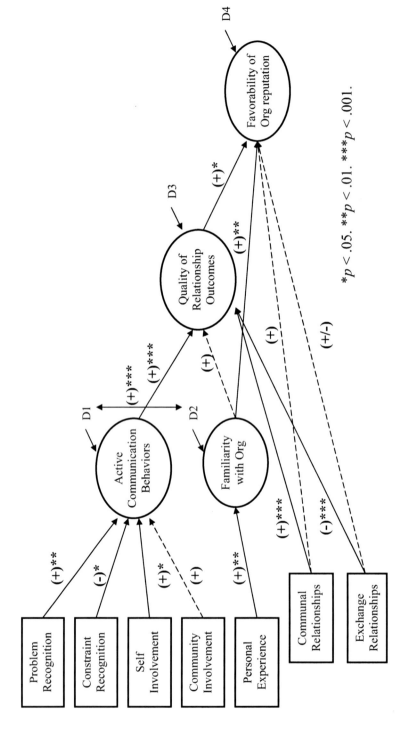

Figure IV.9. Overall results of the hypothesized structural equation model across the four organizations studied. Latent variables are shown in ellipses, and measured variables are shown in rectangles. Note paths of *p* value stronger than .05 are in bold arrow. Plus or minus sign indicates the direction of the structural relations.

Figure IV.13 illustrates the overall results of the hypothesized structural model for all organizations studied. Focusing on *structural* relations (direct and indirect effects) and controlling for correlations between exogenous variables, I extracted the following routes to predict organizational reputation, all of which were highly significant at least at $p < .05$:

1. A "communication-based" route: Three exogenous variables predicting communication behaviors (positive effect of problem recognition, negative effect of constraint recognition, and positive effect of self involvement) → Active communication behaviors → The quality of organization-public relationship outcomes → The favorability of organizational reputation.

2. A "communitarian" route: Types of organization-public relationships (positive effect of communal relationships and negative effect of exchange relationships) → The quality of organization-public relationship outcomes → The favorability of organizational reputation.

3. A "familiarity-based" route: Personal experience → Familiarity → The favorability of organizational reputation.

To summarize, the results of this study showed that organization-public relationships, including organization-public relationship outcomes and relationship types, highly affected organizational reputation for all organizations studied. In addition, the findings of this study suggested that favorable organizational reputation can be obtained under specific conditions through familiarity alone, although familiarity was embedded in the (direct) experience of publics. Last, as shown in Figure IV.13, familiarity generally was also meaningfully associated with communication behaviors above and beyond covariances between exogenous variables hypothesized in the model.

First, for what I have called the communication-based route, communication behaviors of publics significantly affected the quality of relationship outcomes and, in turn, influenced the favorability of organizational reputation. Among the three variables predicting communication behaviors, the quality of relationship outcomes most significantly mediated the effect of problem recognition on organizational reputation.

Secondly, for what I have called the communitarian route, the quality of relationship outcomes significantly mediated the effect of types of organization-public relationships on organizational reputation. I named this path the "communitarian" route because it reflects the importance of communal relationships. I will discuss the reasons for calling it a communitarian path in greater detail in the next chapter. The results of structural equation modeling revealed that the direct effect of types of relationships on reputation generally was minimal and not significant; when the quality of relationship outcomes mediated, however, there were significant effects of types of relationships on reputation. This suggests that when participants evaluated the quality of relationship outcomes with the organizations studied, they were affected by perceived types of organization-public relationships and, in turn, when they formed reputations of the organizations studied.

Finally, although the direct effect of familiarity on the quality of relationship outcome generally was minimal, the third path could be identified as a familiarity-based route to reputation formation. Also, familiarity significantly mediated the effect of personal experience on organizational reputation.

CHAPTER V: Conclusions

Overview of the Study

The purpose of this study was to investigate the link between organization-public relationships and organizational reputation. In particular, I examined how organization-public relationships affect organizational reputations in a causal model. For this purpose, I conducted a survey to collect data. I used structural equation modeling (SEM) to empirically test the causal effect of organization-public relationships on organizational reputation for the four different types of organizations. I hypothesized a causal model in which organization-public relationship outcomes and organization-public relationship types (communal and exchange relationships) predict organizational reputation with exogenous influences of communication behaviors of publics, experience, and familiarity with the organizations studied.

The statistical program AMOS 4.0 was used examine the causal relationships between organization-public relationship outcomes, a latent variable with four indicators (control mutuality, trust, satisfaction, and commitment), organizational reputation, a latent variable with three indicators (net positive representations, overall personal rating, and perceived media rating), communication behaviors of publics, a latent variable with two indicators (information seeking and information processing), and familiarity, a latent variable with two indicators (overall personal familiarity and familiarity with media coverage of the organization). Also, included in the analysis were the exogenous variables of problem recognition, constraint recognition, self-involvement, perceived community involvement, experience, and organization-public relationship types (communal and exchange relationships).

In this study, I tested nine hypotheses. Additionally, I posited a research question about the effects of types of organization-public relationships on organization-public relationship outcomes and organizational reputation. I answered

the research question by means of a nested (or hierarchical) model comparison

between competing structural equation models: between a structural model with the

causal inputs from types of organization-public relationships and a structural model

without them. To put it another way, I checked whether addition of causal inputs from

types of organization-public relationships significantly improved the data-model fits

of the hypothesized structural model for all organizations studied.

This chapter first discusses conclusions based on the results of the study. For

conclusions, I will discuss important findings of this study and the results that I did

not expect and emerged from the data. Then, the implications for the study and

practice of public relations are discussed. Finally, I discuss limitations of this study

and provide suggestions for future research.

Discussion

The purpose of this study was to examine the effect of organization-public

relationships on organizational reputation. For this purpose of this study, I found the

following important results:

1. The significant effects of the quality of *organization-public relationship outcomes* on the favorability of organizational reputation for all organizations studied.

2. The importance of *types of organization-public relationships* in conceptualizing the quality of organization-public relationships and organizational reputation.

3. The relevance of the *antecedents* of organization-public relationships and organizational reputation proposed in this study, such as communication

behaviors of publics, personal experience, familiarity, and types of organization-public relationships.

4. The stronger effect of *communication behaviors* on the quality of organization-public relationship outcomes than the effect of familiarity on relationship outcomes.

5. A similar distribution of *cognitive representations* for the same type of organization.

First, this study found the significant effect of organization-public relationships on organizational reputation for all organizations studied, analyzing the data of a survey using structural equation modeling (SEM). The effect sizes of path coefficients in the hypothesized model were large or, at least, moderate across the four different types of organizations studied (such as a domestic corporation, a multinational corporation, a nonprofit sports association, and a nonprofit social service organization).

In contemporary public relations, the concepts of relationships and reputation have emerged as the key concepts that most influence the study and practice of and education for public relations. Many public relations writers have pointed out that there are divergent approaches existing between public relations professionals and scholars to demonstrate the value of public relations, using either relationships or reputation. However, public relations theorists (e.g., Coombs, 2000; J. Grunig & Hung, 2002; L. Grunig, J. Grunig, and Dozier, 2002) have suggested that the quality of organization-public relationships affects organizational reputation. In Chapter II, I reviewed the literature from different perspectives, such as public relations, business, and psychology, which suggest the effect of relationships on reputation.

I suggested, like many public relations theorists, that the concepts of relationships and reputation should be intertwined in conceptualizing the value of public relations, rather than focusing on one of the concepts alone. I reasoned that there would be synergy effects from elucidating a big picture of the value of public relations when the concepts of relationships and reputation are integrated in a model. The findings of this study clearly demonstrate that favorable organizational reputation can be obtained by quality relationship management between an organization and its publics. This conclusion was consistently supported by the results for the four types of organizations studied.

Secondly, this study found significant effects of types of organization-public relationships on organization-public relationship outcomes and organizational reputation. Public relations scholars, including L. Grunig, J. Grunig, and Dozier (2002) and Hon and J. Grunig (1999), have suggested the importance of types of organization-public relationships for relationship management. However, there has been minimal research testing the effects of types of organization-public relationships in the literature of public relations.

Rather than a hypothesis, I proposed a research question and compared two nested structural equation models: a model with the effects of types of organization-public relationships and the other model without them. The results of this study suggest that types of organization-public relationships should be regarded as one of the key antecedents for the quality of relationship outcomes and the favorability of organizational reputation. For all organizations studied, the inclusion of the causal paths from types of organization-public relationships significantly improved the data-model fits. Especially, the results showed that including types of organization-public relationships critically improved the data-model fits for nonprofit organizations, suggesting that the concept of types of relationships is more relevant for nonprofit organizations than for profit organizations.

Third, one of the important findings of this study was the relevance for key antecedents of organization-public relationship outcomes and organizational reputation. The existing literature of public relations and other fields has suggested some antecedents for relationship outcomes and reputation. For example, J. Grunig and Huang (2000) suggested that the communication behaviors of publics would affect the quality of relationship outcomes; J. Grunig's situational theory of publics (e.g., J. Grunig, 1997; J. Grunig and Hunt, 1984) provides predictor variables of communication behaviors (problem recognition, constraint recognition, and level of involvement). Many business scholars have claimed that familiarity is the most important antecedent of organizational reputation; Bromley (1993) and J. Grunig and Hung (2002) have suggested personal experience as the key antecedent of familiarity of a public with an organization. As noted previously, Hon and J. Grunig (1999) and L. Grunig et al. (2002) suggested types of relationships as one of key antecedents of the quality of relationship outcomes.

I connected these antecedents, identified in the existing literature, in a causal model. Multiple fit indexes of the proposed model suggest that the proposed model can be retained as a valid model. Therefore, the results of the data-model fits supported the relevance of the antecedents of relationship outcomes and reputation used in this study, such as communication behaviors, predictor variables of communication behaviors, personal experience, familiarity, and types of relationships.

Fourth, this study found a stronger effect of communication behaviors on the quality of relationship outcomes than the effect of familiarity. The effect of familiarity on the quality of relationship outcomes generally was minimal and insignificant.

However, communication behaviors of publics played a critical role in predicting the quality of relationship outcomes. The effect sizes were large for all organizations studied and the causal path was one of the strongest paths imposed in the proposed causal model. This suggests that, as opposed to familiarity, communication behaviors of publics are critical in predicting organization-public relationship outcomes because of the behavioral orientation of the concept. Also, this study found that the link between communication behaviors and familiarity is very strong. Putting those findings together, familiarity alone does not seem to be enough to obtain quality organization-public relationship outcomes; and the effect of active communication behaviors or the combined effects of communication behaviors and familiarity is the key predictor of quality relationship outcomes. This conclusion supports the conclusions from a great deal of previous public relations research. For example, Rhee (2004) and Youngmeyer (2002) found that active communication behaviors of publics resulted in quality relationship outcomes between an organization and its publics. For public relations practice, in particular for relationship management, this finding suggests that public relations needs to identify publics that engage in active communication behaviors and to strategically manage communications with them, rather than conduct a publicity-related practice to gain organizational visibility.

Finally, this study found a similar distribution of cognitive representations depending on the type of organization. More specifically, for the profit organizations studied, cognitive representations centered on object-attribute associations—in particular, the quality of products and services. On the other hand, for the nonprofit organizations studied, behavioral representations (e.g., social contribution or transparent use of donations) were most shared by the participants. This suggests that the validity of common reputation surveys should be seriously questioned: Survey respondents seem to hold reputations of organizations based on their individual experiences. The participants also shared both "positive" and "negative" representations about the quality of products and services for the profit organizations, based on their individual experiences, which also suggests that standard questionnaire items might miss the most relevant questions. Common reputation measurement systems generally are driven by financial performance of an organization; however, most participants did not mention financial performance of the organizations studied.

Now that I have discussed the most important findings of this study, I will explain the findings that I did not expect but learned from the data. The three biggest surprises that I found in this study are:

1. Three distinct routes predicting organizational reputation: communication-based, communitarian, and familiarity-based routes.

2. The differential effect of types of organization-public relationships on organizational reputation between profit and nonprofit organizations: "positive" effects of exchange relationships on reputation for profit organizations and "negative" effects of exchange relationships on reputation for nonprofit organizations.

3. A specific situation in which familiarity alone had an effect on organizational reputation: the "negative" effect of familiarity on the quality of relationship outcomes and the "positive" effect of familiarity on reputation for the KFA.

After I summarized the findings of the proposed causal model (Figure IV.13) for all organizations studied, I found three distinct routes that predict organizational reputation, based on significant structural relationships in the model (controlling for correlations between exogenous variables and excluding insignificant relationships in the model): a communication-based route, a "communitarian" route (J. Grunig, personal communication, March 29, 2005), and a familiarity-based route (Figure V.1).

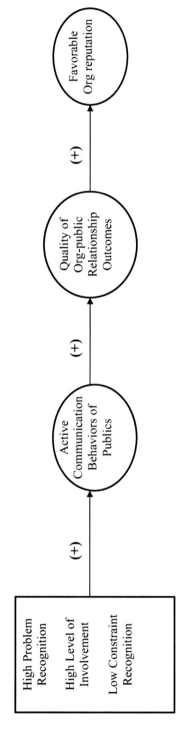

A. A communication-based route of reputation formation

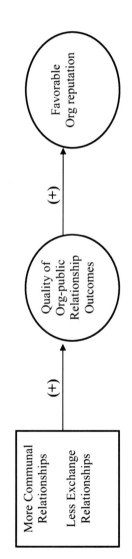

B. A communitarian route of reputation formation

(Figure V.1 continued)

(Figure V.1 continued)

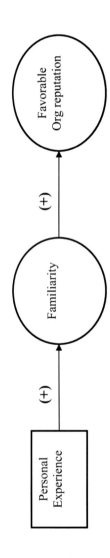

C. A familiarity-based route of reputation formation

Figure V.1. A conceptual framework of organizational reputation formation. Controlling for correlations between exogenous variables, I found that all paths were significant at least at the .05 level for all organization studied.

I named the first causal route the "communication-based route" of reputation formation (Figure V.1). I derived this name, first, from the literature of public relations from which I constructed a theoretical bridge between the situational theory of publics (e.g., J. Grunig, 1997), the Excellence theory (e.g., L. Grunig, J. Grunig, & Dozier, 2002), and organization-public relationships (e.g., Bruning & Ledingham, 2000; Hon & J. Grunig, 1999; Hung, 2002; J. Grunig & Huang, 2000) and organizational reputation (e.g., J. Grunig & Hung, 2002; Kim, 2002).

More specifically, the findings of this study supported the Excellence theory, which maintained that for public relations to be valued by an organization, the function of public relations should 1) identify strategic publics, those publics who engage in active communication behaviors, and 2) help the organization to cultivate good behavioral relationships. Consequently, an organization can obtain favorable reputation, as one of its public relations goals (Kim, 2002), by means of quality relationships with publics (J. Grunig & Hung, 2002; L. Grunig, J. Grunig, & Dozier, 2002).

Secondly, in addition to the value of public relations at the organizational level through the communication-based route, a second route, which I call the communitarian route, suggested that public relations has value to society in general through its contribution to cultivation of quality relationships between an organization and its publics in communities (J. Grunig, personal communication, March 29, 2005; Figure V.1).

In particular, this study demonstrated the important effects of communal relationships on the quality relationship outcomes and on favorable reputation. As the "communitarian" approach suggests (e.g., Kruckeberg & Starck, 1988; Culbertson & Chen, 1997), an organization should be responsible to all members of the community by behaving in a way that goes beyond immediate organizational interests (J. Grunig & L. Grunig, 2002). When it does, these results suggest, a member of a public will be more likely to evaluate his or her relationships with the organization positively and to hold a favorable reputation of the organization.

Other intriguing findings suggesting the communitarian path were the relatively high correlations between community involvement and types of organization-public relationships (positively with communal relationships and negatively with exchange relationships) for the nonprofit organizations studied but not for the profit organizations studied. Also, among the independent variables that predict communication behaviors, "community involvement" generally was most significantly associated with types of organization-public relationships. Such findings also suggested a communitarian approach: Participants cared about how each of the organizations studied was involved with the community as well as how responsible it was to the community in forming reputations of the organizations studied.

Third, this study also shed light on theories from perspectives other than public relations, such as familiarity and corporate reputation from business (e.g., Fombrun & Van Riel, 2003), interpersonal relationship types (e.g., Clark & Mills, 1979, 1993), personal impressions (Bromley, 1993; Carlston & Smith, 1996), and cognitive representations (e.g., Anderson, 1983, 1996, 2000; Ashcraft, 2002; Carlston & Smith, 1996; Smith, 1998) from social and cognitive psychology.

Along with communication-based route and communitarian route predicting organizational reputation, this study also showed the importance of familiarity in creating a favorable organizational reputation, under some conditions, as many business scholars have suggested (e.g., Deephouse, 2000; Fombrun & Van Riel, 2003; Pollack & Rindova, 2002). Also, the findings of this study suggested that theories of mere exposure and attitude (e.g., Zajonc, 1968) in social psychology can be important in some situations. I named this causal path the "familiarity-based route" of reputation formation (Figure V.1).

In this study, I embedded the concept of familiarity in actual interactions of the participants with the organizations studied. This conceptualization differed from the common approach of low-involvement familiarity[35] (i.e., "top-of-mind awareness[36]" that is not based on actual involvement in organizational activities; see Fombrun and Van Riel, 2003, pp. 103-109). Nevertheless, the findings of this study did show that the claims of business scholars can sometimes hold when people have little direct experience with an organization.

Another interesting, and unexpected, result was the differential effect of types of organization-public relationships on organizational reputation for profit and nonprofit organizations: "positive" effects of exchange relationships on reputation for profit organizations and "negative" effects of exchange relationships on reputation for nonprofit organizations (Figure V.2).

---

[35] J. Grunig, personal communication, March 29, 2005.

[36] According to Fombrun and Van Riel (2003), familiarity as top-of-mind awareness is "the probability that a company comes to mind when a consumer is prompted on a specific topic" (p. 104).

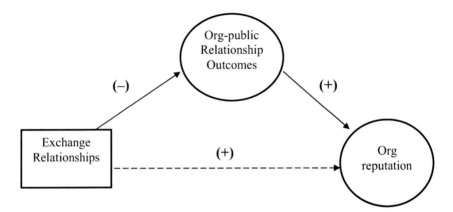

A. Profit organizations studied: Samsung Electronics and Sony Korea

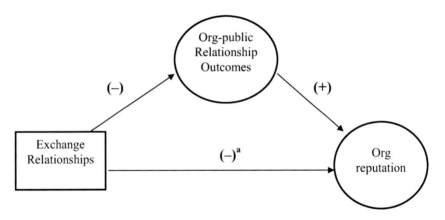

B. Nonprofit organizations studied: the KFA and the KNRC

Figure V.2. The causal links between exchange relationships, organization-public

relationship outcomes, and organizational reputation. Note paths of *p* value stronger

than .05 are in bold arrow. [a]For the KNRC, the standardized path coefficient was -.38

($p < .01$); for the KFA, the value was -.11 (*ns*).

This unexpected finding emerged when I summarized the findings of the proposed structural equation model (SEM) for all organizations studied and found differing effects of exchange relationships on organizational reputation. For the profit organizations studied, Samsung Electronics and Sony Korea, the direct effect of exchange relationships on organizational reputation was insignificant. On the other hand, the direct effect of exchange relationships on organizational reputation was "negative" and relatively significant for the nonprofit organizations studied. However, the mediating effect of organization-public relationships outcomes on reputation revealed that the effect of exchange relationships on organizational reputation was negative and significant, even for the profit organizations studied.

Therefore, these results suggest: 1) The effect of types of organization-public relationships was greater for the nonprofit organizations studied than for the profit organizations studied; 2) the more communal are organization-public relationships and the less they are exchange, the more favorable the reputation of an organization, regardless of organizational type; and 3) such effects were meaningfully mediated by the quality of organization-public relationship outcomes.

Finally, the specific situation in which familiarity alone has an effect can be seen in the intriguing finding of a "negative" effect of familiarity on organization-public relationship outcomes for the KFA. The direct effect of familiarity on organization-public relationship outcomes was "negative," whereas the direct effect of familiarity on organizational reputation was "positive" for the KFA (Figure V.3).

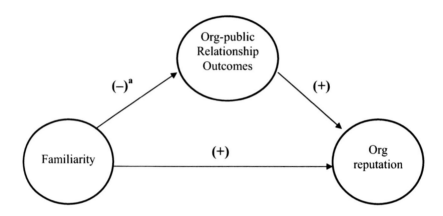

Figure V.3. The causal links between familiarity, organization-public relationship

outcomes, and organizational reputation for the KFA. Note the "negative" effect of

familiarity on organization-public relationship outcomes. Paths of *p* value stronger than

.05 are in bold arrow. [a]Standardized path coefficient was -.21 (significant at *p* < .05).

This suggests that the concept of organizational reputation is relatively more "superficial" (Bromley, 1993) than organization-public relationships; the concept of organization-public relationships is more behaviorally oriented (J. Grunig, 1993) than familiarity. Also, this finding demonstrates risks related with practitioners' common focus on familiarity-centered reputation management rather than focusing on the cultivation of behavioral relationships.

Familiarity alone, however, has an effect only when members of a public do not have an experiential relationship with an organization. J. Grunig (1993) distinguished symbolic relationships (e.g., image, reputation, or other associated terms) from behavioral relationships, a type of relationships that organizations build with publics through long-term interactive behaviors. The relationship with the KFA seemed to be mostly symbolic, as most participants had little direct experience with the KFA. In addition, the descriptive statistics indicated that participants reported poor quality organization-public relationship outcomes for the KFA compared with other organizations studied; consequently, the results of this study revealed: The more familiar with the KFA, the lower the quality of relationships with the KFA.

Implications

The purpose of this study was to investigate how organization-public relationships affect organizational reputation, from the perspective of publics. To this end, I also included communication behaviors of publics and familiarity (explained by personal experience) in the hypothesized causal model as antecedents of organization-public relationships and organizational reputation. In this section, I will explain the implications of this study for the study and practice of public relations.

Relevance of the Research Problem to Public Relations

In recent years, organizations have demanded evidence that public relations is effective. Consequently, professionals and scholars alike in the field of public relations have looked for the key concepts to establish the value of public relations. The terms "relationships" and "reputation" have emerged as the focal concepts in the study and practice of public relations.

Along with the emphasis on such concepts, leading public relations scholars have suggested a "management" perspective in defining public relations (e.g., Cutlip et al., 2000; J. Grunig & Hunt, 1984) and in conducting research (e.g., L. Grunig, J. Grunig, & Dozier, 2002). By bridging the terms "relationships" and "reputation" with the management perspective, both scholars and professionals in public relations now use the terms "relationship management" or "reputation management" regularly to describe the contemporary practice of public relations.

For example, Ledingham and Bruning (2000) maintained that "relationship management" has emerged as a "paradigm" for public relations scholarship and practice. Similarly, Hutton, Goodman, Alexander, and Genest (2001) said: "… 'reputation management' is gaining ground as a driving philosophy behind corporate public relations." (p. 247).

Interestingly, many public relations scholars (e.g., Heath, 2001; Hutton et al., 2001; J. Grunig & Hung, 2002) have pointed out that public relations professionals and scholars have demonstrated the value of public relations differently using the concepts of relationships and reputation. More specifically, influenced by *Fortune* reputation surveys and business scholars studying corporate reputation, public relations professionals have widely embraced reputation management to show economic effects of public relations. For example, public relations scholar, Kim (2001) examined the "economic value of public relations" by testing causal relations between public relations expenses, organizational reputation, and revenue increase.

On the other hand, public relations scholars, in general, have suggested that public relations can have value because it helps the organization cultivate good relationships with strategic publics (e.g., L. Grunig, J. Grunig, & Dozier, 2002). Ferguson (1984), the IABC Excellence Study (J. Grunig et al., 1992; Dozier et al., 1995; L. Grunig et al., 2002), and Hon and J. Grunig (1999) also have shed light on relationship management in public relations.

In this study, I hold that divergent approaches to relationships and reputation are not necessary. The concepts of organization-public relationships and organizational reputation can be integrated within a theoretical framework of public relations effectiveness. When those concepts are integrated in a model, the role of public relations for its effectiveness can be more clearly captured than separate focus on each of the concepts.

Implications for Public Relations Theory

To discuss the implications of this study for public relations theory, I will explain 1) theories on the link between organization-public relationships and reputation, 2) limited existing empirical research supporting such theoretical claims, and 3) this study's contribution to public relations theory by filling the gap between theories and empirical demonstration.

Theoretical Claims

Several public relations theorists have suggested that organization-public relationships and reputation are closely linked. For example, Coombs (2000) explained that relationships and reputation are closely linked because both concepts are built from past interactions between an organization and its publics. Similarly, J. Grunig and Huang (2000) said: "… corporate reputation is highly connected with behavioral relationships because reputation essentially consists of the corporate behaviors that publics remember" (p. 35). Moreover, these scholars suggested that there are causal effects of organization-public relationships on organizational reputation.

The concept of organizational reputation is most commonly defined as "cognitive representations" of an organization that are shared by publics. By cognitive representations, I mean how members of publics actually conceptualize an organization in their minds, following Bromley (1993) and J. Grunig and Hung (2002). In this regard, Coombs (2000) maintained, "… reputation arises from the relational history" (p. 77) because organizational reputation is based on past experiences of publics with an organization. Likewise, L. Grunig et al. (2002) and J. Grunig and Hung (2002) also argued that organizational reputation is a product of organization-public relationships. For example, J. Grunig and Hung (2002) said: "We also theorize that reputation is a direct product of organization-public relationships and that relationships should be the focal variable for measuring the value of public relations" (p. 1).

Limited Existing Empirical Research

Despite significant implications that resulted from studying this research problem (the link between relationships and reputation) for public relations research, there has been minimal research like this in the literature of public relations. Existing studies have limitations. First, most studies that found an effect of relationships on reputation, except for a few experimental studies, were correlational in nature. Secondly, the experimental studies conceptualized the concepts of relationships and reputation as symbolic concepts, such as crisis response strategies used in hypothetical media coverage of fictitious organizations. Since the essence of the relationship concept is in its behavioral orientation—the actual past and ongoing interdependence and consequences of such interdependence between an organization and its publics—such experimental research based on fictitious organizations has limited theoretical and empirical implications. Third, like Rhee (2004) and J. Grunig and Huang (2000), I consider communication behaviors of publics to be the key antecedent of organization-public relationships. Also, I believe that personal experience of a public is the key antecedent of the effect of familiarity on organizational reputation. Previous research did not include these important antecedents in examining the link between relationships and reputation.

More specifically, public relations research investigating the effects of relationships on reputation included Coombs and Holladay (2001), J. Grunig and Hung (2002), Hagan (2003), Lyon and Cameron (2004), and Yang and J. Grunig (2005). Although such studies contributed to a body of knowledge in public relations, these scholars did not test causal effects of organization-public relationships on organizational reputation, except for Coombs and Holladay's (2001) experimental study. In addition, only few studies (J. Grunig and Hung, 2002; Yang & J. Grunig, 2005) examined *communication behaviors* of publics, which I consider to be key antecedents of organization-public relationships and organizational reputation as J. Grunig and Huang (2000) and Rhee (2004) pointed out.

Among them, Coombs and Holladay (2001) and Lyon and Cameron (2004)

conducted experimental research. Lyon and Cameron's (2004) research was more about

the (interaction) effects of organizational reputation and crisis response on attitudes and

behavioral intentions of publics (toward "fake" companies studied), than the effect of

organization-public relationships on organizational reputation. More specifically, they

studied the effects of organizational reputation and crisis response (defensive and

apologetic responses) on attitudes and behavioral intentions of participants toward

companies appeared in four "fictitious" news stories about crises. By a "relational

approach," they meant *crisis response* (whether the crisis response was "defensive or

apologetic") as described in news stories; consequently, they used a *symbolic* approach to

organization-public relationships rather than behavioral relationships.

Coombs and Holladay (2001) came closer to investigating the effect of

organization-public relationships on organizational reputation, than Lyon and Cameron

(2004). They hypothesized that performance history (including relationship history and

crisis history) affects both organizational reputation and crisis response.

I believe that the key constructs in this study, organization-public relationships

and organizational reputation, are difficult to manipulate in experimental research.

Experimental research is not feasible, if not completely impossible, for studying

"behavioral" relationships built between an organization and its publics. Consequently,

Coombs and Holladay's (2002) research was limited to effects of the symbolic approach

to crisis situation on organizational reputation[37]; they found significant effects only of

---

[37] Coombs and Holladay (2002) measured the quality of organization-public relationships
using two items, "The organization has done a lot to help the community" and "The

"negative" relationship history on organizational reputation. Also, their experiment excluded communication behaviors of publics.

J. Grunig and Hung (2002) and Hagan (2003) did not directly study causal effects of organization-public relationships on organizational reputation. Finally, Yang and J. Grunig (2005) used structural equation modeling (SEM) for the similar research problem but did not include personal experience and types of organization-public relationships in the model. More specifically, in this study, I took a step further from the model presented in Yang and J. Grunig (2005) by 1) including the links between communication behaviors of publics (information seeking and processing) and the exogenous variables predicting communication behaviors, 2) taking account of the effect of experience on familiarity, and 3) hypothesizing the effects of types of organization-public relationships on relationship outcomes and reputation.

Filling the Gap Between Theories and Empirical Research

Therefore, this study contributes to a theoretical body of knowledge in public relations by filling the gap between existing theoretical claims and empirical research to support such theories: demonstrating how organization-public relationships affect organizational reputation in a causal model.

Methodologically, I believe that I chose appropriate methods for the purpose of this study. First, structural equation modeling (SEM) allowed me to test a causal model with nonexperiemental data. Consequently, I assessed organization-public relationships and organizational reputation, based on past interactions of research participants with the organizations studied. Secondly, I aligned the theoretical definition of organizational

---

organization tries to provide workers a quality place to work" (p. 330), based on descriptions of an organization in news stories.

reputation and its operationalization by measuring the distribution and valence of cognitive representations that participants held of the organizations studied. Finally, I compared the hypothesized causal model across the four different types of organizations studied.

Summary. By connecting such relevant theories from different perspectives, this study empirically demonstrated the effect of organization-public relationships on organizational reputation: Organizational reputation is a direct product of organization-public relationships, so management of quality organization-public relationships tends to produce favorable reputation for an organization. By clearly demonstrating a causal link between organization-public relationships and organizational reputation, this study contributes to public relations theory since the contemporary literature of pubic relations has increasingly focused on "relationships" or "reputation" as the primary vehicle of public relations value, or the key role of public relations at the organizational level (Bruning & Ledingham, 2000; Hutton et al., 2001).

Implications for Public Relations Practice

The New Trend in Practice

Now that I have discussed the implications of this study for public relations theory, I will explain implications for public relations practice. Although *PR Week* once said: "… reputation management products are becoming as ubiquitous as hot-dog vendors in Manhattan" ("PR Week," 1999, November 15), an increasing number of professionals have valued relationship management (J. Grunig & Huang, 2000) and conceptualized the effect of organization-public relationships on organizational reputation. For example, public relations practitioners Stephanie Feldwicke (2003,

August) wrote an article titled "Every Good Reputation Needs a Good Relationship." Hill & Knowlton, a public relations firm, publicized a case about the effect of relationships on reputation on its website, which was about the firm's practice to enhance reputation of Shell International by means of relationship management including stakeholder dialogue and social responsibility ("Shell: Reputation, Relationships, Results," Hill & Knowlton, n.d.).

Theoretical Frameworks of Reputation Formation

Overview of practical implications. This study contributes to the practice of public relations in several ways. Although practitioners have increasingly embraced "reputation management" (Hutton et al., 2001; Griffin, 2002), it is imperative that public relations research demonstrate a sound theoretical framework of reputation formation. This study shed light on the causal link between organization-public relationship outcomes and organizational reputation, which include key antecedents of organization-public relationships and organizational reputation, such as communication behaviors of publics, experience, familiarity, and types of organization-public relationships. After connecting relevant theories to hypothesize a causal model, this study compared the hypothesized model across different types of organizations.

Bad behaviors of organizations produce bad relationships with publics and in turn a negative reputation of an organization (J. Grunig & Hung, 2002). As the Excellence study suggested, for public relations to be valued, public relations practitioners should practice strategic management of public relations: They should be included in the dominant coalition to influence organizational behaviors and to bring the voices of publics into the decision-making process (L. Grunig, J. Grunig, & Dozier, 2002). In particular, for effective management of relationships and reputation, the findings of this study suggest that practitioners need to 1) implement strategic management of communication by identifying publics with active communication behaviors and 2) help the organization to behave responsibly to value the interests of publics and communities.

A conceptual framework of reputation formation. In this study, I suggested three conceptual routes of reputation formation based on empirical results of this study: 1) a communication-based route, 2) a communitarian route, and 3) a familiarity-based route. Among them, I consider that public relations professionals have often focused on the "familiarity-based" route of reputation formation, influenced by business scholars specializing in reputation management.

For public relations professionals, the link between reputation and financial returns of corporations is attractive (Griffin, 2002), assuming a viable role that public relations has in reputation management (Kim, 2002). Especially today, when organizational demands for public relations accountability have drastically increased because of recent budget cuts in the public relations industry, practitioners need to have appropriate measures of public relations value. This task has been difficult because the value of public relations is almost impossible to measure since most of its elements are intangible (Lesley, 1991). In addition, the function of public relations traditionally has been considered to be a means of reducing costs rather than a means of generating org revenues (L. Grunig, J. Grunig, & Dozier, 2002). Consequently, reputation management can be the "Holy Grail" for practitioners (J. Grunig & Hung, 2002).

Nonetheless, it is ironic that by embracing reputation management practitioners can "devalue" the function of public relations by marginalizing the practice into a publicity-oriented technical function, rather than the strategic management of organizational communication. Reputation scholars (e.g., Dowling, 2001; Fombrun, 1996) often have viewed pubic relations as a technical function used to manipulate symbolic reputations through publicity so as to increase familiarity, or top-of-mind awareness of corporations. For example, Dowling (2001) said that reputation management is too important to be outsourced to public relations firms, but should be handed by corporate managers.

Even if these reputation scholars have stressed quality stakeholder-organization relationships and "good citizenship" of corporations as critical antecedents of favorable reputation (e.g., Fombrun, 1996; Fombrun & Van Riel, 2003), they have public relations practitioners pigeonholed into publicity-makers at the cost of behavioral relationship management. For example, Fombrun and Van Riel explained that corporate citizenship is a key precursor of organizational visibility and in turn favorable reputation: "Corporate citizenship is a label that is increasingly attached to companies that take public positions as 'good citizens'—and claim to behave responsibly, to safeguard communities and the environment, and to serve the best interests of consumers" (p. 118). And, Fombrun (1996) emphasized the effect of quality relationships on favorable reputation: "To acquire a reputation that is positive, enduring, and resilient requires managers to invest heavily in building and maintaining good relationships with their company's constituents" (p. 57).

Therefore, the findings of this study are useful for practitioners to understand the importance of quality organization-public relationships and responsible organizational behaviors on the acquisition of favorable reputation. In contrast to the common focus on the familiarity-based route to reputation formation, this study suggests more focus on the "communication-based" and "communitarian" routes to reputation formation. Indeed, those conceptual frameworks are almost identical to reputation scholars' claims about the role of good stakeholder-organization relationships and corporate citizenship in reputation management.

Additionally, the findings of Fombrun and Shanley (1990) were strongly supportive of these conclusions. They found "negative" effects of media visibility on reputations of 292 corporations sampled in *Fortune*'s 1985 study.[38] Literally speaking, the findings indicated that the more visibility of a company in the media, the less favorable corporate reputation. Thus, Fombrun and Shanley's study suggested risks associated with a publicity-centered practice for reputation management.

Lattimore, Baskin, Heiman, Toth, and Van Leuven (2004) warned against a manipulative, symbolic management of public relations practice as follows: "Public relations was born as a manipulative art… Stunts, sensationalism, and embellished, highly selective truth were the hallmarks of the trade. Such crass manipulation made for short-term rather than long-term impact, thereby limiting the effectiveness of public relations." (p. 387). In this regard, for public relations effectiveness, the findings of this study suggest that practitioners need to focus on quality behavioral relationship management with publics, who engage in active communication behaviors, and to help their organizations behave responsibly.

---

[38] Fombrun and Shanley (1990) developed hypotheses regarding the effects of visibility and favorability of media coverage on reputation: (a) the greater a firm's current media visibility, the better its reputation, (b) the more nonnegative a firm's current media coverage, the better its reputation, and (c) nonnegative coverage and visibility have a positive, interactive effect on reputation. From testing these hypotheses, the most surprising finding was that visibility has an "adverse" strong effect on reputation (at $p <$ .001). They did not get supportive results from favorability and the interaction between visibility and favorability.

Limitations of the Study

Although this study contributed to the study and practice of public relations in a number of ways, there are several limitations that characterize this study. In this section, I will discuss the potential methodological problems that might have occurred in the process of data collection and analysis. By doing so, I can suggest how future studies can address the limitations of this study. I recognize the following limitations of this study:

1. Potential cultural influences on the measurement items of this study.

2. Possible misspecification in the hypothesized causal model.

3. Risks in the validity of the measure of experience.

4. Unnecessary cues for participants' reporting cognitive representations in the survey questionnaire.

5. Low construct reliability of familiarity and communication behaviors.

6. Low construct validity of some latent variables.

7. One-way evaluations of organization-public relationships limited in the perspective of publics.

8. Limited generalizability of the results because of nonprobability sampling.

9. Possible limited application of the proposed model for activist publics.

10. Possible influences of the media in research context and participants' educational level on organizational reputation.

I will discuss such limitations of this study with suggestions for future studies. Then, I will add some additional suggestions for future studies.

Potential Cultural Influences on the Measurement Items

First, I used Western measurement instruments and translated them into Korean for data collection. In particular, the measurement items for "organization-public relationships" might have risks of reliability and validity resulting from both language problems and cultural implications. Other measurement items, such as communication behaviors, experience, familiarity, and organizational reputation, were probably affected less by cultural influences because all measurement items were explicitly stated and translated well into Korean. For example, the overall personal familiarity measure stated: "On a scale from 1 to 5, please indicate overall how familiar you are with each of these organizations." Especially, the open-end measure of reputation was strictly based on participants' individual cognitive representations.

Thus, my concern over cultural influences on the measurement system lies in the measurement of organization-public relationships, since the construct of "relationship" can be defined differently with variant dimensions of relationships across different cultures (Jo, 2003). Since Ferguson (1984) called for more public relations research about organization-public relationships, a few public relations scholars have developed culture-specific dimensions to assess organization-public relationships (Huang, 2001; Jo, 2003).

Among them, first, Huang (2001) introduced "face and favor" to reflect Eastern culture. Secondly, Jo (2003) introduced "personal network" to reflect South Korean culture. Jo also initially used Huang's (2001) "face and favor" but later statistically subsumed the dimension into the concept of "personal network."

I believe these dimensions of organization-public relationships (i.e., face and favor and personal network) can be generic across different cultures. Huang (2001) conceptualized "face and favor," reflecting Eastern culture, as "the viewpoint of resource exchange … a person can present to others as a gift in the course of social exchange" (p. 271). Face and favor to foster interpersonal relationships would be common in American culture (J. Grunig, L. Grunig, Sriramesh, Lyra, & Huang, 1995). J. Grunig et al. (1995) suggested that public relations, using face and favor, also is practiced in the United States.

According to Jo (2003), a personal network is defined as "an established personal network through blood tie (hyulon), school tie (hakyon), and regional hometown (jiyon)" (p. 27). Later, he subsumed Huang's (2002) four-item construct, "face and favor," into a sub-dimension of "personal network" in his study. The sub-dimension of personal network was called *chae-myun*, which he defined as "showing concern and interest to partners and giving favors to maintain a harmonious relationship" (p. 39). I consider that *chae-myun*, based on Jo's (2003) definition, is also common in Western culture, like gift giving to foster an interpersonal relationship.

Public relations scholars have conceptualized the dimensions of organization-public relationships (Bruning & Ledingham, 1999; Ferguson, 1984; L. Grunig et al., 1992; Huang, 1997, 2001; Hon & J. Grunig, 1999; Jo, 2003; Kim, 2001; Ledingham & Bruning, 1998).[39] Among them, I used the scale developed by Hon and J. Grunig (1999)

---

[39] Public relations scholars have conceptualized the dimensions of organization-public relationships as follows: 1) Ferguson (1984): dynamic vs. static, open vs. closed, mutual satisfaction, distribution of power, mutual understanding, and mutual agreement; 2) L. Grunig, J. Grunig and Ehling (1992): reciprocity, trust, credibility, mutual legitimacy, openness, mutual satisfaction, and mutual understanding; 3) Huang (1997): trust, control mutuality, commitment, and relational satisfaction; 4) Ledingham and Bruning (1998): openness, trust, involvement, investment, and commitment; 5) Bruning and Ledingham (1999): professional relationship, personal relationship, and community relationship; 6) Hon and J. Grunig (1999): trust, control mutuality, commitment, satisfaction, communal relationships, and exchange relationships; 7) Huang (2001): trust, control mutuality, commitment, satisfaction, and face and favor; 8) Kim (2001): trust, commitment, local

since this measure is one of the most widely replicated measure, even in research settings of Eastern countries (Huang, 2002; Han, 2001). For example, Han (2001) used Hon and J. Grunig's scale with a South Korean sample. Babbie (2001) recommended using methods that have been reliable in previous research to ensure reliability of the measurement items in a current survey. Additionally, as shown in Ledingham and Bruning (1998) and Kim (2001), some measures conflicted with theories that I used for this study. For example, they used "involvement" and "reputation" as dimensions of organization-public relationships.

In this study, I found good construct reliability (Coefficient H values higher than .90, across all indicators, throughout all organizations studied) and construct validity (average variance extracted greater than .70, across all indicators, throughout all organizations studied) of organization-public relationship outcomes. This indicates that this study successfully replicated Hon and J. Grunig's (1999) measure of organization-public relationships with a South Korean sample, as Babbie (2001) suggested.

Nonetheless, despite desirable reliability and validity of the measurement items, I am concerned about theoretical assumptions in the hypothesized causal model. I imposed causal relations in the model based on theories developed by Western theorists. For example, I posited the effect of organization-public relationship outcomes on organizational reputation based on Western theorists such as J. Grunig and Hung (2002), L. Grunig, J. Grunig, and Dozier (2002), and Coombs (2000). Thus, I need to consider whether I can also apply such a theoretical link to data analysis with a South Korean sample. Unfortunately, there was minimal research on the link between organization-

---

and community involvement, and reputation; and 9) Jo (2003): trust, control mutuality, commitment, satisfaction, face and favor, and personal networks.

public relationships and organizational reputation in the Korean literature of public

relations except for my previous study (S. K. Yang & S. U. Yang, 2004). S. K. Yang and

S. U. Yang (2004) found a moderating effect of involvement in the effect of organization-

public relationships on organizational reputation. Thus, future studies can study cultural

variations of the link between those two constructs.

Possibility of Model Misspecification

Secondly, although I obtained good fits between data and the hypothesized

structural model across the four organizations studied, the model might have been

misspecified to some degree, since a researcher cannot account for all potential causal

elements in a hypothesized model (Whang & Hancock, 1997). I delimited the model to

the perspective of publics. I used communication behaviors of publics, experience,

familiarity and organization-public relationship types (communal and exchange

relationships) as the antecedents of organization-public relationship outcomes and

organizational reputation. Still, there can be more relevant variables affecting

organization-public relationship outcomes and organizational reputation than the

variables that I identified in this study. This study is only "exploratory" or "suggestive"

in this regard; future studies can search for other relevant precursors of organization-

public relationships and organizational reputation than those used in this study.

Risks in the Validity of the Measure of Experience

Third, the measure of experience might have risks of validity. Experiences of

publics, whether first-hand or second-hand experiences, are embedded in "complex"

social contexts. Therefore, I recognize that a few close-end questions in the survey

questionnaire might have not been able to assess experience of participants in a valid way. I revised the questions on experience in the questionnaire since some of participants in the pretest pointed out unclear wordings and directions in the contingent-type questions. For example, I initially separated advertisements and public relations as the dominant sources of indirect experiences. Some of pretest participants mentioned that they could not possibly differentiate advertisements from public relations; I ended up with merging those two categories in the question. Like this, close-end questions had obvious limitations despite my revisions in questions. Thus, I consider that qualitative methods, such as interviews, can be combined with a survey to assess experience of participants for future studies. Along the same line, qualitative methods can deal better with the degree of familiarity or knowledge that participants have of organizational performance than a few close-end questions in a survey questionnaire.

Unnecessary Cues for the Open-end Measure of Cognitive Representations

Fourth, I recognize that there might have been unnecessary cues to participants for the open-end measure of cognitive representations. In the survey questionnaire, I included the open-end question of cognitive representations after the statements that described organizational activities to measure information processing. For example, "Red Cross in Korea will host the fifth ceremony of Family Reunion between South Koreans and North Koreans… a Korean traditional holiday." Thus, I consider that some participants possibly answered cognitive representations based on "that statement" even though they were aware of any organizational activities of the KNRC.

Babbie (1990) suggested that a researcher needs to avoid placing open-end questions at the beginning or the end of the questionnaire because of low response rates. I found from two pretests and a survey that many participants avoided answering the open-end question when I placed it at the beginning or the end of the questionnaire. Additionally, I noticed that overall response-rates also were highly affected depending on the placement of the open-end question.

Also, Babbie (1990) suggested that a survey questionnaire should combine a set of the questions asking about the same variable to facilitate cohesive responses of participants. I had six sets of questions: 1) communication behaviors of publics, 2) the open-end question on cognitive representations (as the first part of organizational reputation questions), 3) organization-public relationships, 4) organizational reputation (as the second part of organizational reputation questions), 5) experience with organizations, and 6) demographic information. Thus, the impasse was to place two sets of organizational reputation items in the middle of the questionnaire while I made a "gap" between the initial part of measures (i.e., the open-end question of cognitive representations) and the subsequent part of organizational reputation question (i.e., "read back through each of thoughts listed" in the open-end question).

However, I consider that potential bias, caused by unnecessary cues for the cognitive representation measure, might have been minimal in this study. For Sony Korea and the KFA, answers such as "I don't know" or "I am not interested" were common as compared to the other organizations studied. For Samsung Electronics and the KNRC, such answers in the open-end question were rare. The results of data analysis were also supportive of minimal bias. The results, regarding communication behavior variables, for example, indicated that participants reported relatively low values of active communication behaviors for Sony Korea and the KFA and high values for Samsung Electronics and the KNRC.

Low Construct Reliability of Familiarity and Communication Behaviors

Fifth, the results concerning several constructs, which might suffer from comparatively low reliability such as communication behaviors and familiarity, should be viewed as "suggestive." Future studies can overcome low reliability of such constructs using more measurement items. For example, to measure familiarity, I used two measurement items: overall personal familiarity and familiarity with media coverage of the organization. Future studies can include more measurement items based on theoretical reasons as well as open-end items assessing the extent to which each participant has knowledge about organizational performance. Also, future studies can include multiple measurement items on the indicators of information seeking and information processing, which can be developed by different types of the media and other dimensions of communication behaviors such as the direction (one-way or two-way), purpose (symmetrical or asymmetrical), and intimacy of the communications.

Low Construct Validity of Some Latent Variables

Sixth, only the latent variable of organization-public relationship outcomes had a desirable level of construct validity in terms of variance extracted: for all organizations studied, more than 70 percent of the total variance was extracted for organization-public relationship outcomes. Ideally, construct validity for the variance extracted should exceed .50. However, the sign and magnitude of the loadings for the latent variables generally was moderate: Most of the loadings were greater than .5 with cohesive sign of loadings between indicators, except for the loading for the net positive representations measuring organizational reputation. In the case of net positive representations, the variable measured individual memory-based representations (the number of positive representations less the number of negative representations in a list of thoughts). Thus, this variable might have not been strongly associated with other variables assessed by the participants directly.

One-way Evaluations of Organization-public Relationships

Seventh, although I clearly delimited the hypothesized causal model to the perspective of publics, a desirable model of organization-public relationships should reflect evaluations of both relational parities: an organization and its publics (Broom et al., 2000; Hon & J. Grunig, 1999). Future studies can assess organization-public relationships from both sides of an organization and its publics using systematic research designs, such as a coorientation approach (Broom et al., 2000) and a gap analysis (Hon & J. Grunig, 1999).

Limited Generalizability of the Study Because of Nonprobability Sampling

Finally, the use of nonprobability sampling may limit generalizability of this study. To mitigate sampling bias, caused by nonprobability sampling, I used quota sampling. The results of quota sampling indicated that the quota of my choice was successfully filled for the sample. Besides, the purpose of this study was to analyze theory-driven causal links, not to report descriptive results of the studied constructs to the sample. Judd, Smith, and Kidder (1991) explained the logic of sampling:

> Some research aims at testing theoretically hypothesized relationships, with no
>
> specific population or setting as the focus of interest ... In such cases, the ability
>
> to extend the research results from the sample to some population is of no interest.
>
> Instead, the applicability of the *theory itself* outside the research context is the
>
> central question... (p. 130)

Possible Limited Application of the Proposed Model for Activist Publics

In this study, I found a positive effect of active communication behaviors of publics on the quality of organization-public relationship outcomes for all organizations studied. This finding might not apply in the case of activist publics. Activist publics engage in active communication behaviors and often maintain negative beliefs toward an organization. According to Fishbein and Ajzen (1976), if beliefs (about attitudinal stimuli) link the attitudinal object to negative attributes, repetition of attitudinal stimuli causes increased disliking of that stimuli. Thus, it could be possible for activist publics to evaluate relationships with an organization more negatively as they engage in increased active communication behaviors with the organization.

This study used the situational theory broadly for organization-public relationships and organizational reputation. For example, problem recognition measured how frequently research participants stop to think about the organizations studied so as to engage in active communication behaviors. If problem recognition were measured about a specific situation in which a negative problem occurred, such as a bribery scandal of an organization, there could be activist publics whose increased active communication behaviors could result in increased negative relationships with an organization.

However, even for activist publics, if two-way (rather than one-way) and symmetrical (rather than asymmetrical) communication behaviors increase with an organization about which they have negative beliefs, positive relationship outcomes could result from active communication behaviors. Following J. Grunig's situational theory of publics, this study used information seeking and processing as the dimensions of communication behaviors. Future research could include other dimensions of communication behaviors, such as the direction of communication behaviors (whether one-way or two-way), the purpose of communication behaviors (whether symmetrical or asymmetrical), and the intimacy of the communication behaviors. By doing so, future research can test whether increased active communication behavior causes more positive relationship outcomes and which dimensions of communication behaviors also are most effective for activist publics.

Possible Influences of the Media in a Research Context and Participants' Educational Level on Organizational Reputation

This study used media influence as a dimension of familiarity (familiarity with the media coverage of an organization) and a dimension of organizational reputation (perceived media reputation). Some scholars (e.g., Deephouse, 2000; Rindova & Kotha, 2001) and practitioners suggest a media-based model of reputation in which the actual frequency and valence of media coverage directly affect reputation formation. Thus, a possible counter argument could be that a media-based model of reputation might fit better in a country where media have greater effects. Hypothetically, reputation as measured in this study might have been minimally affected if the media in South Korea have less effect than the media in another country.

In contrast, I have argued that because of selective exposure and perceptions of media coverage, publics are more affected by individual interactions with an organization that shape perceptions of media coverage than by the actual content of media coverage. Fombrun and Shanley (1990) investigated a link between corporate reputation and the visibility of 292 corporations from *Fortune*'s 1985 study. They found a negative link between the frequency of media coverage and corporate reputation, which contradicts a media-based model of reputation. Future research could investigate this issue by comparing competing models regarding the effects of media in reputation formation. Also, a comparative study could be useful, in which different effects of media in reputation formation are measured and compared across different research contexts.

In addition, the educational level of research participants could affect some variables examined in this study. For example, in previous research, Yang (2004) found that the relation between the educational level of research participants and reputations of organizations studied was negative for all organizations studied, although not all of the negative relations were statistically significant.

In this study, because I did not find relevant theories explaining the link between the education level of publics and organizational reputation, I did not include participants' educational level in the proposed model. Future research could examine this issue by 1) adding the education level of participants to the model—for example, correlations between problem recognition and educational level—and by 2) splitting the sample by the educational level and conducting a multi-sample analysis. I would expect that the first approach would be more relevant than the second because I believe that the education level of publics would affect the mean levels of some variables, rather than education having a moderating effect in the relationships between all variables of interest in the proposed model.

Additional Suggestions for Future Studies

In addition to suggestions for future studies that I have described above, I would like to suggest the following aspects as well:

1. Using organization-public relationship and organizational reputation as mediating variables in specific research context.

2. In-depth investigation of reputation formation.

3. Nonrecursive links between organization-public relationships and organizational reputation.

4. Moderating effects of segmented publics (by communication behaviors) on the link between organization-public relationships and organizational reputation.

First, this study found that the links between organization-public relationships and organizational reputation can be useful for future public relations research, in particular as mediating variables. For example, future studies can investigate the effect of ethical behaviors of an organization or social responsibility, on supportive behaviors of publics toward the organization, mediating by the quality of organization-public relationships and organizational reputation.

Secondly, future studies can investigate reputation formation in more in-depth ways than this study. For example, one can study how organizational reputation has been created through multiple flows of social networks such as interpersonal relations and diverse use of the media (e.g., Web blog or discussion board on the Internet). Another example can be comparisons of the effects of organizational communication activities—such as public relations, advertisements, and marketing communications—on organizational reputation, in particular after organizational crises.

Finally, future studies can examine "nonrecursive" links between organization-public relationships and organizational reputation or "moderating effects" of segmented publics on the link between organization-public relationships and organizational reputation. Although I posited the causal effect of organization-public relationships on organizational reputation, I consider: 1) such causal effects can be reversed depending on characteristics of publics such as involvement and knowledge; and 2) the effect of organization-public relationships on organizational reputation can markedly vary depending on communication behaviors of publics. Earlier, I found from a qualitative research about a case study of a South Korean activist organization (Yang & Mallabo, 2003):

1. When participants were substantially involved in and had knowledge about the case organization, participants tended to hold a reputation of the case organization based on their individual evaluations of organization-public relationships.

2. When participants were not involved and had a little or no knowledge about the case organization, participants tended to speculate the quality of organization-public relationships based on (superficial) reputation, in particular reputation shaped by the media coverage or hearsay from others.

Thus, it will be interesting to conduct a qualitative investigation of the link between organization-public relationships and organizational reputation. Also, future research can posit nonrecursive links between the two constructs ("Organization-public relationships ↔ Organizational reputation") in structural equation modeling and compare the effect sizes of path coefficients. Another possible approach is to design a longitudinal study in which the concepts of relationships and reputation are measured over time (as a panel study) so that the causal effects of relationships and reputation can be compared.

Additionally, with regard to moderating effects of communication behaviors on the link between organization-public relationships and organizational reputation, S. K. Yang and S. U. Yang (2004) found that the effect of organization-public relationship outcomes on organizational reputation varied significantly depending on involvement of participants in the five South Korean-based organizations studied: The more involved, the stronger the effect of organization-public relationship outcomes on organizational reputation. Future research can take a step further by investigating such research problems and contribute to a theoretical body of knowledge in public relations.

References

Aldrich, H. E. (1975). An organization-environment perspective on cooperation and conflict between organizations in the manpower training system. In A. R. Negandhi (Ed.), *Interorganizational Theory* (pp. 49-70). Kent, OH: Kent State University Press.

Aldrich, H. E. (1976). Resource dependence and interorganizational relations: Local employment service sector organizations. *Administration and Society, 7*, 419-453.

Aldrich, H. E. (1979). *Organizations and environments*. Englewood Cliffs, NJ: Prentice-Hall.

Anderson, D. S. (1992). Identifying and responding to activist publics: A case study. *Journal of Public Relations Research, 4*, 151-165.

Anderson, E., & Narus, J. A. (1990). A model of distributor firm and manufacturer firm working partnership. *Journal of Marketing, 54*(1), 42-58.

Anderson, J. R. (1983). *The architecture of cognition*. Cambridge, MA: Harvard University Press.

Anderson, J. R. (1996). ACT: A simple theory of complex cognition. *American Psychologist, 51*, 355-365.

Anderson, J. R. (2000). *Cognitive psychology and its implications* (5th ed.). New York: Worth.

Anderson, J. R., & Lebiere, C. (1998). *The atomic components of thought*. Mahwah, NJ: Lawrence Erlbaum Associates.

Anderson, P. A. (1993). Cognitive schemata in personal relationships. In S. W. Duck (Ed.), *Individuals in relationships* (pp. 1-29). Newbury Park, CA: Sage.

Arbuckle, J. L. (1996). Full information estimation in the presence of incomplete dat. In G. A. Marcoulides & R. E. Schumacker (Eds.), *Advanced structural equation modeling: Issues and techniques* (pp. 243-277). Mahwah, NJ: Lawrence Erlbaum Associates.

Ashcraft, M. H. (2002). *Cognition* (3rd ed.). Upper Saddle River, NJ: Prentice Hall.

Babbie, E. R. (1990). *Survey research method* (2nd ed.). Belmont, CA: Wadsworth Company.

Babbie, E. R. (2001). *The practice of social research* (9th ed.). Belmont, CA: Wadsworth Company.

Baldwin, M. W. (1997). Relational schemas as a source of if-then self-inference procedures. *Review of General Psychology, 1*, 326-335.

Baldwin, M. W. (1999). Relational schemas and cognition in close relationships. *Journal of Social and Personal Relationships, 12*, 547-552.

Barlett, J. (1980). *Familiar quotations* (15th ed.). London: Macmillan.

Baxter, L. A., & Dindia, K. (1990). Marital partners' perceptions of martial maintenance strategies. *Journal of Social and Personal Relationships, 7*, 187-208.

Baxter, L. A. (1994). A dialogic approach to relationship maintenance. In D. J. Canary & L. Stafford (Eds.), *Communication and relational maintenance* (pp. 233-254). San Diego: Academic Press.

Becerra, M. (1998*). Nature, antecedents, and consequence of trust within organizations: A multilevel analysis within multinational corporation.* Unpublished doctoral dissertation, University of Maryland, College Park.

Bell, R. A., Daly, J. A., & Gonzalez, C. (1987). Affinity-maintenance in marriage and its relationship to women's marital satisfaction. *Journal of Marriage and the Family, 49*, 445-454.

Benham, G. (1948). *Benham's book of quotations, proverbs and household words* (Revised ed.). London: Harrap.

Bentler, P. M. (1985). *Theory and implementation of EQS, a structural equation program*. Los Angeles, BMDP Statistical Software.

Bergen, J. (2001). Reputation's return on investment. In A. Jolly (Ed.), *Managing corporate reputations* (pp. 20-26). London: Kogan Page.

Biz360 (n.d.). Success Stories: Sterling commerce. Retrieved April 6, 2005, from www.biz360.com.

Blumer, H. (1946). Elementary collective groupings. In A. M. Lee (Ed.), *New outlines of the principles of sociology* (pp. 178-198). New York: Barnes & Noble.

Blumer, H. (1948). Public opinion and public opinion polling. *American Sociological Review, 13*, 542-554.

Bochner, A. P., Kaminsk, E. P., & Fitzpatrick, M. A. (1977). The conceptual domain of interpersonal communication behavior. *Human Communication Research, 3*, 291-302.

Botan, C. (1993). A human nature approach to image and ethics in international public relations. *Journal of Public Relations Research, 5*, 71-81.

Bromley, D. (2002). Comparing corporate reputations: League tables, quotients, benchmarks, or case studies? *Corporate Reputation Review, 5*(1), 35-50.

Bromley, D. B. (1993). *Reputation, image, and impression management.* Chichester, UK: John Wiley & Sons.

Bromley, D. B. (2000). Psychological aspects of corporate identity, image, and reputation. *Corporate Reputation Review, 3*, 240-252.

Broom, G. M, Casey, S., & Ritchey, J. (2000). Concepts and theory of organization-public relationships. In J. A. Ledingham and S. D. Bruning (Eds.), *Public relations as relationship management: A relational approach to the study and practice of public relations* (pp. 3-22). Mahwah, NJ: Lawrence Erlbaum Associates.

Broom, G. M., & Dozier, D. M. (1990). *Using research in public relations: Applications to program management.* Englewood Cliffs, NJ: Prentice Hall.

Bruning, S. D., & Ledingham, J. A. (1999). Relationships between organizations and publics: Development of a multi-dimensional organization-public relationship scale. *Public Relations Review, 25*, 157-170.

Bruning, S. D., & Ledingham, J. A. (1999). Relationships between organizations and publics: Development of a multi-dimensional organization-public relationship scale. *Public Relations Review, 25*, 157-170.

Bruning, S. D., & Ledingham, J. A. (2000). Perceptions of relationships and evaluations of satisfaction: An exploration of interaction. *Public Relations Review, 26*, 85-95.

Burgoon, J., & Hale, J. (1984). The fundamental topoi of relational communication. *Communication Monograph, 51*, 193-214.

Byrne, B. M. (2001). Structural equation modeling with AMOS: Basic concepts, applications, and programming. Mahwah, NJ: Lawrence Erlbaum Associates.

Byrne, B. M. (1994). *Structural equation modeling with EQS and EQS/Windows: Basic concepts, applications, and programming.* Thousand Oaks, CA: Sage.

Campbell, D. T., & Stanley, J. C. (1963). *Experimental and quasi-experimental designs for research.* Skokie, IL: Rand-McNally.

Canary, D. J., & Cupach, W. R. (1988). Relational and episodic characteristics associated with conflict tactics. *Journal of Social and Personal Relationships, 5*, 305-325.

Canary, D. J., & Sptizberg, B. H. (1989). A model of the perceived competence of conflict strategies. *Human Communication Research, 15*, 630-649.

Canary, D. J., & Stafford, L. (1992). Relational maintenance strategies and equity in marriage. *Communication Monographs, 59*, 243-267.

Carfi, C. (2004, June 23). Reputation management: Many thoughts on a thorny subject. Retrieved April 6, 2005, from http://www.alwayson-network.com/comments.phd?id=4663_0_5_0_C.

Capelin, J. (1999, November 15). Search for reputation management standard is a noble one, but kept figures in perspective. *PR Week.*

Cappella, J. N., & Jamieson, K. H. (1997). *Spiral of cynicism.* New York: Oxford University Press.

Carlston, D. E., & Smith, E. R. (1996). Principles of mental representation. In E. T. Higgins and A. W. Kruglanski (Eds.), *Social psychology: Handbook of basic principles* (pp. 184-210). New York: The Guilford Press.

Carter, R. F. (1979). A journalistic cybernetic. In K. Krippendorff (Ed.), *Communication and control in society* (pp. 475-487). New York: Gordon and Breach Science.

Caruana, A., & Chircop, S. (2000). Measuring corporate reputation: A case example. *Corporate Reputation Review, 3,* 43-57.

Cheaney, G., & Christensen, L. T. (2001). Public relations as contested terrain: A critical response. In R. Heath (Ed.), *Hand book of Public Relations* (167-182). Thousand Oaks, CA: Sage.

Clark, M. S. (1984). Record keeping in two types of relationships. *Journal of Personality and Social Psychology, 47*, 549–557.

Clark, M. S. (1986). Evidence for the effectiveness of manipulations of communal and exchange relationships. *Personality and Social Psychology Bulletin, 12*, 414–425.

Clark, M. S., & Mills, J. (1979). Interpersonal attraction in exchange and communal relationships. *Journal of Personality and Social Psychology, 37*, 12-24.

Clark, M. S., & Mills, J. (1993). The difference between communal and exchange relationships: What it is and is not. *Personality and Social Psychology Bulletin, 19*, 684-691.

Clark, M. S., & Taraban, C. B. (1991). Reactions to and willingness to express emotion in two types of relationships. *Journal of Experimental Social Psychology, 27*, 324–336.

Clark, M. S., & Waddell, B. (1985). Perceptions of exploitation in communal and exchange relationships. *Journal of Social and Personal Relationships, 2*, 403–418.

Clark, M. S., Mills, J., & Corcoran, D. (1989). Keeping track of needs and inputs of friends and strangers. *Personality and Social Psychology Bulletin, 15*, 533–542.

Clark, M. S., Ouellette, R., Powell, M., & Milberg, S. (1987). Recipient's mood, relationship type, and helping. *Journal of Personality and Social Psychology, 53*, 94–103.

Clark, M., Mills, J., Powell, M. (1986). Keeping track of needs in communal and exchange relationships. *Journal of Personality and Social Psychology, 51*, 333–338.

Clarkson, M. B. E. (1991). Defining, evaluating, and managing corporate social performance: The stakeholder management model. In L. E. Preston (Ed.), *Research in corporate social performance and policy*, vol. 12 (pp. 331-358). Greenwich, CT: JAI press.

Cohen, J. (1988). Statistical power analysis for the behavioral science (2nd ed.). New York: Academic Press.

Collins, A. M., & Quillian, M. R. (1969). Retrieval time from semantic memory. *Journal of Verbal Learning and Verbal Behavior, 8*, 240-247.

Collins, A., & Loftus, E. F. (1975). A spreading activation theory of semantic memory. *Psychological Review, 82*, 407-428.

Collins, N. L., & Read, N. J. (1990). Adult attachment, working models, and relationship quality in dating couples. *Journal of Personality and Social Psychology, 58*, 644-663.

Conley, T. D., & Collins, B. E. (2002). Gender, relationship status, and stereotyping about sexual risk. *Personality and Social Psychology Bulletin, 28*(11), 1483-1494.

Cook, K. S. (1977). Exchange and power in networks of interorganizational relations. *The Sociological Quarterly, 18*, 62-82.

Cook, K. S., & Emerson, R. M. (1978). Power, equity and commitment in exchange networks. *American Sociological Review, 43*, 721-739.

Coombs, W. T. (2000). Crisis management: Advantages of a relational perspective. In J. A. Ledingham and S. D. Bruning (Eds.), *Public relations as relationship management: A relational approach to the study and practice of public relations* (pp. 73-94). Mahwah, NJ: Lawrence Erlbaum Associates.

Coombs, W. T., & Holladay, S. J. (2001). An extended examination of the crisis situations: A fusion of relational management and symbolic approaches. *Journal of Public Relations Research, 13*, 321-340.

Cutlip, S. M., Center, A. H., & Broom, G. M. (2000). *Effective public relations* (8th ed.). Upper Saddle River, NJ: Prentice-Hall.

Daft, R. L. (2001). *Essentials of organization theory & design* (2nd ed.). Cincinnati, OH: South-Western College Publishing.

Deephouse, D. (2002). The term "Reputation Management": Users, uses and the trademark tradeoff. *Corporate Reputation Review, 5*, 9-18.

Deephouse, D. L. (2000). Media reputation as a strategic resource: An integration of mass communication and resource-based theories. *Journal of Management, 26*, 1091-1112.

Denzin, N. K., & Lincoln, Y. S. (Eds.). (1998). *The landscape of qualitative research: Theories and issues*. Thousand Oaks, CA: Sage. [Introduction: Entering the field of Qualitative Research]

Dewey, J. (1938). *Logic: The theory of inquiry*. New York: Henry Holt.

Dowling, G. R. (2001). *Creating corporate reputations: Identity, images, and performance*. Oxford, New York: Oxford University Press.

Dozier, D. M., & Lauzen, M. M. (2000). Liberating the intellectual domain from the developing theory for public relations. *Journal of Public Relations Research, 14*(2), 103-126.

Dozier, D. M., Grunig, L. A., & Grunig, J. E. (1995). *Manager's guide to excellence in public relations and communication management*. Mahwah, NJ: Lawrence Erlbaum Associates.

Ferguson, M. A. (1984, August). *Building theory in public relations: Interorganizational relationships as a public relations paradigm*. Paper presented to the Association for Education In Journalism and Mass Communication, Gainesville, FL.

Fishbein, M., & Ajzen, I. (1975). *Beliefs, attitudes, intention, and behavior: An introduction to theory and research*. Reading, MA: Addison-Wesley.

Fombrun, C. J. (1996). *Reputation: Realizing value from the corporate image.* Boston: Harvard Business School Press.

Fombrun, C. J., & Foss, C. B. (2001a, May). The reputation quotient, part 3: Five principles of reputation management. Retrieved August 7, 2004, from http://www.thegauge.com/SearchFolder/OldGauges/Vol14No3/fombrunfossreput ation3.html.

Fombrun, C. J., & Foss, C. B. (2001b, May). The reputation quotient, part 1: Developing a reputation quotient. Retrieved August 7, 2004, from http://www.thegauge.com/SearchFolder/OldGauges/Vol14No3/fombrunfossreput ation1.html.

Fombrun, C. J., & Gardberg, N. (2000). Who's tops in corporate reputation? *Corporate Reputation Review, 3*, 13-17.

Fombrun, C. J., & Rindova, V. (1996). Who's tops and who decides? The social construction of corporate reputations. New York University, Stern School of Business, Working Paper.

Fombrun, C. J., & Rindova, V. P. (2000). The road to transparency: Reputation management at Royal Dutch Shell. In M. Schultz, M. J. Hatch, & M. H. Larsen (Eds.), *The expressive organization: Linking identity, reputation, and the corporate brand* (pp.77-96). Oxford, England: Oxford University Press.

Fombrun, C. J., & Van Riel, C. B. M. (1997). The reputational landscape. *Corporate Reputation Review, 1*, 5-13.

Fombrun, C. J., & Van Riel, C. B. M. (2003). Fame & fortune: How successful companies build winning reputations. Upper Saddle River, NJ: Prentice Hall.

Fombrun, C. J., Gardberg, N. A., & Sever, J. M. (2000). The reputation quotient sm: A multi-stakeholder measure of corporate reputation. *The Journal of Brand Management, 7*(4), 241-255.

Fombrun, C., & Shanley, M. (1990). What's in a name? Reputation building and corporate strategy. *Academy of Management Journal, 33*(2), 233-258.

Fornell, C., & Larcker, D. F. (1981). Evaluating Structural Equation Models with Unobservable Variables and Measurement Error. *Journal of Marketing Research, 18*, 39-50.

Fowler, F. J. (2002). Survey research methods (3rd ed.). Thousand Oaks, CA: Sage.

Freeman, R. E. (1984). *Strategic management: A stakeholder approach.* Boston: Pitman.

Fryxell, G.E. and Wang, J. (1994). The Fortune corporate reputation index: Reputation for what? *Journal of Management, 20*, 1-14.

Gelso, C. J., & Carter, J. A. (1994). Components of the psychotherapy relationship: Their interaction and unfolding during treatment. *Journal of Counseling Psychology*, 41, 296-306.

Goffman, E. (1961). Asylums: Essays on the social situation of mental patients and other inmates. Garden City, NY: Anchor Books.

Gordon, C. G., & Kelly, K. S. (1999). Public relations expertise and organizational effectiveness: A study of US hospitals. *Journal of Public Relations Research, 11*, 143-165.

Griffin, G. (2002). *Reputation management*. Oxford: Capstone Publishing.

Grunig, J. E. (1976a). Communication behaviors occurring in decision and nondecision situations. *Journalism Quarterly, 53*, 252-263.

Grunig, J. E. (1976b). Organizations and public relations: Testing a communication theory. *Journalism Monographs, 46*.

Grunig, J. E. (1978). Defining publics in public relations: The case of a suburban hospital. *Journalism Quarterly*, 55, 109-118.

Grunig, J. E. (1979). A new measure of public opinions on corporate social responsibility. *Academy of Management Journal, 22*, 738-764.

Grunig, J. E. (1983a). Communication behaviors and attitudes of environmental publics: two studies. *Journalism Monographs, 81*.

Grunig, J. E. (1983b). Washington reporter publics of corporate public affairs programs. *Journalism Quarterly, 60*, 603-615.

Grunig, J. E. (1989a). Sierra club study shows who become activists. *Public Relations Review, 15*(3), 3-24.

Grunig, J. E. (1989b). Symmetrical presuppositions as a framework for public relations theory. In C. Botan & V. T. Hazelton (Eds.), *Public relations theory* (pp. 17-44). Hillsdale, NJ: Lawrence Erlbaum Associates.

Grunig, J. E. (1993). Image and substance: From symbolic to behavioral relationships. *Public Relations Review*, 91(2), 121-139.

Grunig, J. E. (1997). A situational theory of publics: Conceptual history, recent challenges, and new research. In D. Moss, T. McManus, & D. Vercic (Eds.),

Public relations research: International Perspectives (pp. 5-47). London: International Thompson Business Press.

Grunig, J. E. (2000). Collectivism, collaboration, and societal corporatism. *Journal of Public Relations Research, 12*, 23-48.

Grunig, J. E. (2001). Two-way symmetrical public relations: Past, present, and future. In R. L. Heath (Ed.), *Handbook of public relations* (pp. 11-32). Thousand Oaks, CA: Sage.

Grunig, J. E. (2002). Qualitative methods for assessing relationships between organizations and publics. Gainesville, FL: The Institute for Public Relations.

Grunig, J. E. (Ed.). (1992). *Excellence in public relations and communication management.* Hillsdale, NJ: Lawrence Erlbaum Associates.

Grunig, J. E., & Childer (a.k.a. Hon), L. (1988). *Reconstruction of a situational theory of communication: Internal and external concepts as identifiers of publics for AIDS.* Paper presented at the meeting of the Association for Education in Journalism & Mass Communication, Portland, OR.

Grunig, J. E., & Disbrow, J. B. (1977). Developing a probabilistic model for communication decision making. *Communication Research, 4*, 145-168.

Grunig, J. E., & Grunig, L. A. (1989). Toward a theory of the public relations behavior of organizations: Review of a program of research. In J. E. Grunig & L. A. Grunig (Eds.), *Public relations research annual* (Vol. 1, pp. 27-63). Hillsdale, NJ: Lawrence Erlbaum Associates.

Grunig, J. E., & Grunig, L. A. (1992). Models of public relations and communication. In J. E. Grunig (Ed.), *Excellence in public relations and communication management* (pp. 285-326). Hillsdale, NJ: Lawrence Erlbaum Associates.

Grunig, J. E., & Grunig, L. A. (1996, May). *Implications of symmetry for a theory of ethics in public relations.* Paper presented to the International Communication Association, Chicago.

Grunig, J. E., & Grunig, L. A. (2000). Public relations in strategic management and strategic management of public relations: Theory and research from the IABC excellence project. *Journalism Studies, 1*, 303-321.

Grunig, J. E., & Grunig, L. A. (2001). *Guidelines for formative and evaluative research in public affairs: A report for the Department of Energy Office of Science.* Washington, DC: U. S. Department of Energy.

Grunig, J. E., & Huang, Y. H. (2000). From organizational effectiveness to relationship indicators: Antecedents of relationships, public relations strategies, and relationship outcomes. In J. A. Ledingham and S. D. Bruning (Eds.), *Public relations as relationship management: A relational approach to the study and practice of public relations* (pp. 23-53). Mahwah, NJ: Lawrence Erlbaum Associates.

Grunig, J. E., & Hung, C. F. (2002, March). *The effect of relationships on reputation and reputation on relationships: A cognitive, behavioral study.* Paper presented at the PRSA Educator's Academy 5th Annual International, Interdisciplinary Public Relations Research Conference, Miami, Florida.

Grunig, J. E., & Hunt, T. (1984). *Managing public relations.* New York: Holt, Rinehart and Winston.

Grunig, J. E., & Repper, F. C. (1992). Strategic management, publics, and issues. In J. E. Grunig (Ed.), *Excellence in public relations and communication management* (pp. 117-158). Hillsdale, NJ: Lawrence Erlbaum Associates.

Grunig, J. E., & White, J. (1992). The effect of worldviews on public relations theory and practice. In J. E. Grunig (Ed.), *Excellence in public relations and communication management* (pp. 31-64). Hillsdale, NJ: Lawrence Erlbaum Associates.

Grunig, J. E., Grunig, L. A., Sriramesh, K., Lyra, A., & Huang, Y. H. (1995). Models of public relations in an international setting. *Journal of Public Relations Research, 7*, 163-186.

Grunig, J. E., Ramsey, S., & Schneider, L. A. (a.k.a., L. Grunig) (1985). An axiomatic theory of cognition and writing. *Journal of Technical Writing and Communication, 15*, 95-130.

Grunig, L. A. (1992). Activism: How it limits the effectiveness of organizations and how excellent public relations departments respond. In J. E. Grunig (Ed.), *Excellence in public relations and communication management* (pp. 503-530). Hillsdale, NJ: Lawrence Erlbaum Associates.

Grunig, L. A. (1992). Matching public relations research to the problem: Conducting a special focus group. *Journal of Public Relations Research 4*(1), 21-43.

Grunig, L. A. (1993). Image and symbolic leadership: Using focus group research to bridge the gap. *Journal of Public Relations Research 5*(3), 95-125.

Grunig, L. A., Grunig, J. E., & Dozier, D. M. (2002). Excellent public relations and effective organizations: A study of communication management in three countries. Mahwah, NJ: Lawrence Erlbaum Associates.

Grunig, L. A., Grunig, J. E., & Ehling, W. P. (1992). What is an effective organization? In J. E. Grunig (Ed.), *Excellence in public relations and communication management* (pp. 65-90). Hillsdale, NJ: Lawrence Erlbaum Associates.

Guba, E. G. (1981). Criteria for assessing the trustworthiness of naturalistic inquiries. *Educational Communication and Technology, 29*(2), 75-91.

Hagan, L. M. (2003). *Public relations, relationships, and reputation: A case study of a safety recall in the U.S. Automotive industry.* Unpublished doctoral dissertation, University of Maryland, College Park.

Hall, R. (1992). The strategic analysis of intangible resources. *Strategic Management Journal, 13,* 135-144.

Hallahan, K. (2000). Inactive publics: The forgotten publics in public relations. *Public Relations Review, 26(4),* 499-515.

Hamilton, D. L. (1981). Cognitive representations of persons. In E. T. Higgins, C. P. Herman, & M. P. Zanna (Eds.), *Social cognition: The Ontario symposium* (Vol. 1, pp. 135-160). Hillsdale, NJ: Erlbaum.

Hamilton, D. L., Katz, L. B., & Leirer, V. (1980). Organizational processes in impression formation. In R. Hastie et al. (Eds.), *Person memory.* Hillsdale, NJ: Erlbaum.

Han, J. H. (2001). *A study on the indicators of organization-public relationships.* Paper presented at the 2001 Convention of Korean Academic Association for Public Relations, South Korea.

Hancock, G. R., & Mueller, R. M. (2004). *Structural equation modeling* [lecture note for EDMS 722: Structural Equation Modeling]. University of Maryland, College Park.

Hancock, G. R., & Mueller, R. M. (2001). Rethinking construct reliability within latent variable systems. In R. Cudeck, S. du Toit, & D. Sörbom (Eds.), *Structural equation modeling: Present and future—A Festschrift in honor of Karl Jöreskog* (pp. 195-216). Lincolnwood, IL: Scientific Software International.

Heath, R. L. (Ed.) (2001). *Handbook of public relations.* Thousand Oaks, CA: Sage.

Heath, R. L., Bradshaw, J., & Lee, J. (2002). Community relationship building: Local leadership in the risk communication infrastructure. *Journal of Public Relations Research, 14,* 317-353.

Hecht, M. L. (1978). The conceptualization and measurement of interpersonal communication satisfaction. *Human Communication Research, 4,* 253-264.

Hendrick, S. S. (1988). A generic measure of relational satisfaction. *Journal of Marriage and the Family, 50,* 93-98.

Holsti, O. R. (1969). *Content analysis for the social sciences and humanities.* Reading, MA: Addison-Wesley.

Hon, L. C. (1997). What have you done for me lately? Exploring effectiveness in public relations. *Journal of Public Relations Research, 9*(1), 1-30.

Hon, L. C. (1998). Demonstrating effectiveness in PR: Goals, objectives and evaluation. *Journal of Public Relations Research, 10,* 103-135.

Hon, L. C., & Grunig, J. E. (1999). *Guidelines for measuring relationships in public relations.* Gainesville, FL: The Institute for Public Relations, Commission on PR Measurement and Evaluation.

Hu, L., & Bentler, P. M. (1999). Cutoff criteria for fit indexes in covariance structure analysis: Conventional criteria versus new alternatives. *Structural Equation Modeling: A Multidisciplinary Journal, 6*(1), 1-55.

Huang, Y. H. (1997). *Public relations strategies, relational outcomes, and conflict management strategies.* Unpublished doctoral dissertation, University of Maryland, College Park.

Huang, Y. H. (1998). *Public relations strategies and organization-public relationships.* Paper presented at the annual conference of the Association for Education in Journalism and Mass Communication, Baltimore.

Huang, Y. H. (2001). OPRA: A cross-cultural, multiple-item scale for measuring organization-public relationships. *Journal of Public Relations Research, 13,* 61-90.

Hung, C. F. (2002). *The interplays of relationship types, relationship cultivation, and relationship outcomes: How multinational and Taiwanese companies public relations and organization-public relationship management in China.* Unpublished doctoral dissertation, University of Maryland, College Park.

Hutton, J. G. (1999). The definition, dimensions, and domain of public relations. *Public Relations Review, 25,* 199-214.

Hutton, J. G., Goodman, M. B., Alexander, J. B., & Genest, C. M. (2001). Reputation management: The new face of corporate public relations? *Public Relations Review, 27,* 247-261.

Jackson, P. (2000, November 17). *Reputation: Assessing nonfinancial measures.* Presentation at the Conference on Corporate Communication, University of Notre Dame, South Ben, IN.

Jeffries-Fox Associates (2000a, March 3). *Toward a shared understanding of corporate reputation and related concepts: Phase I: Content analysis.* Basking Ridge, NJ: Report Prepared for the Council of Public Relations Firms.

Jeffries-Fox Associates (2000b, March 24). *Toward a shared understanding of corporate reputation and related concepts: Phase II: Measurement Systems Analysis.* Basking Ridge, NJ: Report Prepared for the Council of Public Relations Firms.

Jo, S. (2003, August 4). *Measurement of organization-public relationships: validation of measurement using a manufacturer relationship.* A paper submitted to the Institute for Public Relations.

Jo, S., & Kim, Y. (2003). The effect of web characteristics on relationship building. *Journal of Public Relations Research, 15*, 199-224.

Johnson, B. T., & Eagly, A. H. (1989). Effects of involvement on persuasion: A meta-analysis. *Psychological Bulletin, 106*(2), 290-314.

Judd, C. M., Smith, E. R., & Kidder, L. H. (1991). *Research methods in social relations.* (6th ed.). New York: Harcourt Brace Jovanovich College.

Kaid, L. L., & Wadsworth, A. J. (1989). Content analysis. In P. Emmert, & L. L. barker (Eds.), *Measurement of communication behavior* (pp.197-217). New York: Longman.

Karlberg, M. (1996). Remembering the public in public relations research: From theoretical to operational symmetry. *Journal of Public Relations Research, 8*(4), 263-278.

Keller, K. L. (1993). Conceptualizing, measuring, and managing customer-based brand equity. *Journal of Marketing, 57*, 1-22.

Kelley, H. H. (1979). *Personal relationships: Their structure and processes.* Hillsdale, NJ: Lawrence Erlbaum.

Kelley, H. H., & Thibaut, J. W. (1978). *Interpersonal relations.* New York: Wiley.

Kim, Y. (2000). Measuring the bottom-line impact of corporate public relations. *Journalism and Mass Communication Quarterly, 77*, 273-291.

Kim, Y. (2001). Measuring the economic value of public relations. *Journal of Public Relations Research, 13*, 3-26.

Kim, Y., & Hon, L. (1998). Craft and professional models of public relations and their relation to job satisfaction among Korean public relations practitioners. *Journal of Public Relations Research, 10,* 155-175.

Kline, R. B. (1998). *Principles and practice of structural equation modeling.* New York: The Guilford Press.

Knox, S., Maklan, S., & Thompson, K. E. (2000). Building the unique organization value proposition. In M. Schultz, M. J. Hatch, & M. H. Larsen (Eds.), *The expressive organization: Linking identity, reputation, and the corporate brand* (pp.115-1377). Oxford, England: Oxford University Press.

Kruckeberg, D., & Starck, K. (1988). *Public relations and community: A reconstructed theory.* New York: Praeger.

Kruglanski, A. W. (1975). The human subject in the psychology experiment: Fact and artifact. In L. Berkowitz (Ed.). *Advances in experimental social psychology,* Vol. 8. New York: Academic Press.

Kruglanski, A. W. (1989). *Lay epistemics and human knowledge: Cognitive and motivational bases.* New York: Plenum Press.

Krugman, H. E. (1965). The impact of television advertising: learning without involvement. *Public Opinion Quarterly, 29,* 349-356.

Lattimore, D., Baskin, O., Heiman, S. T., Toth, E. L., & Van Leuven, J. K. (2004). Public relations: The profession and the practice (4th ed.). Boston: McGraw Hill.

L'Etang, J., & Pieczka, M. (1996). *Critical perspectives in public relations.* London: International Thomson Publishing Company.

Larzelere, R. E., & Huston, T. L. (1980). The dyadic trust scale: Toward understanding interpersonal trust in close relationships. *Journal of Marriage and the Family, 42,* 595-604.

Ledingham, J. A. (2001). Government-community relationships: Extending the relational theory of public relations. *Public Relations Review, 27,* 285-295.

Ledingham, J. A., & Bruning, S. D. (1998). Relationship management in public relations: Dimensions of an organization-public relationship. *Public Relations Review, 24,* 55-65.

Ledingham, J. A., Bruning, S. D. (Eds.)(2000), *Public relations as relationship management: A relational approach to the study and practice of public relations.* Mahwah, NJ: Lawrence Erlbaum Associates.

Leitch, S., & Neilson, D. (2001). Bringing publics into public relations: New theoretical frameworks for practice. In R. Heath (Ed.), *Hand book of Public* Relations (127-138). Thousand Oaks, CA: Sage.

Lesley, P. (1991). *The Handbook of Public Relations and Communications* (4th ed.). London: McGraw-Hill Book Company.

Levine, S., & White, P. E. (1976). Exchange as a conceptual framework for the study of interorganizational relationships. *Administrative Science Quarterly, 5*, 583-601.

Levinger, G., & Rubin, J. Z. (1994). Bridges and barriers to a more general theory of conflict. *Negotiation Journal*, 201-215.

Lincoln, J. R., & McBride, K. (1985). Resources, homophily, and dependence: Organizational attributes and asymmetric ties in human service networks. *Social Science Research, 14*, 1-30.

Little. R. J. A., & Rubin, D. B. (1987). *Statistical analysis with missing data.* New York: Wiley.

Loehlin, J. C. (1992). *Latent variable models: An introduction to factor, path, and structural analysis* (2nd ed.). Hillsdale, NJ: Lawrence Erlbaum Associates.

Lovelock, C. H. & Weinberg, C. B. (1984). *Marketing for public and nonprofit managers.* New York: Wiley.

Lund, M. (1985). The development of investment and commitment scales for predicting continuity of personal relationships. *Journal of Social and Personal Relationships, 2*, 3-23.

Major, A. M. (1993). Environmental concern and situational communication theory: Implications for communicating with environmental publics. *Journal of Public Relations Research 5*(3), 251-268.

Major, A. M. (1998). The utility of situational theory of publics for assessing public response to a disaster prediction. *Public Relations Review, 24*, 489-508.

McCallum, D. B., Hammond, S. L., & Covello, V. T. (1991). Communicating about environmental risks: How the public uses and perceives information sources. *Health Communication Quarterly, 18*(3), 349-361.

McDonald, G. W. (1981). Structural exchange and martial interaction. *Journal of Marriage and the Family, 43*, 825-839.

McQuail, D. (1985). Sociology of mass communication. *Annual Review of Sociology, 11*, 93-111.

Meyer, J. P., & Allen, N. (1984). Testing the side-best theory or organizational commitment: Some methodological considerations. *Journal of Applied Psychology*, 69, 372-378.

Millar, F. E., & Rogers, L. E. (1987). Relational dimensions of interpersonal dynamics. In M. E. Roloff & G. Miller, (Eds.), *Interpersonal process: New directions in communication research*. Newbury Park, CA: Sage.

Miller, M. B. (1995). Coefficient alpha: A basic introduction from the perspective of classical test theory and SEM. *Structural Equation Modeling, 2*, 255-273.

Mills, J., & Clark, M. (1994). Communal and exchange relationships: Controversies and research. In R. Erber & R. Gilmour (Eds). *Theoretical frameworks for personal relationships* (pp. 29-42). Hillsdale, NJ: Lawrence Erlbaum Associations.

Mills, J., & Clark, M. S. (1982). Communal and exchange relationships. *Review of Personality and Social Psychology, 3*, 121-144.

Mills, J., & Clark, M. S. (1988, July). *Communal and exchange relationships: New research and old controversies*. Invited address at the biannual meeting of the International Society for the Study of Personal Relationships, Vancouver, B.C.

Mintzberg, H. (1983). *Power in and around organizations*. Englewood Cliffs, NJ: Prentice Hall.

Moore, C. W. (1986). *The mediation process*. San Francisco: Jossey-Bass.

Moorman, C., Deshpandè, R., & Zalman, G. (1993). Factors affecting trust in market research relationship. *Journal of Marketing, 57*, 81-101.

Morgan, R. M., & Hunt, S. D. (1994). The commitment-trust theory of relationship marketing. *Journal of Marketing, 58*(3), 20-38.

Mowday, R. T, Steers, R. M., & Porter, L. W. (1979). The measurement of organizational commitment. *Journal of Vocational Behavior, 14*, 224-247.

Murphy, P. (1991). The limits of symmetry: A game theory approach to symmetric and asymmetric public relations. In J. E. Grunig & L. A. Grunig (Eds.), *Public relations research annual* (Vol. 3, pp. 115-132). Hillsdale, NJ: Lawrence Erlbaum Associates.

Murphy, P., & Dee, J. (1996). Reconciling the preferences of environmental activists and corporate policymakers. *Journal of Public Relations Research, 8*, 1-34.

Nardi, P. M. (2003). *Doing survey research: A guide to quantitative methods*. Boston, MA: Allyn and Bacon.

Nielsen, J. (1998, February 8). The reputation manager. Retrieved April 6, 2005, from http://www.useit.com/alertbox/980208.html.

O'Hair, D., Friedrich, G. W., Wiemann, J. M., & Wiemann, M. O. (1995). *Competent communication*. New York: St. Martin's press.

Oxford University Press (1979). *The Oxford dictionary of quotations* (3rd ed.). Oxford: Oxford University Press.

Petty, R. E., & Cacioppo, J. T. (1986). The elaboration likelihood model of persuasion. In L. Berkowitz (Ed.), *Advances in experimental social psychology* (Vol. 19, pp. 123-205). Orlando, FL: Academic Press.

Planalp, S. (1987). Interplay between relational knowledge and events. In R. Burnett & P. McGhee (Eds.), *Accounting for relationships: Explanation, representation and knowledge*. New York: Info Methuen.

Plowman, K. D. (1995). *Congruence between public relations and conflict resolution: Negotiating in the organization*. Unpublished doctoral dissertation, University of Maryland, College Park, MD.

Pollack, T. G., & Rindova, V. P. (2002). *Media legitimation effects in the market for initial public offerings*. Unpublished paper, University of Maryland, College Park.

Preacher, K., & Leonardelli, G. J. (2003). *Calculation for the Sobel Test: An interactive calculation too for mediation tests*. Retrieved January, 30, 2005, from http://www.unc.edu/~preacher/sobel/sobel.htm.

Price, V. (1992). *Public opinion*. Newbury Park, CA: Sage.

Pruzan, P. (2001). Corporate reputation: Image and identity. *Corporate Reputation Review, 4,* 50-64.

Rao, H. (1994). The social construction of reputation: Certification contests, legitimation, and the survival of organizations in the American automobile industry: 1985-1912. *Strategic Management Journal, 15,* 29-44.

Raykov, T., & Widaman, K. F. (1995). Issues in applied structural equation modeling research. *Structural Equation Modeling, 2*(4), 289-318.

Reputation Institute (n.d.a). *Corporate reputations*. Retrieved August 7, 2004, from http://www.reputationinstitute.com/sections/who/rep_mn_2.html.

Reputation Institute (n.d.b). *Corporate reputations*. Retrieved August 7, 2004, from http://www.reputationinstitute.com/sections/who/rep_mn_1.html.

Rhee, Y. (2002). Global public relations: A cross-cultural study of the Excellence theory in South Korea. *Journal of Public Relations Research, 14*(3), 159-184.

Rhee, Y. (2004). *The employee-public-organization chain in relationship management: A case study of a government organization.* Gainesville, FL: The Institute for Public Relations.

Rindova, V. P., & Kotha, S. (2001). *Accumulating reputation through strategic action flows: Lessons from Amazon.com and its competitors in Internet retailing.* Unpublished paper, University of Maryland, College Park.

Rindova, V., & Fombrun, C. J. (1999). Constructing competitive advantage. *Strategic Management Journal, 20*, 691-710.

Rips, L. J., Shoben, E. J., & Smith, E. E. (1973). Semantic distance and the verification of semantic relations. *Journal of Verbal Learning and Verbal Behavior, 12*, 1-20.

Rubin, D. B. (1976). Inference and missing data. *Biometrika, 63*, 581-592.

Rusbult, C. E. (1983). A longitudinal test of the investment model: The development (and deterioration) of satisfaction and commitment in heterosexual involvements. *Journal of Personality and Social Psychology, 45*, 101-117.

Sabatelli, R. M. (1984). The marital comparison index: A measure for assessing outcomes relative to expectations. *Journal of Marriage and the Family, 46*, 651-662.

Sabatelli, R. M., & Cecil-Pigo, E. F. (1985). Relational interdependence and commitment in marriage. *Journal of Marriage and the Family, 47*, 931-937.

Saxton, M, K. (1998). Where do reputations come from? *Corporate Reputation Review, 1*(4), 393-399.

Schacter, D. L. (1987). Implicit memory: History and current status. Journal of Experimental Psychology: *Learning, Memory, and Cognition, 13*, 501-518.

Schacter, D. L. (1994). Priming and multiple memory systems: Perceptual mechanisms of implicit memory. In D. L. Schacter & E. Tulving (Eds.), *Memory systems 1994* (pp. 233-268). Cambridge, MA: MIT Press.

Schultz, M., Hatch, M. J., & Larsen, M. H. (2000). Introduction: Why the expressive organization? In M. Schultz, M. J. Hatch, & M. H. Larsen (Eds.), *The expressive organization: Linking identity, reputation, and the corporate brand* (pp.1-7). Oxford, England: Oxford University Press.

Schultz, M., Mouritsen, J., & Gabrielsen, G. (2001). Sticky reputation: Analyzing a ranking system. *Corporate Reputation Review, 4,* 24-41.

Scott, W. A., Osgood, D. W., & Peterson, C. (1979). *Cognitive structure: Theory and measurement of individual differences.* New York: John Wiley & Sons.

Shadish, W., Cook, T. D., & Campbell, D. T. (2002). *Experimental and Quasi-experimental designs for generalized causal inference.* Boston, MA: Houghton Mifflin.

Shapiro, S. P. (1983). Premiums for high-quality products as returns to reputations. *Quarterly Journal of Economics, 98*, 659-681.

Sherif, C. W., Sherif, M., & Nebergall, R. E. (1965). *Attitude and attitude change: The social judgment-involvement approach.* Westport, CT: Greenwood.

Smith, E. E., Rips, L. J., & Shoben, E. J. (1974). Semantic memory and psychological semantics. In G. H. Bower (Ed.), *The psychology of learning and motivation* (Vol. 8, pp. 1-45). New York: Academic Press.

Smith, E. R. (1998). Mental representation and memory. In D. Gilbert, S. Fiske, and G. Lindzey (Eds.), *The handbook of social psychology* (4th ed.) (pp. 391-445). New York: Oxford University Press.

Sobel, M. E. (1982). Asymptotic intervals for indirect effects in structural equations models. In S. Leinhart (Ed.), *Sociological methodology 1982* (pp. 290-312). San Francisco: Jossey-Bass.

Spicer, C. (1997). *Organizational public relations: A political perspective.* Mahwah, NJ: Lawrence Erlbaum Associates.

SPSS FAQ (n.d.): *What does Cronbach's alpha mean?* Retrieved March, 9, 2005, from http://www.ats.ucla.edu/stat/spss/faq/alpha.html.

Sriramesh, K., Grunig, J. E., & Dozier, D. M. (1996). Observation and measurement of two dimensions of organizational culture and their relationship to public relations. *Journal of Public Relations Research, 8*(4), 229-261.

Sriramesh, K., Kim, Y., & Takasaki, M. (1999). Public relations in three Asian cultures: An analysis. *Journal of Public Relations Research*, 11, 271-292.

Staff (1999, November 15). Corporate reputation: Are we close to "Holy Grail" of reputation? *PR Week.*

Stafford, L., & Canary, D. J. (1991). Maintenance strategies and romantic relationship type, gender, and relational characteristics. *Journal of Social and Personal Relationships, 8,* 217-242.

Starck, K., & Kruckeberg, D. (2001). Public relations and community: A reconstructed theory revisited. In R. L. Heath (Ed.), *Handbook of public relations* (pp. 51-60). Thousand Oaks, CA: Sage.

Sterns, T. M., Hoffman, A. N., & Heide, J. G. (1987). Performance of commercial television stations as an outcome of interorganizational linkage and environmental conditions. *Academy of Management Journal, 30,* 71-90.

Stevenson, B. (1949). *Stevenson's book of proverbs, maxims and familiar phrases.* London: Routledge & Kegan Paul.

Stevenson, B. (1974). *Stevenson's book of quotations.* (10th ed). London: Cassell.

Stewart, D. W., Pavlou P., & Ward, S. (2002). Media influences on marketing communications. In J. Bryant and D. Zillmann (Eds.), Media effects: Advances in theory and research (pp. 353-396). Mahwah, NJ: Lawrence Erlbaum Associates.

Surra, C. A.. & Ridley, C. A. (1991). Multiple perspectives on interaction: Participants, peers, and observers. In B. M. Montgomery & S. Duck (Eds.), *Studying interpersonal interaction* (pp. 35-55). New York: Guilford.

Sykes, J. B. (Ed.) (1976). *The concise oxford dictionary of current English* (6th ed). Oxford: Clarendon Press.

Korean National Statistical Office (2002). *The 2002 census of district and age.* Retrieved September, 1, 2002, from http://culture.cyberarts.kwangju.kr/cgi-bin/sws_999.cgi.

Tabachnick, B. G., & Fidell, L. S. (2001). *Using multivariate statistics* (4th ed.). Boston; Allyn and Bacon.

Thayer, L. (1968). *Communication and communication systems.* Homewood, IL: Irwin.

Thomas L. Harris/Impulse Research (1999, June 4). *Corporate communications spending & reputations of Fortune 500 companies.* Los Angeles: Impulse Research Corporation.

Toth, E. L. (2000). From personal influence to interpersonal influence: A model for relationship management. In J. A. Ledingham and S. D. Bruning (Eds.), *Public relations as relationship management: A relational approach to the study and practice of public relations* (pp. 205-219). Mahwah, NJ: Lawrence Erlbaum Associates.

Trumbo, C. W., & McComas, K. A. (2003). The information of credibility in information processing for risk perception. *Risk Analysis, 23*(2), 343-353.

Vasquez, G. M. (1996). Public relations as negotiation: An issue development perspective. *Journal of Public Relations Research, 8*(1), 57-77.

Vasquez, G. M., & Taylor, M. (2001). Research perspectives on "the public." In R. L. Heath (Ed.), *Handbook of public relations* (pp. 139-154). Thousand Oaks, CA: Sage.

Verčič, D. (1997). Toward fourth wave public relations: A case study. In D. Moss, T. MacManus, & D. Verčič (Eds.), *Public relations research: An international perspective* (pp. 264-279). London: International Thomson Business Press.

Verčič, D. (2000, June). *Reputation: A new public relations fad?* Session handout abstract, International Association of Business Communicators International Conference, Vancouver.

Wakefield, R. I. (1997). *International PR: A theoretical approach to excellence Based on a worldwide Delphi study.* Unpublished doctoral dissertation, University of Maryland, College Park.

Wakefield, R. I. (2000). World-class PR: A model for effective PR in the multinational. *Journal of Communication Management, 5*(1), 59-71.

Wallack, L., Dorfman, L., Jenigan, D., & Themba, M. (1993). *Media advocacy and public health.* Newbury Park, CA: Sage.

Weigelt, K., & Camerer, C. (1988). Reputation and corporate strategy: A review of recent theory and applications. *Strategic Management Journal, 9*, 443-454.

Weisberg, H. F., Krosnick, J. A., & Bowen, B. D. (1996). *An introduction to survey research, polling, and data analysis.* Thousand Oak, CA: Sage.

Whang, P. A., & Hancock, G. R. (1997). Modeling the mathematics achievement of Asian-American elementary students. *Learning and Individual Differences, 9*(1), 63-68.

Wilson, R. (1985). Reputations in games and markets in A. E. Roth (Ed.), Game-theoretic models of bargaining. Cambridge University Press.

Wood, D. (1991). Corporate social performance revisited. *Academy of Management Review, 16*, 691-718.

Yang, S. U., & Grunig, J. E. (2005). The Effects of Organization-Public Relationships Outcomes on Cognitive Representations of Organizations and Overall Evaluations of Organizational Performance. *Journal of Communication Management 9*(4), 305-326.

Yang, S. U. (2004, October). *The effects of organization-public relationships, organizational visibility, and media coverage in reputation formation.* Paper presented at the Public Relations Society of America (PRSA) International Conference, New York City.

Yang, S. U., & Mallabo, J. (2003, May). *Exploring the link between organization-public relationships and organizational reputation in PR management: A relational approach.* Paper presented at the Public Relations Division, 53rd Annual Conference of ICA, San Diego, CA.

Yang, S. K., & Yang, S. U. (2003). Organization-public relationships and organizational reputation: The interaction effect with involvement in organizational performance. *Korean Journal of Communication & Information, 21*, 114-146.

Youngmeyer, D. R. (2002). *Measuring organization-public relationships: The case of a university department of communication and its undergraduate student public.* Paper presented at the Educators' Academy, Public Relations Society of America International Conference, November 16-19, San Francisco.

Zajonc, R. B. (1968). Attitudinal effects of mere exposure. *Journal of Personality and Social Psychology, 9*(No. 2, pt. 2).

Lightning Source UK Ltd.
Milton Keynes UK

173607UK00002B/19/A

9 783836 429160